# Statistical Analysis "In Focus"

## *Third Edition*

Sara Miller McCune founded SAGE Publishing in 1965 to support the dissemination of usable knowledge and educate a global community. SAGE publishes more than 1000 journals and over 800 new books each year, spanning a wide range of subject areas. Our growing selection of library products includes archives, data, case studies and video. SAGE remains majority owned by our founder and after her lifetime will become owned by a charitable trust that secures the company's continued independence.

Los Angeles | London | New Delhi | Singapore | Washington DC | Melbourne

# Statistical Analysis "In Focus"

*Alternate Guides for R, SAS®, and Stata®
for Statistics for the Behavioral Sciences,
Third Edition*

**Gregory J. Privitera**
*St. Bonaventure University*

**Kristin Lee Sotak**
*SUNY Oswego*

**Yu Lei**
*SUNY Old Westbury*

Los Angeles | London | New Delhi
Singapore | Washington DC | Melbourne

FOR INFORMATION:

SAGE Publications, Inc.
2455 Teller Road
Thousand Oaks, California 91320
E-mail: order@sagepub.com

SAGE Publications Ltd.
1 Oliver's Yard
55 City Road
London EC1Y 1SP
United Kingdom

SAGE Publications India Pvt. Ltd.
B 1/I 1 Mohan Cooperative Industrial Area
Mathura Road, New Delhi 110 044
India

SAGE Publications Asia-Pacific Pte. Ltd.
3 Church Street
#10-04 Samsung Hub
Singapore 049483

Acquisitions Editor:  Lara Parra
Editorial Assistant:  Zachary Valladon
Content Development Editor:  Lucy Berbeo
Production Editor:  Kelly DeRosa
Copy Editor:  Liann Lech
Typesetter:  C&M Digitals (P) Ltd.
Proofreader:  Theresa Kay
Indexer:  Beth Nauman-Montana
Cover Designer:  Michael Dubowe
Marketing Manager:  Katherine Hepburn

Printed in the United States of America

ISBN 978-1-5443-0560-8

This book is printed on acid-free paper.

MIX
Paper from
responsible sources
FSC® C012947

17 18 19 20 21 10 9 8 7 6 5 4 3 2 1

# Contents

## PART II. ANALYSIS IN FOCUS: SAS

## SAS in Focus

Page numbers for corresponding sections in the third edition of
Privitera's *Statistics for the Behavioral Sciences* are included in parentheses.

## PART III. ANALYSIS IN FOCUS: STATA

### Stata in Focus

Page numbers for corresponding sections in the third edition of
Privitera's *Statistics for the Behavioral Sciences* are included in parentheses.

# About the Authors

**Gregory J. Privitera** is a professor and chair of the Department of Psychology at St. Bonaventure University, where he is a recipient of their highest teaching honor, the Award for Professional Excellence in Teaching, and their highest honor for scholarship, the Award for Professional Excellence in Research and Publication. Dr. Privitera received his PhD in behavioral neuroscience in the field of psychology at the State University of New York at Buffalo and continued to complete postdoctoral research at Arizona State University. He is an author of multiple books on statistics, research methods, and health psychology, in addition to authoring more than three dozen peer-reviewed scientific articles aimed at advancing our understanding of health and well-being. He oversees a variety of undergraduate research projects at St. Bonaventure University, where dozens of undergraduate students, many of whom are now earning graduate degrees at various institutions, have coauthored research in his laboratories. For his work with students and fruitful record of academic and research advisement, Dr. Privitera was honored as Advisor of the Year by St. Bonaventure University in 2013. In addition, he is the award-winning author of *Research Methods for the Behavioral Sciences*, for which he received the Most Promising New Textbook Award from the Textbook & Academic Authors Association in 2014. In addition to his teaching, research, and advisement, Dr. Privitera is a veteran of the U.S. Marine Corps and is married with two children: a daughter, Grace Ann, and a son, Aiden Andrew.

**Kristin Lee Sotak** is an Assistant Professor of Management at SUNY Oswego and a former faculty member at SUNY Farmingdale. She received her PhD from the State University of New York at Binghamton in organizational behavior with a concentration in advanced research methods. She earned her MBA and her bachelor's degree in psychology from St. Bonaventure University. She has many years of teaching experience for survey courses in her discipline and statistical concepts. Her research interests include leadership, motivation, and dynamic models, where she bridges knowledge creation across business and psychology fields. Dr. Sotak oversees a variety of faculty-mentored research projects with undergraduate students, many of whom are now earning graduate degrees at various institutions. She has a diverse record of publication in leading journals across psychological and management fields in addition to national and international conference presentations. In addition to her passion for teaching and research, she played professional soccer in Iceland and enjoys traveling.

**Yu Lei** is an Assistant Professor of Management in the School of Business, SUNY College at Old Westbury. He received his PhD in management of information systems and a master's degree in accounting, both from State University of New York at Binghamton. His research interests include information systems strategy, consumer behaviors in e-commerce, and the societal impacts of information technology. Yu Lei has been teaching courses in quantitative areas for many years. His teaching interests include advanced spreadsheet, business analytics, and operations management.

# About This Supplemental Guide

This guide is written to support students who are using the third edition of Gregory J. Privitera's *Statistics for the Behavioral Sciences* but require resources for statistical programs not taught in the book. A unique feature of engaging in data analysis is the technological choices we have to compute and analyze data. By far, the most common statistical program used to analyze data in the behavioral sciences is IBM® SPSS® Statistics. SPSS (Statistical Package for the Social Sciences) is the statistical program introduced with each of the data analysis techniques taught in Privitera's *Statistics for the Behavioral Sciences*, Third Edition.

However, statistics is not something static or antiquated that we used to do in times past; statistics is an ever-evolving discipline with relevance to our daily lives. There are statistical programs that are increasingly popular, depending on the discipline you study in the behavioral sciences; thus, this *Statistical Analysis "In Focus"* guide was written to provide students with a supplemental text that can be used as a replacement for the SPSS in Focus sections in Privitera's *Statistics for the Behavioral Sciences*, Third Edition. Three quite common alternatives to SPSS today are the following statistical programs:

- R
- SAS® (Statistical Analysis System)
- Stata

In this book, there are three parts, and each part stands alone as a step-by-step statistical guide that replaces the SPSS in Focus sections in Privitera's *Statistics for the Behavioral Sciences*, Third Edition. In Part I, you learn how to use R to compute each of the "In Focus" sections; in Part II, you learn how to use SAS to compute each of the "In Focus" sections; and in Part III, you learn how to use Stata to compute each of the "In Focus" sections—all through the use of the following key themes, features, and pedagogy.

---

SPSS is a registered trademark of International Business Machines Corporation.

SAS and all other SAS Institute Inc. product or service names are registered trademarks or trademarks of SAS Institute Inc. in the USA and other countries. ® indicates USA registration.

# Emphasis on Student Learning

**Conversational writing style.** We write in a conversational tone that speaks to the reader as if he or she is the researcher. It empowers students to view statistics as something they are capable of understanding and using. It is a positive psychology approach to writing that involves students in the process of statistical analysis and making decisions using statistics. The goal is to motivate and excite students about the topic by making the book easy to read and follow without "dumbing down" the information they need to be successful.

**Additional features.** For each statistical program (R, SAS, and Stata), we provide a "To the Student" introduction to allow students to get familiar with each statistical program prior to computing the "In Focus" sections. We also provide a General Instruction Guide (GIG) for each statistical program and even provide the code you will enter as an ancillary resource, where appropriate. These additional sections and ancillary materials provide students with necessary resources to make this book a valuable reference guide, even beyond your studies.

# Looking Beyond SPSS

**Guide to using R, SAS, and Stata with Privitera's** *Statistics for the Behavioral Sciences,* **Third Edition.** For professors who teach statistics and statistical programs other than SPSS, it can be difficult to teach from a textbook and a separate manual written by another author where the examples and language between texts can often be inconsistent. This guide changes all of that by creating a guide that exactly corresponds to the SPSS in Focus sections in Privitera's *Statistics for the Behavioral Sciences,* Third Edition but for use with three common alternative statistical programs: R, SAS, and Stata.

In addition, there is one more overarching feature that we refer to as *teachability*. While this book is comprehensive for using R, SAS, and Stata for the tests taught in Privitera's *Statistics for the Behavioral Sciences,* Third Edition and a great reference for any undergraduate student, it is likely too difficult to teach every statistical program described in this book. For this reason, each statistical program (R, SAS, and Stata) is organized into parts, each of which stands alone. This gives professors the ability to more easily manage course content by choosing which part or parts they wish to assign in a way that will be easy to follow. Thus, this book was not only written with the student in mind, but also with the instructor in mind.

Thank you for choosing *Statistical Analysis "In Focus": Alternate Guides for R, SAS, and Stata* as a supplemental text to Privitera's *Statistics for the Behavioral Sciences,* Third Edition. Best wishes for a successful semester!

Gregory J. Privitera
*St. Bonaventure, New York*

Kristin Lee Sotak
*Oswego, New York*

Yu Lei
*Old Westbury, New York*

# PART I

# Analysis in Focus: R

# R in Focus

## Sections for Privitera, *Statistics for the Behavioral Sciences,* Third Edition

Page numbers for corresponding sections in the third edition of Privitera's *Statistics for the Behavioral Sciences* are included in parentheses.

# To the Student—How to Use R With This Book

R is a free, open-source programming language that can be used for statistical analysis. Though it has the benefit of being free, the downside is that it has a steep learning curve. It takes users longer to learn because instead of pointing and clicking to get results, users have to learn how to code and program in order to run analyses and create graphs. However, there are many online resources and a large, supportive community where users can get help (e.g., Stack Overflow, Quick-R). The fact that it is open source is also helpful because users can see all the code used for analyses and creating graphs, which users can then adapt to meet their needs. Thus, R is popular because it is free and flexible to use, and because of its graphing capabilities. Though R is widely used in academia, it is also used by large corporations, such as Google and *The New York Times*.

This preface provides you with an overview to familiarize you with how to use R. The output and screenshots in this book show R Version 3.3.1 "Bug in Your Hair" (R has some pretty cool names for the different versions) for a PC. Still, even if you use a Mac or different version, the figures and instructions should provide a rather effective guide for helping you use this statistical software (with some minor differences, of course). One thing to remind yourself is to be patient when learning R! There are a lot of commands and new terminology to learn, especially if you are not familiar with programming. Be patient! In addition to understanding how to compute a mean or plot a bar graph by hand, knowing how to enter, analyze, and interpret statistics using R is equally important for no other reason than you will need it. This is an essential complement to your readings in the textbook. By knowing how and why you compute certain statistics, you will better understand and interpret the output from R.

## Downloading and Installing R and RStudio

To download R, go to the R website and select the Comprehensive R Archive Network (CRAN) Mirror closest to you for your operating system (Linux, Mac, or Windows): https://cran.r-project.org/mirrors.html. Once it has downloaded, open R. You will notice a simple user interface (see Figure P.1).

**Figure P.1**  Simple User Interface in R

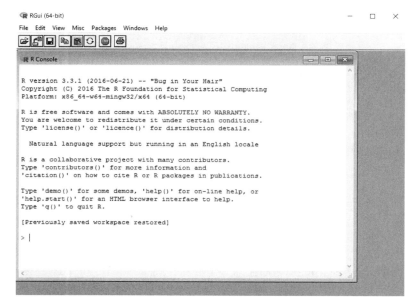

This is a basic view of R, where you see the Console to type commands and view output.

RStudio and Shiny are trademarks of RStudio, Inc.

To make R easier to use, you can download RStudio, an integrated development environment (IDE): https://www.rstudio.com/. Once RStudio is downloaded, open it and notice a more detailed environment. Compared to the original R user interface, RStudio has four separate windows that serve different functions (see Figure P.2).

**Figure P.2** View of R Using RStudio

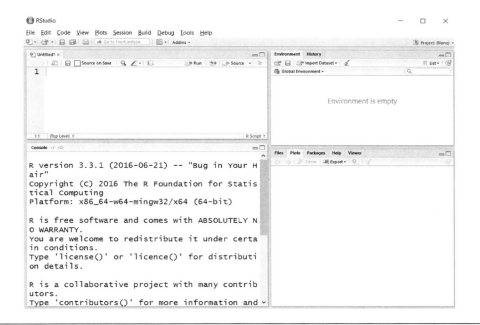

This is the view of R in RStudio, where there are four separate windows to type commands and view output, history, help options, and other objects loaded in your session.

First, the "Console" is where you can type commands and view output. Right now, your Console is displaying information about R, such as the version you are using, how to cite R, and how to close the program. Second, your "Workspace" shows all the objects you have loaded, such as your data and functions. This should be empty now. Once you begin working with R, your history will also be saved here under the "History" tab. Third, you will see an area for Files, Plots, Packages, and Help. If you create graphs or other visual aids, they will appear here (under "Plots"). Packages are add-ons that you can download to help you run more analyses and create more plots. We will download some later. Once you download more packages, they will all be listed here, as well as more information on what they do and the various functions they come with. The "Help" tab will give you more information on a function. For example, you will notice, in the "Help" tab, information about the mean function when you type (see Figure P.3):

```
> help(mean)
```

The fourth window is currently not in view. Go to "File," "New File," and then "R Script" and a new window will appear. (Also note that this is one of very few times where you will point and click in R to get something done!) An R Script is a file where you can type code and save it for future use. This is a lot to take in! Once you start using R, these views, new concepts, and new terminology will make sense and become easier to understand. Let us get started with R!

**Figure P.3**   Help Output

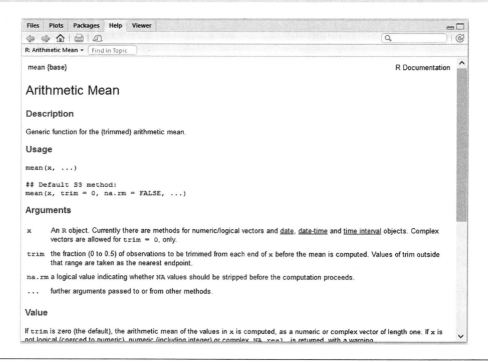

The Help menu shows information such as what the mean function does, what arguments it takes, and examples of how to use the function.

## Getting Started With R—A Brief Tutorial

First, we need to get comfortable with the R language. If you are familiar with programming, some of this may be review. In R, you can create a **vector**, which is a group of data **elements** that are all the same. For example, we can create a numeric vector (note that you do not have to type the "greater than" symbol, >; that should already appear in the R Console):

```
> c(1,2,3)

[1] 1 2 3
```

In this example, we created a vector composed of all numeric elements: numbers 1, 2, and 3. However, we can assign a name to that vector and save it for later use. To do this, we use the **assignment operator:**

```
> v.example <- c(1,2,3)
```

In this example, we called the vector "v.example," but you can name it whatever you want. The assignment operator is the "less than" symbol immediately followed by the dash (<-).

The c stands for **concatenate,** which means to link things together, which is what we are doing. Now, when we type the name of this object we just created (a numeric vector), we get output: our three data elements, 1, 2, and 3.

```
> v.example

[1] 1 2 3
```

We can also create a **dataframe** of data. You can think of a dataframe as a file of data that has rows and columns of different variables and information for those variables. It is similar to an Excel file of data. One way we can create the dataframe is by combining vectors of equal length. For example, we may want to have a dataframe of students' ID values and their test scores. We already have a vector of ID values (1, 2, 3), so let us make another vector of test scores:

```
> scores <- c(88,92,71)

> scores

[1] 88 92 71
```

Now, let us put those together:

```
> df <- data.frame(v.example,scores)

> df

 v.example scores

1        1     88

2        2     92

3        3     71
```

In this example, Student 1 received an 88, Student 2 received a 92, and Student 3 received a 71. Our label of students as "v.example" does not make sense, so let us change the name of the label to "Student ID":

```
> names(df) <- c("Student ID", "Scores")

> df

 Student ID Scores

1         1     88

2         2     92

3         3     71
```

We can add another column of variables to our dataframe. Let us add another column that lists students' gender:

```
> df$Gender <- c("M","F","F")

> df

  Student ID Scores Gender

1          1     88      M

2          2     92      F

3          3     71      F
```

Notice the dollar sign symbol. We can use this to add a new variable, like we just did, or we can use it to select a variable from a dataframe:

```
> df$Scores

[1] 88 92 71
```

Importantly, note that R is case sensitive, which means for our example that df$Scores is not the same as df$scores (the s is lowercase, not uppercase). When typing in R, be aware of this.

We can also obtain information about our dataframe with the structure function:

```
> str(df)

'data.frame':   3 obs. of 3 variables:

 $ Student ID: num 1 2 3

 $ Scores    : num 88 92 71

 $ Gender    : chr "M" "F" "F"
```

First, we see df is a dataframe. The structure function also lists each variable and tells us what type of data elements the variable vectors consist of. In our dataframe, both Student ID and Scores are numeric, but Gender is a **character,** which is a "string" value rather than a number or integer. This is important because R treats different types of vectors differently. Therefore, we need to know how to identify **class type** and how to convert vectors of data elements to different classes:

```
> class(scores)

[1] "numeric"

> scores.2<-as.character(scores)

> scores.2

[1] "88" "92" "71"

> scores.2+3

Error in scores.2 + 3 : non-numeric argument to binary operator
```

In this example, we used the "class" function to confirm our Scores vector is numeric. Then, we created a new object called "scores.2" to create a new vector of scores that are now characters (notice the quotes around each individual value). In this example, we wanted to add 3 points to each student's score, but R would not let us do this because the vector consisted of characters instead of numeric elements. Let us fix this:

```
> scores.2<-as.numeric(scores.2)
> scores.2
[1] 88 92 71
> scores.2+3
[1] 91 95 74
```

Now that the vector consists of numeric elements, we can add 3 points to each score.

In R, you can use—and write!—**functions** to execute a specific action. A function is what you use to perform tasks in R, such as to create a plot or to run an analysis. A function can also take specific **arguments,** which are more information that is needed or can be used to execute the function. An example may help:

```
mean()
```

This is a function that computes the mean. Inside the function, a user can specify arguments. In order to find out what arguments the function takes, see the Help menu:

```
> help(mean)
```

In the Help menu, you will see the mean function takes at least three arguments. For example, the function takes $x$, which is the data it uses to compute the mean, and na.rm, which tells the mean function what to do with missing data. Let us see how this works by creating a vector of height values, which has one missing value (NA), and computing the mean:

```
> height <- c(165,179,NA,142)
> height
[1] 165 179 NA 142
> mean(height)
[1] NA
```

Notice we do not get a value for the mean. This is because of the one missing value. We need to tell the function what to do with that missing value. In this case, we want to remove it from the calculation by using the na.rm argument (which stands for **remove na** values):

```
> mean(height,na.rm=TRUE)
[1] 162
```

In this case, we told the function to set the na.rm argument to TRUE. The default, as you can see in the Help menu, is set to na.rm = FALSE. To make sure R did what we wanted it to do, you can calculate the mean by hand:

```
> (165+179+142)/3

[1] 162
```

As you can see, R does a lot, and what we covered so far does not even cover the basics of an introductory tutorial! As we continue, we will learn more. For now, let us finish this section by learning how to import data, save our code, and write files.

In the beginning of this tutorial, you opened a new **R Script,** which should be the upper left window (note, you can move your windows around). An R Script is a document of your saved code and functions, which is useful because you can save your code in it and come back to it later, rather than having to type everything again. For future work, it is best to type your code in your R Script window and **Run it** from that window rather than to type it in the Console. Once you exit R, you will lose the code you wrote in the Console; however, you can save all your code in your R Script for later use. Type this in your new R Script:

```
new <- data.frame(ID=c(1,2,3,4), Score=c(94,83,72,89),
Gender=c("M","F","F","F"))

new
```

Now, you can "Run" this code one of two ways. First, you can highlight all of it and hit the "Run" button in the R Script window. Or, you can put your cursor in the first line of code and then hold down the ctrl key and then hit the enter key (or the R letter key; for Mac, hold down the command key and then hit the enter key). Notice that these commands get executed in the Console window. Let us save our code by saving this R Script. You can do this by going to the File tab and selecting Save As . . . Or, you can hold down the ctrl key and then hit the S letter key (for a Mac, hold down the command key and then hit the S letter key). We saved the file as "CodeForManual," but you can name it whatever you would like. Close R by hitting the X button in the top left corner of the program, or type:

```
> q()
```

Now, reopen R. Your R Script should load. If it does not, go to the folder where the R Script is saved and open it. Also notice your History tab—you should see the code you ran before you closed R (see Figure P.4). If you want to erase your history, you can click on the broom symbol in the History window.

You can save output, such as figures, tables, and dataframes. For example, let us assume we want to share with our friends our "new" dataframe we created. First, you may have to rerun your code, so practice doing that. Now, look in your Environment tab and notice that under "Data" the "new" dataframe is listed there (see Figure P.4). Click on it to view your data (see Figure P.5).

**Figure P.4**   View of Environment and History Tabs, and Broom

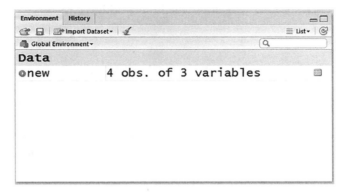

In the Environment tab, you will see your data as well as variables and functions (if you have them). The History tab shows commands you have previously executed. Notice the broom button, which you can use to delete your History or other objects, such as your data.

**Figure P.5**   View of R Script Tab and Data

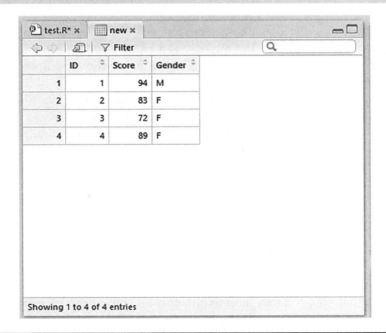

View of the R Script (CodeForManual.R) and the dataframe titled "new."

To save this dataframe, you need to use the **write.csv** function, but you also have to know where you want to save your dataframe. We can find out the location from which R is reading data and to which it is saving data, which is called the **working directory**:

```
> getwd()

[1] "C:/Users/ExampleUser/Desktop"
```

This function is asking R to get us the working directory (thus, *wd*). In this example, if we were to save our dataframe right now, it would be saved to the Desktop. You can change the directory in one of two ways. First, you can click on Session, Set Working Directory, and Choose Directory. Alternatively, you can type where you want things saved by using the following function:

```
> setwd("C:/Users/Dropbox/RPractice")
```

For a Mac computer, you do not need to write "C:"; otherwise, the directory is the same.

Finally, let us save the "new" dataframe using the write.csv function. In this function, we have to use two arguments. First, we have to tell R what to "write" or save, and second, we have to tell R where it should be saved (note: change your directory to where you want your dataframe saved) and what we should call the saved file (this is the very last part: df.csv):

```
> write.csv(new, "C:/Users/Dropbox/RPractice/df.csv")
```

Now go to your directory, and you should be able to open an Excel file with your "new" dataframe, which should be saved as df.csv. Notice we saved this file as a **.csv** (which stands for comma-separated values) file. R does not directly read Excel file extensions, such as .xlsx, so we need to save our data as .csv files. Excel can open .csv files, so others can open this dataframe we saved for them, even if they do not use R.

Now that we know R needs .csv files, let us practice opening saved data files in R. If you have an Excel file with a .xlsx extension, that is okay. You can convert it to a .csv file or simply save the data as a .csv file. For example, open the df.csv file you saved. Copy and paste the dataframe into a new Excel file. Go to File, Save As, and save the file as a .csv file by selecting CSV (comma delimited) (*.csv) under Save as type. You can rename the file to "PracticeCSV" and save it to your Desktop. Now, we need to read that file into R:

```
> read.csv(file.choose())
```

This command will prompt a window to open where you can go through your directory to find the .csv file to open. In this case, go to your Desktop and select the "PracticeCSV" file. If a window does not immediately appear, look for a blinking box in your taskbar at the bottom of your computer. Alternatively, you may have to minimize all your opened windows until you see it.

Related to this, it is possible you know someone who uses SPSS, a statistical program that is popular among social scientists. You can open SPSS files in R, but you need the foreign package. Remember, **packages** are add-ons that allow users to carry out more functions. To download this package in R:

```
> install.packages("foreign")
```

This may take a minute to download. Once a package is downloaded, you have to load it in R *every* session before you can use it:

```
> library(foreign)
```

Once it is loaded, now you can use its functions to read an SPSS file into R:

```
> SPSS.File <- read.spss("C:\PathToFile\MyDataFile.sav", to.data.
frame=TRUE)
```

In this example, we called the SPSS file "SPSS.File" but remember, you can name it whatever is easiest for you. You will also have to change the directory to wherever you have the SPSS file saved. The read.spss function takes many arguments for reading files; see the Help menu for more information.

At this point, you have a solid foundation for navigating various views and commands in R, as will be further discussed in this guide for many statistical tests and analyses. There are also many online resources to help you if you get lost along the way. And remember, be patient when learning R! There is a steep learning curve, but with time and practice, you will be able to master the skills needed to utilize R to analyze data and create visual outputs that convey your results.

## Preview of R in Focus

This book is unique in that you will learn how to use R to perform statistical analyses as they are taught in this book. Most statistics textbooks for behavioral science omit such information, include it in an appendix separate from the main chapters in the book, include it at the end of chapters with no useful examples or context, or include it in ancillary materials that often are not included with course content. Instead, this book provides instructions for using R in each chapter as statistical concepts are taught using practical research examples and screenshots to support student learning. You will find this instruction in the R in Focus sections. These sections provide step-by-step instructions for how the concepts taught in each chapter can be applied to research problems using R.

The reason for this inclusion is simple: Most researchers use some kind of statistical software to analyze statistics, and in the social sciences, R is rapidly becoming popular. This textbook brings statistics in research to the 21st century, giving you both the theoretical and computational instruction needed to understand how, when, and why you perform certain statistical analyses under different conditions and the technical instruction you need to succeed in the modern era of data collection, data entry, data analysis, and statistical interpretation using R. This preface was written to familiarize you with this environment. Subsequent R in Focus sections will show you how to use R to perform the applications and statistics taught in this book.

# 1.7 R IN FOCUS

## Entering and Defining Variables

Privitera's *Statisics for the Behavioral Sciences,* Third Edition (p. 23)

Throughout this book, we present instructions for using R by showing you how you can use functions and code to solve problems instead of doing them by hand. Before you read this section, please take the time to read the section titled "How to Use R With This Book" at the beginning of this book. That section provides an overview of what R is and how to use it.

In this chapter, we discussed how variables are defined, coded, and measured. We can expand on what we learned in the introductory section of "How to Use R With This Book" to reinforce the different ways we can get data into R. We first talked about entering data into Excel, saving it as a .csv file, and reading it into R. We can also import data from other software programs, such as SPSS, by using the foreign package. Last, we also discussed how we can create our own dataframe by typing our data in R. The biggest challenge is making sure you enter the data correctly. Entering even a single value incorrectly can alter your results. For this reason, always double-check the data to make sure the correct values have been entered.

Let us create a dataframe of data again, but this time using a different example and a different approach. Suppose you record the average GPA of students in one of three statistics classes. You record the following GPA scores for each class, given in Table 1.4.

**Table 1.4   GPA Scores in Three Statistics Classes**

| Class 1 | Class 2 | Class 3 |
|---------|---------|---------|
| 3.3 | 3.9 | 2.7 |
| 2.9 | 4.0 | 2.3 |
| 3.5 | 2.4 | 2.2 |
| 3.6 | 3.1 | 3.0 |
| 3.1 | 3.0 | 2.8 |

There are two ways you can enter these data: by column or by row. To enter data by *column,* use the following code:

```
GPA.Scores <- data.frame("Class 1" = c(3.3,2.9,3.5,3.6,3.1), "Class 2"
= c(3.9,4.0,2.4,3.1,3.0), "Class 3" = c(2.7,2.3,2.2,3.0,2.8))

GPA.Scores
```

In this example, remember you should be typing your code in your R Script instead of typing directly into the Console. If you did this, and then ran the code from the R Script, your output should look identical (or nearly identical) to the output below. Notice the "+" sign. In R, if you execute a function (in this case, the data.frame function) and all the code does not fit on one line in the Console window, R will let you know by using this symbol. In other words, you should not type the "+" sign in your code.

```
> GPA.Scores <- data.frame("Class 1" = c(3.3,2.9,3.5,3.6,3.1),
+ "Class 2" = c(3.9,4.0,2.4,3.1,3.0),
+ "Class 3" = c(2.7,2.3,2.2,3.0,2.8))
> GPA.Scores
  Class.1 Class.2 Class.3
1     3.3     3.9     2.7
2     2.9     4.0     2.3
3     3.5     2.4     2.2
4     3.6     3.1     3.0
5     3.1     3.0     2.8
```

Notice the output—the data for each group are now listed down each column. Also, notice how R changed "Class 1" to Class.1. It does this to get rid of any spaces, which may cause confusion. Alternatively, you could have used the following code to label your Class variable:

```
> GPA_Scores <- data.frame(Class1 = c(3.3,2.9,3.5,3.6,3.1),
+                          Class2 = c(3.9,4.0,2.4,3.1,3.0),
+                          Class3 = c(2.7,2.3,2.2,3.0,2.8))
> GPA_Scores
  Class1 Class2 Class3
1    3.3    3.9    2.7
2    2.9    4.0    2.3
3    3.5    2.4    2.2
4    3.6    3.1    3.0
5    3.1    3.0    2.8
```

There is another way to enter these data in R: You can enter data by *row*. This requires coding the data:

```
> GPA.Scores.Row <- data.frame(Class = c(rep(1,5),rep(2,5),rep(3,5)),
GPA = c(3.3,2.9,3.5,3.6,3.1,3.9,4.0,2.4,3.1,3.0,2.7,2.3,2.2,3.0,2.8))

> GPA.Scores.Row
   Class GPA
1      1 3.3
2      1 2.9
3      1 3.5
4      1 3.6
5      1 3.1
6      2 3.9
7      2 4.0
8      2 2.4
9      2 3.1
10     2 3.0
11     3 2.7
12     3 2.3
13     3 2.2
14     3 3.0
15     3 2.8
```

In this example, we introduced a new function, rep(). This is the repeat function, and we supplied it with two arguments. First, we told it what number to repeat, and second, we told it how many times to repeat that number. So rep(1,5) means, repeat the number 1, five times:

```
> rep(1,5)

[1] 1 1 1 1 1
```

This is a shortcut and saves us time so we do not have to type out a lot of numbers. For this example, we are not saving ourselves too much time, but imagine if we had a dataset with 500 observations! That most certainly will save us time.

# 2.4 R IN FOCUS

## Frequency Distributions for Quantitative Data

Privitera's *Statisics for the Behavioral Sciences,* Third Edition (p. 46)

R can be used to construct frequency distributions. In this section, we will construct a frequency distribution table for the business safety data first listed in Table 2.3, which are reproduced here for reference.

**Data reproduced from Table 2.3.**

| | | | | |
|---|---|---|---|---|
| 45 | 98 | 83 | 50 | 86 |
| 66 | 66 | 88 | 95 | 73 |
| 88 | 55 | 76 | 115 | 66 |
| 92 | 110 | 79 | 105 | 101 |
| 101 | 85 | 90 | 92 | 81 |
| 55 | 95 | 91 | 92 | |
| 78 | 66 | 73 | 58 | |
| 86 | 92 | 51 | 63 | |
| 91 | 77 | 88 | 86 | |
| 94 | 80 | 102 | 107 | |

Create a dataframe in R called "complaints" that has the above safety data observations listed in one column:

```
> complaints <- data.frame(Complaints=c(45,98,83,50,86,66,66,88,
+ 95,73,88,55,76,115,66,92,
+ 110,79,105,101,101,85,90,
+ 92,81,55,95,91,92,78,66,
+ 73,58,86,92,51,63,91,77,
+ 88,86,94,80,102,107))
```

First, let us order the data to see which businesses filed the fewest and most complaints by using the order function on the Complaint column data from the complaint dataframe:

```
> order(complaints$Complaints)
 [1]  1  4 36 12 26 33 37  6  7 15 31 10 32 13 39 30 18 43 25  3 22
[22]  5 34 41  8 11 40 23 28 38 16 24 29 35 42  9 27  2 20 21 44 19
[43] 45 17 14
```

The order function shows us that business observation 1 filed the fewest complaints, and business number 14 filed the most. This might be helpful for us if we knew which businesses those were. However, we may be more interested to know the most and fewest number of complaints filed. For that, we can use the sort function:

```
> sort(complaints$Complaints)
 [1] 45 50 51 55 55 58  63  66  66  66  66  73  73 76 77 78
[17] 79 80 81 83 85 86  86  86  88  88  88  90  91 91 92 92
[33] 92 92 94 95 95 98 101 101 102 105 107 110 115
```

We can go a step further and create a table that shows us, for each number of complaints filed, how many businesses filed that number:

```
> table(complaints$Complaints)

 45 50 51 55 58 63 66  73  76  77  78  79  80 81 83 85 86

  1  1  1  2  1  1  4   2   1   1   1   1   1  1  1  1  3

 88 90 91 92 94 95 98 101 102 105 107 110 115

  3  1  2  4  1  2  1   2   1   1   1   1   1
```

In the above output, we see that the most common numbers of complaints filed are 66 and 92: Four businesses filed 66 complaints and four businesses filed 92 complaints over the previous 3 years.

Next, we may want to know, for each value of number of complaints filed, what percentage of all of the values each represents. We can do this by using the prop.table (proportion) function:

```
> prop.table(table(complaints$Complaints))

        45          50          51          55          58          63
0.02222222  0.02222222  0.02222222  0.04444444  0.02222222  0.02222222
        66          73          76          77          78          79
```

```
0.08888889 0.04444444 0.02222222 0.02222222 0.02222222 0.02222222
        80         81         83         85         86         88
0.02222222 0.02222222 0.02222222 0.02222222 0.06666667 0.06666667
        90         91         92         94         95         98
0.02222222 0.04444444 0.08888889 0.02222222 0.04444444 0.02222222
       101        102        105        107        110        115
0.04444444 0.02222222 0.02222222 0.02222222 0.02222222 0.02222222
```

This output shows us that the value 45 makes up 2.22% of all the values. Of course, this output looks sloppy. First, there are too many values, and we can make it easier to read by rounding our output with the round() function:

```
> round(prop.table(table(complaints$Complaints)),4)

    45     50     51     55     58     63     66     73     76
0.0222 0.0222 0.0222 0.0444 0.0222 0.0222 0.0889 0.0444 0.0222
    77     78     79     80     81     83     85     86     88
0.0222 0.0222 0.0222 0.0222 0.0222 0.0222 0.0222 0.0667 0.0667
    90     91     92     94     95     98    101    102    105
0.0222 0.0444 0.0889 0.0222 0.0444 0.0222 0.0444 0.0222 0.0222
   107    110    115
0.0222 0.0222 0.0222
```

In the above code, we gave the round() function two arguments. First, we gave it the data that we wanted rounded, and second, we told it how many places we wanted our data rounded to (in this case, 4). We can make our data easier to read by multiplying our output by 100 to get the percentage:

```
> round(prop.table(table(complaints$Complaints)),4)*100

  45   50   51   55   58   63   66   73   76   77   78   79   80
2.22 2.22 2.22 4.44 2.22 2.22 8.89 4.44 2.22 2.22 2.22 2.22 2.22
  81   83   85   86   88   90   91   92   94   95   98  101  102
2.22 2.22 2.22 6.67 6.67 2.22 4.44 8.89 2.22 4.44 2.22 4.44 2.22
 105  107  110  115
2.22 2.22 2.22 2.22
```

Finally, let us assume we want to know the cumulative percentage for our values. We can use the cumsum() function. First, I saved our output and work so far by assigning it the name safety. data, and then I applied the cumsum() function to that object:

```
> safety.data <- round(prop.table(table(complaints$Complaints)),4)*100

> cumsum(safety.data)

   45     50     51     55     58     63     66     73     76     77     78
 2.22   4.44   6.66  11.10  13.32  15.54  24.43  28.87  31.09  33.31  35.53

   79     80     81     83     85     86     88     90     91     92     94
37.75  39.97  42.19  44.41  46.63  53.30  59.97  62.19  66.63  75.52  77.74

   95     98    101    102    105    107    110    115
82.18  84.40  88.84  91.06  93.28  95.50  97.72  99.94
```

You may notice that our cumulative percent does not equal 100%, and it should. Can you guess why? If you said it is due to rounding, you are correct! Remember, we rounded our data to four decimal places, which influenced how the data added up.

## 2.7 R IN FOCUS

### Frequency Distributions for Categorical Data

Privitera's *Statisics for the Behavioral Sciences,* Third Edition (p. 51)

R can be used to summarize categorical data that are ungrouped. We can use R to create a frequency distribution for the following hypothetical example: A group of health practitioners wants to classify children in public schools as being lean, healthy, overweight, or obese; this type of classification is common (Centers for Disease Control and Prevention, 2013; Privitera, 2016). To do this, the researchers calculated the body mass index (BMI) score of 100 children. Based on the BMI scores, they classified 15 children as lean, 30 as healthy, 35 as overweight, and 20 as obese.

As usual, let us begin by creating our dataframe:

```
> BMI <- data.frame(BMI=c("lean","healthy","overweight",
+ "obese"), Total=c(15,30,35,20))
> BMI
         BMI    Total
1       lean       15
2    healthy       30
3 overweight       35
4      obese       20
```

Similar to the previous section, we can calculate the percent (out of 100) for each category, convert that calculation to a number out of 100 (to make it easier to read), and then calculate the cumulative percentage:

```
> prop.table(BMI$Total)
[1] 0.15 0.30 0.35 0.20
> prop.table(BMI$Total)*100
[1] 15 30 35 20
> cumsum(prop.table(BMI$Total)*100)
[1] 15 45 80 100
```

As another example, instead of having the number of children classified as either lean, healthy, overweight, or obese, we may simply have classification types for each child, which we can enter into a dataframe:

```
> BMI.2 <-data.frame(BMI=c("lean","lean","healthy","overweight",
+ "lean","obese","obese","obese","lean",
```

```
+ "healthy","lean","obese","lean",
+ "overweight","lean"))
> BMI.2
           BMI
1         lean
2         lean
3      healthy
4   overweight
5         lean
6        obese
7        obese
8        obese
9         lean
10     healthy
11        lean
12       obese
13        lean
14  overweight
15        lean
> table(BMI.2)
BMI.2
  healthy      lean     obese overweight
        2         7         4          2
> prop.table(table(BMI.2))
BMI.2
   healthy       lean      obese overweight
 0.1333333 0.4666667 0.2666667  0.1333333
> cumsum(c(.47,.13,.13,.27))
[1] 0.47 0.60 0.73 1.00
```

In this example, we see that there are 7 lean children, 2 healthy children, 2 overweight children, and 4 obese children. The prop.table() function calculates the percentage for each of these categories, and we can again use the cumsum() function to calculate the cumulative percentage.

# 2.12 R IN FOCUS

## Histograms, Bar Charts, and Pie Charts

Privitera's *Statisics for the Behavioral Sciences,* Third Edition (p. 65)

To review, histograms are used for continuous or quantitative data, and bar charts and pie charts are used for discrete, categorical, or qualitative data. As an exercise to compare histograms, bar charts, and pie charts, we can construct these graphs for the same data by treating the data as a simple set of general values. Suppose we measure the data shown in Table 2.16.

**Table 2.16**   A Sample of 20 Values

| | | | |
|---|---|---|---|
| 1 | 4 | 5 | 7 |
| 2 | 3 | 6 | 8 |
| 3 | 6 | 7 | 9 |
| 2 | 6 | 5 | 4 |
| 4 | 5 | 8 | 5 |

Because we are not defining these values, we can just call the variable "numbers."

Creating a histogram in R is super simple! Of course, we are going to take advantage of this and learn some new tricks in R. First, create the dataframe:

```
> numbers <- data.frame(numbers=c(1,4,5,7,2,3,6,8,3,6,7,9,2,6,5,
+ 4,4,5,8,5))
```

Next, create a histogram using the hist() function:

```
hist(numbers$numbers)
```

This does the job, but the labels are not professional. For example, the *x*-axis label is numbers$numbers, which can be changed to our variable name, Numbers. We can also change the title of our histogram. These changes can be done by passing more information to the arguments of the hist() function. You can see the various arguments that the hist() function takes by looking them up in the help menu:

```
> help(hist)
```

Let us now improve our histogram:

```
> hist(numbers$numbers, n=20, main="Histogram",xlab="Numbers")
```

23

The "main" argument tells the hist() function what the title of the histogram should be, and the "xlab" argument renames the *x*-axis label. Experiment with the "n=20" argument by changing it to different values, such as "n=5" (note that the argument "break=5" will give you the same results). What do you notice? This argument can be used to specify the width of what are called bins. Be careful using this argument, because it can distort your histogram and therefore visualization of your data. There is no best value to use; experiment with it to see what best illustrates your data.

Finally, let us say we want to compare two histograms to see how different bin width values affect our histogram. We can divide our Plots window into two, where we see two plots in this one window:

```
> par(mfrow=c(2,1))
```

Now run this code:

```
> hist(numbers$numbers, n=2, main="Histogram",xlab="Numbers")
> hist(numbers$numbers, n=15, main="Histogram",xlab="Numbers")
```

Now we have two histograms in one window to compare (see Figure 2.1)! To change our window back to its original view, type:

```
> par(mfrow=c(1,1))
```

To become a better R user, it is important that you practice and experiment. Try using different functions and arguments to see how they influence your results. For example, can you change the colors of the bar graph using the arguments in the hist() function?

**Figure 2.1**   Two Histograms With Different Bin Widths

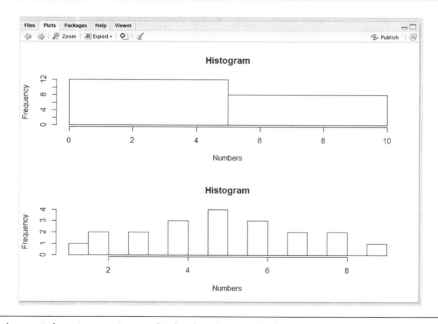

We can use the par() function to view multiple plots in one window.

# 3.6 R IN FOCUS

## Mean, Median, and Mode

Privitera's *Statisics for the Behavioral Sciences,* Third Edition (p. 98)

R can be used to measure the mean, the median, and the mode for all sorts of data. In this section, we will work through a new example to compute each measure of central tendency. Suppose you want to study creativity using a paper clip, as has been used in prior studies on the topic (Chatterjea & Mitra, 1976; Piffer, 2012). You give students a paper clip, and the time (in seconds) it takes the students to list 10 uses for the paper clip is recorded. Faster times are presumed to reflect greater creativity. Using the data shown in Table 3.11, we can use R to compute the mean, the median, and the mode.

**Table 3.11** The Time (in seconds) That It Took 20 Participants to Write Down 10 Uses for a Paper Clip on a Creativity Test

| | |
|---|---|
| 41 | 80 |
| 65 | 80 |
| 123 | 64 |
| 46 | 59 |
| 48 | 51 |
| 87 | 36 |
| 38 | 80 |
| 90 | 143 |
| 132 | 122 |
| 115 | 100 |

To calculate the mean and median, the functions are very simple:

```
> clips <- data.frame(Time=c(41,65,123,46,48,87,38,90,132,115,
+ 80,80,64,59,51,36,80,143,122,100))
> mean(clips$Time)
```

```
[1] 80

> median(clips$Time)

[1] 80
```

You may think that typing "mode()" will give you the mode central tendency measure, but this is not the case!

```
> mode(clips$Time) # Does not give you the mode you want!

[1] "numeric"
```

Indeed, mode() is a function, but it does not give us the mode we want. Instead, it tells us an object's type. In fact, R does not have a standard function that comes with the base R that you downloaded. So, we need to be creative with how we can determine the mode. Before we do that, note the pound symbol (#) after the function. We can use this to type notes in R, especially in the R Script. We may want to write what analyses we are running or make other notes so when we return to our R Script at a later time, we can be reminded about decisions we made or thoughts we had. The symbol tells R to ignore anything that is written after it on that line of code, so do not worry that R will misinterpret your notes as code.

To find the mode we want, we can actually use functions we learned in Chapter 2. First, we can sort the data and look through them to see which values are repeated the most:

```
> sort(clips$Time)

 [1]   36  38  41  46  48  51  59  64  65  80  80  80  87  90  100  115  122  123
[19] 132 143
```

Here, we can see 80 is repeated the most. This was not hard to determine with only 20 observations, but what if we had over 100 observations? To help make this easier, we can use the table() function:

```
> table(clips$Time)

 36 38 41 46 48 51 59 64 65 80 87 90 100 115 122 123 132 143
  1  1  1  1  1  1  1  1  1  3  1  1   1   1   1   1   1   1
```

Still, we can sort this table such that the last column and value is the value that appears the most (the mode):

```
> sort(table(clips$Time))

 36 38 41 46 48 51 59 64 65 87 90 100 115 122 123 132 143 80
  1  1  1  1  1  1  1  1  1  1  1   1   1   1   1   1   1  3
```

Another option that allows us to quickly view some descriptive statistics about the data is the describe() function in the psych package. First, install the psych package, and then use the describe() function:

```
> install.packages("psych")

> library(psych)

> describe(clips$Time)
   vars  n mean    sd median trimmed   mad min max range skew kurtosis   se
X1    1 20   80 33.42     80   78.19 45.22  36 143   107 0.35    -1.24 7.47
```

# 4.11 R IN FOCUS

## Range, Variance, and Standard Deviation

Privitera's *Statisics for the Behavioral Sciences,* Third Edition (p. 129)

In the R in Focus section of Chapter 3, we computed the mean, the median, and the mode for creativity, measured as the time (in seconds) it took participants to list 10 uses for a paper clip. The data for this example, originally given in Table 3.11, are reproduced here in Table 4.10. In this section, we will use these same data to compute the range, variance, and standard deviation.

This table originally appeared as Table 3.11 in Chapter 3.

**Table 4.10** The Time (in seconds) That It Took a Group of 20 Participants to Write Down 10 Uses for a Paper Clip on a Creativity Test

| | |
|---|---|
| 41 | 80 |
| 65 | 80 |
| 123 | 64 |
| 46 | 59 |
| 48 | 51 |
| 87 | 36 |
| 38 | 80 |
| 90 | 143 |
| 132 | 122 |
| 115 | 100 |

There are several ways we can compute the range, variance, and standard deviation. Each has its own function, or we can use the describe() function in the psych package (which we did in Chapter 3) or the stat.desc() function in the pastecs package. Hopefully you saved your code from Chapter 3 in an R Script, so you can reload the clips object rather than having to type it again! If you have it saved, you can run your code, or retype the dataframe:

```
> clips <- data.frame(Time=c(41,65,123,46,48,87,38,90,132,115,
+ 80,80,64,59,51,36,80,143,122,100))
```

Calculate the standard deviation with the sd() function, the variance with the var() function, and the range with the range() function. The range gives the min and max values of all observations.

We can also calculate the min and max separately, and then calculate the range by getting the difference between the max and min:

```
> sd(clips$Time)

[1] 33.42234

> var(clips$Time)

[1] 1117.053

> range(clips$Time)

[1] 36 143

> max(clips$Time) - min(clips$Time)

[1] 107
```

The describe() function calculates the min, max, range, and standard deviation all at once, but not the variance:

```
> library(psych)

> describe(clips$Time)

   vars  n mean    sd median trimmed  mad min max range skew kurtosis   se
X1    1 20   80 33.42     80   78.19 45.22  36 143   107 0.35    -1.24 7.47
```

The stat.desc() function can also calculate the standard deviation, min, max, and range, in addition to the variance. Remember, you have to install the pastecs package and load the library before you can use the function:

```
> install.packages("pastecs")

> library(pastecs)

> stat.desc(clips$Time)

      nbr.val      nbr.null       nbr.na          min          max        range
   20.0000000     0.0000000    0.0000000   36.0000000  143.0000000  107.0000000
          sum        median         mean      SE.mean CI.mean.0.95          var
 1600.0000000    80.0000000   80.0000000    7.4734618   15.6421354 1117.0526316
      std.dev      coef.var
   33.4223373     0.4177792
```

# 5.6 R IN FOCUS

## Probability Tables

Privitera's *Statisics for the Behavioral Sciences,* Third Edition (p. 152)

Table 5.5 displayed a crosstabulation for the frequency of births based on the type of hospital (public versus private) and insurance status (insured versus uninsured) of mothers. We will use R to convert these data to a conditional probability table. In R, there is not always one way to do things, as we learned in the previous section when we were calculating the range, variance, and standard deviation. In this section, we will create probability tables one way so that we can learn more about R, but do know that there are alternative approaches.

## Construct a Probability Table

First, we need to create Table 5.5. This table shows us a nice summary of the data. For example, assume we were gathering data on 200 women. For each woman, we would want to know whether she was insured or uninsured, and whether she gave birth in a public or private hospital. We could keep track of the data in an Excel file, where each row represented a woman and each column represented information about her (her ID number, insurance status, and hospital type). Generally, this is how data are organized, whether you are using Excel, R, SPSS, or another type of software: Rows represent participants, and columns represent variables (see Figure 5.1).

**Figure 5.1**   Excel File Preview of Data

|   | A | B | C |  |
|---|---|---|---|---|
| 1 | Woman # | Insurance | Hospital | |
| 2 | 1 | Insured | Public | |
| 3 | 2 | Uninsured | Private | |
| 4 | 3 | Uninsured | Public | |
| 5 | 4 | Insured | Private | |
| 6 | 5 | Insured | Public | |
| 7 | | | | |

Each row represents one subject, and each column represents information about each variable.

In Figure 5.1, the first woman is insured and gave birth in a public hospital. The entire second row in Excel is data on one woman, and each column represents data on different variables. Once we had all that data, we could count up how many women

1. were insured and who gave birth in a public hospital,

2. were insured and who gave birth in a private hospital,

3. were uninsured and who gave birth in a public hospital, and

4. were uninsured and who gave birth in a private hospital.

This would give us our data for Table 5.5. Let us first create a dataframe in R that displays the data similar to how the data are displayed in an Excel file in Figure 5.1:

```
> hosp.ins <- data.frame(hospital=c(rep("A.public",130),rep("B.
private",70)),
+ insurance=c(rep("insured",50),rep("uninsured",80),
+ rep("insured",40),rep("uninsured",30)))
> head(hosp.ins)
  hospital insurance
1 A.public   insured
2 A.public   insured
3 A.public   insured
4 A.public   insured
5 A.public   insured
6 A.public   insured
```

The head() function displays the first few observations instead of the entire dataframe, just to give you a preview of what it looks like. Go ahead and display the entire dataframe:

```
> hosp.ins
```

You can see how those data match up with the summary data in Table 5.5 (e.g., there are 50 women who are insured and who gave birth in a public hospital).

Now we can use the table() function to create Table 5.5:

```
> table(hosp.ins)
           insurance
hospital    insured uninsured
  A.public       50        80
  B.private      40        30
```

Notice how we titled the hospital types as "A.public" and "B.private." This is because R will, by default, arrange the words alphabetically. Therefore, if we did not put the "A" and "B" in the description, private would have come before public and our table would have been different from

Table 5.5. However, the order does not influence our calculations and results, it only influences their arrangement in the output.

The addmargins() function gives us the row and column totals:

```
> addmargins(table(hosp.ins))
```

```
            insurance
hospital  insured uninsured    Sum
  A.public      50        80    130
  B.private     40        30     70
  Sum           90       110    200
```

We can calculate conditional probabilities with the prop.table() function:

```
> round(prop.table(table(hosp.ins),1),3) # by row; conditional upon
hospital
```

```
            insurance
hospital  insured uninsured
  A.public   0.385     0.615
  B.private  0.571     0.429
```

In this example, prop.table() takes two arguments. First, it takes data (our table). Second, the "1" argument tells R to calculate the conditional probability for the row. In this case, the rows represent hospital type. For example, what is the probability of selecting a woman who is uninsured, given (conditional upon) she gave birth in a public hospital? In this example, we need to know a probability, conditional upon hospital type. In this case, hospital type is represented by the rows in the table, so we have to tell R to make the calculations based on rows. If we look at the table, the answer to this example is 61.5% (look at the row for public hospital, and the column for uninsured). When we computed this by hand, our answer was 62%, so our results converge (there are minor differences due to rounding).

If we wanted to know conditional probabilities based on columns instead of rows, we would use the same code, but would use the argument of "2" instead of "1" to specify this:

```
> round(prop.table(table(hosp.ins),2),3) # by column; conditional upon
insurance
```

```
            insurance
hospital  insured uninsured
  A.public   0.556     0.727
  B.private  0.444     0.273
```

# 6.8 R IN FOCUS

## Converting Raw Scores to Standard *z* Scores

Privitera's *Statisics for the Behavioral Sciences,* Third Edition (p. 193)

R can be used to compute a *z* transformation for a given dataset. To demonstrate how R computes *z* scores, suppose you evaluate the effectiveness of an SAT remedial tutoring course with 16 students who plan to retake the standardized exam. Table 6.2 lists the number of points that each student gained on the exam after taking the remedial course. We will use R to convert these data into *z* scores.

Table 6.2 The Number of Points Gained on the SAT Exam After Taking a Remedial Course (for 16 students)

| | | | |
|---|---|---|---|
| +500 | +950 | +780 | +800 |
| +750 | +880 | +800 | +680 |
| +600 | +990 | +800 | +550 |
| +900 | +560 | +450 | +600 |

To create *z* scores, we can use the scale() function. In addition to the data argument, the function takes two other arguments, which both have to be set to TRUE:

```
> SAT <- data.frame(SAT=c(500,750,600,900,950,880,990,560,780,800,
+ 800,450,800,680,550,600))

> scale(SAT$SAT,center=T, scale=T)
        [,1]
 [1,] -1.3515688
 [2,]  0.1543574
 [3,] -0.7491983
 [4,]  1.0579131
 [5,]  1.3590984
 [6,]  0.9374391
 [7,]  1.6000466
```

```
 [8,]  -0.9901465

 [9,]   0.3350686

[10,]   0.4555427

[11,]   0.4555427

[12,]  -1.6527540

[13,]   0.4555427

[14,]  -0.2673019

[15,]  -1.0503835

[16,]  -0.7491983
```

To have a better understanding of what these arguments mean and why we set them to TRUE, let us look at the help menu:

```
> help(scale)
```

In the details section, we can see when center is set to TRUE, R subtracts the column's mean (the mean of our data) from each individual observation value. This is the equivalent to the calculation of the numerator for the $z$ scores formula. When scale is set to TRUE, R takes the centered values (that were just calculated) and divides them by the standard deviation of the data. This is the denominator for the $z$ scores formula. We can check to make sure this is what happens by doing the calculations "by hand" in R:

```
> SAT$SAT-mean(SAT$SAT) # numerator for z score
 [1] -224.375   25.625 -124.375   175.625 225.625 155.625   265.625 -164.375

 [9]   55.625   75.625   75.625 -274.375   75.625 -44.375 -174.375 -124.375

> scale(SAT$SAT, center=T, scale=F) #equivalent to the numerator for z
score

       [,1]

 [1,] -224.375

 [2,]   25.625

 [3,] -124.375

 [4,]   175.625

 [5,]   225.625

 [6,]   155.625
```

```
 [7,]   265.625
 [8,]  -164.375
 [9,]    55.625
[10,]    75.625
[11,]    75.625
[12,]  -274.375
[13,]    75.625
[14,]   -44.375
[15,]  -174.375
[16,]  -124.375
```

We see these results converge.

```
> (SAT$SAT-mean(SAT$SAT))/sd(SAT$SAT)
 [1] -1.3515688  0.1543574 -0.7491983  1.0579131 1.3590984  0.9374391
 [7]  1.6000466 -0.9901465  0.3350686  0.4555427 0.4555427 -1.6527540
[13]  0.4555427 -0.2673019 -1.0503835 -0.7491983
```

This last step is equal to setting both the scale and center arguments to TRUE, and we see our results converge. It is good to check your work from time to time in R, if possible, to make sure you understand what the arguments mean and how they work. These simple checks also reinforce your understanding of the material.

## Estimating the Standard Error of the Mean

Privitera's *Statisics for the Behavioral Sciences,* Third Edition (p. 227)

Researchers rarely know the value of the population standard deviation, which is in the numerator of the formula for standard error. It is more common to estimate the standard error by substituting the sample standard deviation in place of the population standard deviation in the formula for standard error. The formula, which is discussed further in Chapter 9, is as follows:

$$s_M = \frac{s}{\sqrt{n}}.$$

To illustrate, suppose we measure the individual reaction times (in seconds) for a team of 10 firefighters to respond to an emergency call. The reaction times are 93, 66, 30, 44, 20, 100, 35, 58, 70, and 81. We can use the describe() function in R in the psych package to find the standard error:

```
> e.call <- data.frame(reaction=c(93,66,30,44,20,100,35,58,70,81))

> library(psych)

> describe(e.call) # last output, "se"
         vars  n mean    sd median trimmed  mad min max range skew kurtosis
reaction    1 10 59.7 27.18     62   59.62 34.1  20 100    80 0.03    -1.57
            se
reaction 8.6
```

The R output above gives the value for the standard error as 8.6 (see the last output, se). We can double-check that the value of the standard error is correct because the R output also gives us the value of the sample standard deviation and sample size. When we enter these values into the formula for standard error, we obtain the same result from R (differences due to rounding, of course):

```
> 27.18/sqrt(10) # sample sd divided by the square root of sample size
[1] 8.595071
```

# 9.6 R IN FOCUS

## One-Sample *t* Test

Privitera's *Statisics for the Behavioral Sciences,* Third Edition (p. 286)

R can be used to compute the one-sample *t* test. To illustrate how to compute this test in R and how the R output matches with the data we computed by hand, let us compute this test using the same data given for Example 9.1 in Table 9.3. For reference, the social functioning scores in the sample of 18 relatives who care for patients with OCD were 20, 60, 48, 92, 50, 82, 48, 90, 30, 68, 43, 54, 60, 62, 94, 67, 63, and 85. We will compare these scores to the mean in the general healthy population ($\mu$ = 77.43) using a .05 level of significance ($\alpha$ = .05).

The t.test() function in R can be used for several *t* tests. The function takes several arguments, so use the help() function to see what options you have:

```
> help(t.test)
```

The t.test() function requires the data. For a one-sample *t* test, we have to specify the mean of the general healthy population. We can also specify the level of significance. Note, however, that the .05 value is the default. We can specify it for practice, though:

```
> OCD <- data.frame(SF.Score=c(20,60,48,92,50,82,48,90,30,68,
+ 43,54,60,62,94,67,63,85))

> t.test(OCD$SF.Score,mu=77.43, conf.level=.95)

        One Sample t-test

data: OCD$SF.Score
t = -3.1259, df = 17, p-value = 0.006153
alternative hypothesis: true mean is not equal to 77.43
95 percent confidence interval:
 51.58554 72.41446
sample estimates:
mean of x
      62
```

The results give us the *t* value, *df* ($n - 1 = 18 - 1 = 17$), *p* value, the confidence interval (confidence intervals will be described in Chapter 11), and the mean of the sample.

Note we can compute the effect size for the *t* test because we have or can get all the information needed to do so. For example, to estimate Cohen's *d*, we can calculate the mean difference because we have the comparison value (77.43), and the output gives us the sample mean (62):

```
> 62-77.43

[1] -15.43
```

We previously learned how to calculate the standard deviation, which is the denominator:

```
> library(psych)

> describe(OCD$SF.Score)

   vars  n mean    sd median trimmed   mad min max range  skew kurtosis   se
X1    1 18   62 20.94     61   62.62 19.27  20  94    74 -0.12    -0.89 4.94

> round((62-77.43)/20.94,3)

[1] -0.737
```

These results converge with those we did by hand.

When we run a *t* test, we can find out the structure of the output with the str() function. First, we need to give our analysis a name:

```
> output<-t.test(OCD$SF.Score,mu=77.43, conf.level=.95)

> str(output)

List of 9
 $ statistic : Named num -3.13
 ..- attr(*, "names")= chr "t"
 $ parameter : Named num 17
 ..- attr(*, "names")= chr "df"
 $ p.value   : num 0.00615
 $ conf.int  : atomic [1:2] 51.6 72.4
 ..- attr(*, "conf.level")= num 0.95
 $ estimate  : Named num 62
 ..- attr(*, "names")= chr "mean of x"
 $ null.value : Named num 77.4
 ..- attr(*, "names")= chr "mean"
 $ alternative: chr "two.sided"
 $ method    : chr "One Sample t-test"
 $ data.name : chr "OCD$SF.Score"
 - attr(*, "class")= chr "htest"
```

Instead of typing numbers into formulas in R (which can lead to errors!), we can specify to R exactly what values we want in order to avoid such errors. We do this by using the $ function we learned about in the introduction section. For example, to get the *t* value:

```
> output$statistic # gives us t value, -3.1259
        t
-3.12589
```

Now, to calculate eta-squared, we can plug the values into the formula using this notation:

```
> output$statistic^2/(output$statistic^2+output$parameter)
0.364989
```

Note our results converge with those we calculated by hand. Try calculating omega-squared on your own. The formulas are restated here:

$$\text{Estimated Cohen's } d = \frac{\text{Mean Difference}}{\text{Std. Deviation}}.$$

$$\text{Proportion of variance } \eta^2 = \frac{(t)^2}{(t)^2 + df}.$$

$$\omega^2 = \frac{(t)^2 - 1}{(t)^2 + df}.$$

# 9.9 R IN FOCUS

## Two-Independent-Sample *t* Test

Privitera's *Statisics for the Behavioral Sciences,* Third Edition (p. 297)

R can be used to compute the two-independent-sample *t* test. To illustrate how to compute this test in R and how the output matches with the data we computed by hand, let us compute this test using the same data originally given for Example 9.2 in Table 9.7. For reference, Table 9.11 restates the original data for this example, which we will enter into R. We will compare these data between groups using a .05 level of significance ($\alpha$ = .05).

**Table 9.11**   The Number of Calories Consumed in a Meal Between Groups Asked to Eat Slowly or Fast

| Group Eating Slowly | Group Eating Fast |
|---------------------|-------------------|
| 700 | 450 |
| 450 | 800 |
| 850 | 750 |
| 600 | 700 |
| 450 | 550 |
| 550 | 650 |

These data for Example 9.2 are restated here from data originally given in Table 9.7.

To compute a two-independent-sample *t* test, we can again use the t.test() function. There are two ways we can enter the data. First, we can re-create Table 9.11, or we can put all values in one column, and in a separate column specify to which group the values belong. Either way is fine, but it will influence how we use the t.test() function:

```
> calories<-data.frame(Speed=c(rep("Slow",6),rep("Fast",6)),

+ Calories=c(700,450,850,600,450,550,

+ 450,800,750,700,550,650))

> calories

  Speed Calories

1 Slow      700

2 Slow      450

3 Slow      850
```

```
4   Slow        600

5   Slow        450

6   Slow        550

7   Fast        450

8   Fast        800

9   Fast        750

10  Fast        700

11  Fast        550

12  Fast        650
```

```
> t.test(calories$Calories~calories$Speed, var.equal=T)

        Two Sample t-test

data: calories$Calories by calories$Speed

t = 0.60486, df = 10, p-value = 0.5587

alternative hypothesis: true difference in means is not equal to 0

95 percent confidence interval:

 -134.1868 234.1868

sample estimates:

mean in group Fast mean in group Slow

                650                600
```

In this example, we have to use the tilde symbol (~) to tell R to conduct the *t* test, where the two conditions are specified in the "Speed" column. We are also assuming equal variances, so we need to tell R this. This is important because the default in R is set to false. We can also specify the alpha value, but the default is the value we want, so we do not have to include this argument in our code. Alternatively, we can enter our data as in Table 9.11:

```
> calories.2<-data.frame(Slow=c(700,450,850,600,450,550),

+ Fast=c(450,800,750,700,550,650))

> calories.2

 Slow Fast

1 700  450
```

```
2 450   800

3 850   750

4 600   700

5 450   550

6 550   650

> t.test(calories.2$Slow,calories.2$Fast,var.equal=T)

        Two Sample t-test

data: calories.2$Slow and calories.2$Fast

t = -0.60486, df = 10, p-value = 0.5587

alternative hypothesis: true difference in means is not equal to 0

95 percent confidence interval:

 -234.1868 134.1868

sample estimates:

mean of x mean of y

      600       650
```

Notice the code is the same, except now we separate the two groups with a comma (,). This is our way of telling R that both columns are numeric. In the previous example, we entered our data such that only one column was numeric. However, both ways give us the same results. The output includes the test statistic ($t$ value), the degrees of freedom, the $p$ value, the confidence intervals (to be discussed in Chapter 11), and the mean values for both groups. Again, though the effect size is not given, we can use these data and get the other information we need to compute it.

## 10.4 R IN FOCUS

### The Related-Samples *t* Test

Privitera's *Statistics for the Behavioral Sciences,* Third Edition (p. 317)

In Example 10.1, we tested whether teacher supervision influences the time it takes elementary school children to read. We used a two-tailed test at a .05 level of significance and decided to reject the null hypothesis. Thus, we concluded that elementary school children spent significantly more time reading in the presence of a teacher than when the teacher was absent, $t(7) = 2.804$, $p < .05$. We can confirm this result using R, using the t.test() function:

```
> supervision<-data.frame(present=c(220,245,215,260,300,280,250,310),
+ absent=c(210,220,195,265,275,290,220,285))

> supervision
```

|   | present | absent |
|---|---------|--------|
| 1 | 220     | 210    |
| 2 | 245     | 220    |
| 3 | 215     | 195    |
| 4 | 260     | 265    |
| 5 | 300     | 275    |
| 6 | 280     | 290    |
| 7 | 250     | 220    |
| 8 | 310     | 285    |

```
> t.test(supervision$present,supervision$absent,var.equal=F,paired=T)

        Paired t-test
data: supervision$present and supervision$absent
t = 2.8062, df = 7, p-value = 0.02629
alternative hypothesis: true difference in means is not equal to 0
95 percent confidence interval:
 2.360552 27.639448
sample estimates:
mean of the differences
```

15

Again, we use similar arguments, except now we have to tell R that the two samples are not independent; they are paired. Thus, the "paired" argument has to be set to TRUE, as the default is FALSE. Note that in R you can write "T" or "TRUE." R understands both.

Notice that the calculations we made match the results from the output. Also, note that R gives the confidence intervals for this test (confidence intervals are described in Chapter 11).

# 11.5 R IN FOCUS

## Confidence Intervals for the One-Sample *t* Test

Privitera's *Statisics for the Behavioral Sciences,* Third Edition (p. 347)

In Chapter 9, we computed a one-sample *t* test using R for the data given in Example 11.2. The R output lists the 95% confidence interval for the outcome we observed. To change the confidence interval, use the conf.level argument of the t.test() function to choose any level of confidence. By default, R gives a 95% confidence interval with the *t* test. Let us compare these results to those with a 90% confidence interval:

```
> OCD <- data.frame(SF.Score=c(20,60,48,92,50,82,48,90,30,68,
+ 43,54,60,62,94,67,63,85))
> conf.95<-t.test(OCD$SF.Score,mu=77.43, conf.level=.95)
> conf.90<-t.test(OCD$SF.Score,mu=77.43, conf.level=.90)

> conf.95$conf.int
[1] 51.58554 72.41446
attr(,"conf.level")
[1] 0.95
> conf.90$conf.int
[1] 53.41296 70.58704
attr(,"conf.level")
[1] 0.9
```

In this example, we see that our confidence interval is wider at the 95% level:

```
> 72.41446-51.58554 # 95% confidence interval
[1] 20.82892
> 70.58704-53.41296 # 90% confidence interval
[1] 17.17408
```

This makes sense, intuitively, because if we want to be more confident (95% versus 90%) that the actual population mean is between two values, we should make the range of possible values for the mean larger! Clearly, the difference in our 95% confidence level range is larger (20.83, rounded) than that of the 90% confidence level (17.17, rounded).

# 11.7 R IN FOCUS

## Confidence Intervals for the Two-Independent-Sample *t* Test

Privitera's *Statisics for the Behavioral Sciences,* Third Edition (p. 350)

In Chapter 9, we computed a two-independent-sample *t* test using R for the data given in Example 11.3. The R output lists the 95% confidence interval for the mean difference between the groups:

```
> calories<-data.frame(Speed=c(rep("Slow",6),rep("Fast",6)),
+ Calories=c(700,450,850,600,450,550,
+ 450,800,750,700,550,650))
> t.test(calories$Calories~calories$Speed, var.equal=T)

        Two Sample t-test
data: calories$Calories by calories$Speed
t = 0.60486, df = 10, p-value = 0.5587
alternative hypothesis: true difference in means is not equal to 0
95 percent confidence interval:
 -134.1868 234.1868
sample estimates:
mean in group Fast mean in group Slow
              650                600
```

Using these 95% confidence limits, we conclude that it is likely that there is no difference in calories consumed between groups instructed to eat slowly or fast because zero falls within the interval (−134.19 to 234.19, rounded).

### Confidence Intervals for the Related-Samples *t* Test

Privitera's *Statisics for the Behavioral Sciences,* Third Edition (p. 353)

In Chapter 10, we computed a related-samples *t* test using R for the data given in Example 11.4. The R output lists the 95% confidence interval for the mean difference in time spent talking:

```
> supervision<-data.frame(present=c(220,245,215,260,300,280,250,310),
+ absent=c(210,220,195,265,275,290,220,285))
> t.test(supervision$present,supervison$absent,var.equal=F,paired=T)
        Paired t-test

data:  supervision$present and supervision$absent
t = 2.8062, df = 7, p-value = 0.02629
alternative hypothesis: true difference in means is not equal to 0
95 percent confidence interval:
 2.360552 27.639448
sample estimates:
mean of the differences
                 15
```

We can determine the effect size of the confidence interval using the confidence limits given in the R output. The lower and upper confidence limits in the R output match those we already computed, give or take rounding.

# 12.8 R IN FOCUS

## The One-Way Between-Subjects ANOVA

Privitera's *Statisics for the Behavioral Sciences,* Third Edition (p. 389)

There are two ways for computing a one-way between-subjects ANOVA using R—the One-Way ANOVA and the GLM Univariate approach. We will use both to analyze Example 12.1. Using the data given in Table 12.10, which is reproduced from data originally given in Table 12.4, we will confirm our conclusion.

Table 12.10   Data for Example 12.1

| Perceived Stress Level of Workplace | | |
|---|---|---|
| Low | Moderate | High |
| 3.4 | 3.5 | 2.9 |
| 3.2 | 3.6 | 3.0 |
| 3.0 | 2.7 | 2.6 |
| 3.0 | 3.5 | 3.3 |
| 3.5 | 3.8 | 3.7 |
| 3.8 | 2.9 | 2.7 |
| 3.6 | 3.4 | 2.4 |
| 4.0 | 3.2 | 2.5 |
| 3.9 | 3.3 | 3.3 |
| 2.9 | 3.1 | 3.4 |

First, let us use the One-Way ANOVA approach using the aov() function (**Analysis of Variance**):

```
> stress<-data.frame(stress=c(rep("Low",10),rep("Moderate",10),

+ rep("High",10)), score=c(3.4,3.2,3.0,3.0,3.5,

+ 3.8,3.6,4.0,3.9,2.9,

+ 3.5,3.6,2.7,3.5,3.8,

+ 2.9,3.4,3.2,3.3,3.1,

+ 2.9,3.0,2.6,3.3,3.7,
```

```
+ 2.7,2.4,2.5,3.3,3.4))

> head(stress)

  stress score

1  Low    3.4

2  Low    3.2

3  Low    3.0

4  Low    3.0

5  Low    3.5

6  Low    3.8

> stress.a <-aov(score~stress, data=stress)
```

The aov() function is pretty simple. We first give R our dependent variable (score), and then the independent variable (stress level). In this case, we did not have to type "stress$score" to tell R that the score data come from the stress dataframe. Instead, we told R that all data come from the stress dataframe by using the "data" argument. Note you can do this with other functions, too. In fact, you can use both approaches and R will understand.

To get the R output for the One-Way ANOVA:

```
> stress.a

Call:

  aov(formula = score ~ stress, data = stress)


Terms:

                  stress Residuals

Sum of Squares  1.072667   4.117000

Deg. of Freedom        2         27


Residual standard error: 0.3904888

Estimated effects may be unbalanced
```

Our results give us some information, but not everything we need. To get more information about the results, use the summary() function:

```
> summary(stress.a)
```

```
           Df  Sum Sq   Mean Sq F value    Pr(>F)
stress      2   1.073    0.5363    3.517 0.0439 *
Residuals  27   4.117    0.1525
---
Signif. codes:  0 '***' 0.001 '**' 0.01 '*' 0.05 '.' 0.1 ' ' 1
```

The output now shows us the degrees of freedom, sum of squares, mean squares, our test statistic (F value), and the p value. In this example, we see that p is less than .05, so we can conclude that there is a statistically significant difference between the groups. However, where exactly are the differences? In order to find out which groups statistically differ from one another, we need post hoc analyses. There are several types, but we can illustrate a post hoc analysis with Tukey's HSD (Honestly Significant Difference) test:

```
> TukeyHSD(stress.a)

 Tukey multiple comparisons of means

  95% family-wise confidence level

Fit: aov(formula = score ~ stress, data = stress)

$stress
                diff         lwr       upr     p adj
Low-High        0.45  0.01701461 0.8829854 0.0404540
Moderate-High   0.32 -0.11298539 0.7529854 0.1782828
Moderate-Low   -0.13 -0.56298539 0.3029854 0.7395178
```

Each row represents a comparison between two groups, and the results tell us three things. First, we get the mean differences between groups (diff column). Second, we get the lower and upper confidence levels. Finally, we get the p value. Notice that the only statistically significant difference is between the low and high groups: The p value is less than .05, and the confidence interval does not include zero.

When running ANOVAs, certain assumptions must be met. One assumption that has to be met is equal variances across groups. Let us look at the group variances:

```
> library(psych)

> by(stress$score, stress$stress, describe)

stress$stress: High
```

| | vars | n | mean | sd | median | trimmed | mad | min | max | range | skew | kurtosis | se |
|---|---|---|---|---|---|---|---|---|---|---|---|---|---|
| X1 | 1 | 10 | 2.98 | 0.43 | 2.95 | 2.96 | 0.52 | 2.4 | 3.7 | 1.3 | 0.16 | −1.55 | 0.14 |

```
-----------------------------------------------------------------
```

```
stress$stress: Low
```

| | vars | n | mean | sd | median | trimmed | mad | min | max | range | skew | kurtosis | se |
|---|---|---|---|---|---|---|---|---|---|---|---|---|---|
| X1 | 1 | 10 | 3.43 | 0.4 | 3.45 | 3.42 | 0.59 | 2.9 | 4 | 1.1 | 0.04 | -1.7 | 0.13 |

```
-------------------------------------------------------
```

```
stress$stress: Moderate
```

| | vars | n | mean | sd | median | trimmed | mad | min | max | range | skew | kurtosis | se |
|---|---|---|---|---|---|---|---|---|---|---|---|---|---|
| X1 | 1 | 10 | 3.3 | 0.33 | 3.35 | 3.31 | 0.3 | 2.7 | 3.8 | 1.1 | -0.32 | -1.13 | 0.11 |

The by() function tells R to use the describe() function (the last argument) for the score values in the stress dataframe (the first argument, stress$score). The second argument (stress$stress) tells R to use the describe() function for the score values *for each stress group*. The output above illustrates this. We see the describe() function output for each stress group (High, Low, Moderate) for the stress scores. In order to calculate the variance, we can square the standard deviation scores:

```
> .43^2 #High

[1] 0.1849

> .4^2 #Low

[1] 0.16

> .33^2 #Moderate

[1] 0.1089
```

We can also directly ask R to compute the variance score using the by() function we just learned!

```
> round(by(stress$score, stress$stress, var),4)

stress$stress: High

[1] 0.1884

-----------------------------------------------------------

stress$stress: Low

[1] 0.1579

-----------------------------------------------------------

stress$stress: Moderate

[1] 0.1111
```

Notice the results converge, with minor differences due to rounding. By looking at these values, do you think there are equal variances across groups? Statistical analyses help us answer these types of questions; statistics takes the subjectivity out of making decisions and tries to make things more objective and consistent for research. Therefore, let us use a statistical test, called the Levene test, to see if there are equal variances across groups. To do this, we need to install the lawstat package:

```
> install.packages("lawstat")

> library(lawstat)

> levene.test(stress$score, stress$stress)

        modified robust Brown-Forsythe Levene-type test based on the

        absolute deviations from the median

data: stress$score

Test Statistic = 0.64991, p-value = 0.5301
```

The test function takes two arguments. The first argument is the scores for each condition, and the second argument is the group label. The function also takes other arguments that you can change. For example, the default is to run this analysis based on the median (see the description in the output), because it is supposed to be more robust (stronger) compared to other approaches. However, you could change the default to run the analysis based on the mean by using this argument: center=mean.

The results are not significant ($p$ is greater than .05), which tells us that the variances across groups are *not* statistically different from one another. Therefore, we are not violating the equal variances assumption and we can safely use the One-Way ANOVA aov() function in R. If, however, the Levene test was significant, we would have to account for unequal variances in our One-Way ANOVA by using the one.way() function in R:

```
> oneway.test(score~stress, data=stress)

        One-way analysis of means (not assuming equal variances)

data: score and stress

F = 2.9559, num df = 2.000, denom df = 17.773, p-value = 0.07794
```

Results now tell us that there are no significant differences between the groups. Thus, it is important to make sure you are checking assumptions and using the correct tests. If not, you could make mistakes in your conclusions!

Something to be aware of is that R packages can sometimes "interfere" with other packages. For example, run the by() function we ran earlier and compare the output:

```
> by(stress$score, stress$stress, describe)

stress$stress: High
```

```
dd[x, ]

     n missing unique  Info  Mean
    10        0      9  0.99  2.98

          2.4 2.5 2.6 2.7 2.9   3 3.3 3.4 3.7
Frequency   1   1   1   1   1   1   2   1   1
%            10  10  10  10  10 10  20  10  10
----------------------------------------------------------
stress$stress: Low

dd[x, ]

     n missing unique  Info  Mean
    10        0      9  0.99  3.43

          2.9   3 3.2 3.4 3.5 3.6 3.8 3.9   4
Frequency   1   2   1   1   1   1   1   1   1
%            10  20  10  10  10  10  10  10 10
----------------------------------------------------------
stress$stress: Moderate

dd[x, ]

     n missing unique  Info  Mean
    10        0      9  0.99   3.3

          2.7 2.9 3.1 3.2 3.3 3.4 3.5 3.6 3.8
Frequency   1   1   1   1   1   1   2   1   1
%            10  10  10  10  10  10  20  10  10
```

That output is different from the output we got before we loaded the lawstat package! Be aware that this may happen. To find out what packages are running in your current session, use the search() function:

```
> search()
  [1]       ".GlobalEnv" "package:lawstat"        "package:VGAM"
  [4]  "package:splines"   "package:stats4"    "package:mvtnorm"
  [7]  "package:Kendall"    "package:Hmisc"    "package:Formula"
 [10] "package:survival"  "package:lattice"   "package:ggplot2"
```

```
[13]      "package:psych"      "tools:rstudio"    "package:stats"
[16]  "package:graphics" "package:grDevices"   "package:utils"
[19]  "package:datasets"   "package:methods"       "Autoloads"
[22]      "package:base"
```

To remove the lawstat package from your current working environment, use the detach() function:

```
> detach(package:lawstat)

> search()
 [1]        ".GlobalEnv"      "package:VGAM"    "package:splines"
 [4]    "package:stats4"   "package:mvtnorm"   "package:Kendall"
 [7]     "package:Hmisc"   "package:Formula"  "package:survival"
[10]   "package:lattice"   "package:ggplot2"     "package:psych"
[13]     "tools:rstudio"     "package:stats"  "package:graphics"
[16]  "package:grDevices"     "package:utils"  "package:datasets"
[19]   "package:methods"         "Autoloads"      "package:base"
```

Notice that the lawstat package is now gone. Do this for all the other packages that come before the psych package (e.g., VGAM, splines, stats4 . . . ). Once you have done that, now try running the by() function:

```
> by(stress$score, stress$stress, describe)
stress$stress: High
   vars  n mean   sd median trimmed  mad min max range skew kurtosis   se
X1    1 10 2.98 0.43   2.95    2.96 0.52 2.4 3.7   1.3 0.16    -1.55 0.14
-----------------------------------------------------------
stress$stress: Low
   vars  n mean   sd median trimmed  mad min max range skew kurtosis   se
X1    1 10 3.43  0.4   3.45    3.42 0.59 2.9   4   1.1 0.04     -1.7 0.13
-----------------------------------------------------------
stress$stress: Moderate
   vars  n mean   sd median trimmed mad min max range  skew kurtosis   se
X1    1 10  3.3 0.33   3.35    3.31 0.3 2.7 3.8   1.1 -0.32    -1.13 0.11
```

Problem solved!

Finally, remember one of R's strengths is its visual and graphic abilities. We can visualize our data to inspect for equal variances using the plot() function:

```
> par(mfrow=c(2,2))

> plot(stress.a)
```

The par() function sets up our Plot window so that we can see all four plot outputs from the plot() function in one window rather than four (note: we only show the plot in the upper left corner for illustrative purposes). When observing variances across groups, the figure shown in Figure 12.1 is most useful. It shows the points on the plot across the three groups are fairly similar, which converges with the Levene test results.

**Figure 12.1**   Plot() Function to Inspect Equal Variances Across Groups

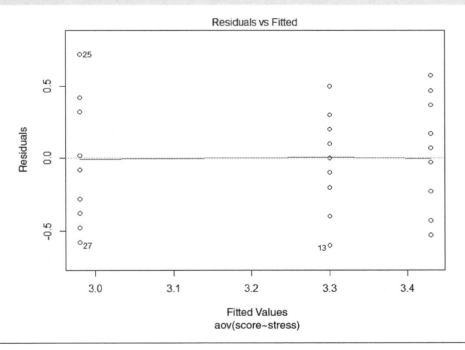

The second approach to conducting a one-way between-subjects ANOVA using R is by using the anova() function and lm() function (linear model):

```
> stress.lm<-lm(stress$score~stress$stress)

> summary(stress.lm)

Call:
```

```
lm(formula = stress$score ~ stress$stress)

Residuals:
   Min     1Q   Median    3Q    Max
-0.600 -0.355   0.010 0.315 0.720

Coefficients:
                      Estimate Std. Error t value   Pr(>|t|)
(Intercept)             2.9800     0.1235  24.133    <2e-16 ***
stress$stressLow        0.4500     0.1746   2.577    0.0158 *
stress$stressModerate   0.3200     0.1746   1.832    0.0779 .
---
Signif. codes:  0 '***' 0.001 '**' 0.01 '*' 0.05 '.' 0.1 ' ' 1

Residual standard error: 0.3905 on 27 degrees of freedom
Multiple R-squared: 0.2067,     Adjusted R-squared: 0.1479
F-statistic: 3.517 on 2 and 27 DF, p-value: 0.0439
```

The output suggests that there may be some differences between the Low group compared to the High group, and possibly between the Moderate group and the High group at the $p < .10$ level. Let us follow up by using the anova() function:

```
> stress.anova<-anova(stress.lm)

> stress.anova

Analysis of Variance Table

Response: stress$score
              Df Sum Sq Mean Sq F value Pr(>F)
stress$stress  2 1.0727 0.53633  3.5174 0.0439 *
Residuals     27 4.1170 0.15248
---
Signif. codes:  0 '***' 0.001 '**' 0.01 '*' 0.05 '.' 0.1 ' ' 1

> confint(stress.lm)
```

```
                           2.5 %    97.5 %

(Intercept)              2.72663301 3.233367

stress$stressLow         0.09168496 0.808315

stress$stressModerate   -0.03831504 0.678315
```

The ANOVA output confirms the differences, and the confint() function tells us that the Low versus High condition is significant (zero is not included in the confidence interval). However, the Moderate to High conditions are not significant, as zero is included in the confidence interval.

Finally, let us use one more visualization, the boxplot:

```
> par(mfrow=c(1,1))

> boxplot(stress$score~stress$stress)
```

We can clearly see in Figure 12.2 that the largest difference is between the High versus Low group, and there is possibly a difference between the High versus Moderate group. However, the overall data between the High and Moderate groups overlap a lot more than the data between the High and Low groups.

**Figure 12.2   Boxplots of Data**

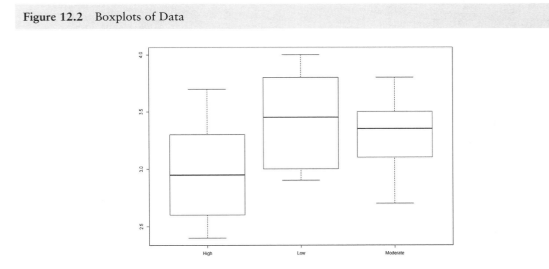

The boxplot shows (from the bottom line to the top) the minimum value, the first quartile, the median, the third quartile, and the maximum value. This helps us visualize the data and differences between groups.

In Example 13.1, we concluded that ratings of effectiveness for the three advertisements significantly varied, $F(2, 12) = 17.38$, $p < .05$. A Bonferroni procedure showed that participants rated the effectiveness of an ad with smoking-related cues higher compared to an ad with no cues and compared to an ad with generic cues. We will use R to confirm the calculations we computed in Example 13.1.

First, we have to create our dataframe. However, our dataframe has to look different from the data table in Table 13.3. Instead, we have to have all data values in one column, and have two other columns to link those data values to both the subject (Person) and condition (Cues):

```
> ads <- data.frame(Person=c(rep(c("A","B","C","D","E","F","G"),3)),
+ Cues=c(rep("NoCues",7),rep("Generic",7),rep("Smoking",7)),
+ Values=c(2,3,1,4,4,5,2,5,5,4,5,3,4,2,5,6,5,7,6,7,6))
> ads
```

|    | Person | Cues    | Values |
|----|--------|---------|--------|
| 1  | A      | NoCues  | 2      |
| 2  | B      | NoCues  | 3      |
| 3  | C      | NoCues  | 1      |
| 4  | D      | NoCues  | 4      |
| 5  | E      | NoCues  | 4      |
| 6  | F      | NoCues  | 5      |
| 7  | G      | NoCues  | 2      |
| 8  | A      | Generic | 5      |
| 9  | B      | Generic | 5      |
| 10 | C      | Generic | 4      |
| 11 | D      | Generic | 5      |
| 12 | E      | Generic | 3      |
| 13 | F      | Generic | 4      |
| 14 | G      | Generic | 2      |
| 15 | A      | Smoking | 5      |

```
16          B Smoking        6

17          C Smoking        5

18          D Smoking        7

19          E Smoking        6

20          F Smoking        7

21          G Smoking        6
```

We can use the tapply() function to calculate both the means and standard deviations of the data scores (Values) for the different conditions (Cues):

```
> tapply(ads$Values,ads$Cues,mean)

Generic NoCues Smoking

      4      3       6

> tapply(ads$Values,ads$Cues,sd)

  Generic    NoCues   Smoking

1.1547005 1.4142136 0.8164966
```

We see the means are different and the standard deviations are not large, but we need to figure out if these mean differences are statistically significant with the analysis of variance function. Similar to a one-way between-subjects ANOVA (12.8 R in Focus), we use the aov() function and save the model output as an object. However, there is one difference. With the within-subjects ANOVA, we have to account for the additional error source (between-subjects, or between-persons). Thus, the code for the within-subjects ANOVA is the same as the between-subjects ANOVA, except the former has the additional error source added to the code:

```
> aov.ads<-aov(Values~Cues+Error(Person),data=ads)

> summary(aov.ads)

Error: Person

          Df Sum Sq Mean Sq F value Pr(>F)

Residuals  6  12.67   2.111

Error: Within

          Df Sum Sq Mean Sq F value   Pr(>F)

Cues       2  32.67  16.333   17.29 0.000292 ***

Residuals 12  11.33   0.944

---

Signif. codes: 0 '***' 0.001 '**' 0.01 '*' 0.05 '.' 0.1 ' ' 1
```

Our results converge with those we calculated by hand. The $F$ statistic is 17.29 and the $p$ value is less than .05. Next, we need to find out which group means are different statistically. In other words, we want to compare the mean of the No Cues group to the mean of the Generic Cues group, and the mean of the No Cues group to the mean of the Smoking-Related Cues group, and so on. The pairwise.t.test() function allows us to do this. The function does different post hoc tests, but we can use the Bonferroni procedure by specifying this in the p.adjust="bonf" argument. Specifically, we ask to find the differences in the means of the different groups (Cues) for the data observations (Values). Remember, this is a within-subjects design, so our data observations are not completely independent (think of independent versus related $t$ tests). Therefore, we have to specify paired tests with the paired=T argument:

```
> pairwise.t.test(ads$Values, ads$Cues, p.adjust="bonf", paired=T)

        Pairwise comparisons using paired t tests

data: ads$Values and ads$Cues

        Generic NoCues

NoCues  0.5325 -

Smoking 0.0288 0.0002

    P value adjustment method: bonferroni
```

The R output gives us $p$ values for the different group comparisons. The means of the Generic and No Cues groups are not statistically different from one another. However, the means of the Generic versus Smoking-related groups are statistically different from one another, as are the means of the Smoking-related and No Cues groups.

# 14.8 R IN FOCUS

## The Two-Way Between-Subjects ANOVA

Privitera's *Statisics for the Behavioral Sciences,* Third Edition (p. 474)

In Example 14.1, we tested whether levels of exposure to sugars interfered with the time it took participants to complete a computer task in the presence or absence of a buffet of sugary foods. We concluded that participants with more exposure to sugars took longer to complete the computer task when the buffet of sugary foods was present. Using the same data as in Example 14.1, we will use R to confirm the calculations that we computed for these data.

First, create the dataframe:

```
> sugars <- data.frame(buffet=c(rep("Absent",18),rep("Present",18)),
+ exposure=c(rep("Low",6),rep("Mod",6),rep("High",6),
+ rep("Low",6),rep("Mod",6),rep("High",6)),
+ times=c(8,7,9,10,12,8,10,12,15,8,6,9,
+ 13,9,11,8,13,12,5,8,5,6,5,7,
+ 15,10,8,9,7,11,15,12,15,16,12,14))
> sugars
```

```
   buffet exposure times

1  Absent      Low     8

2  Absent      Low     7

3  Absent      Low     9

4  Absent      Low    10

5  Absent      Low    12

6  Absent      Low     8

7  Absent      Mod    10

8  Absent      Mod    12

9  Absent      Mod    15

10 Absent      Mod     8

11 Absent      Mod     6

12 Absent      Mod     9

13 Absent     High    13
```

| 14 | Absent | High | 9 |
| 15 | Absent | High | 11 |
| 16 | Absent | High | 8 |
| 17 | Absent | High | 13 |
| 18 | Absent | High | 12 |
| 19 | Present | Low | 5 |
| 20 | Present | Low | 8 |
| 21 | Present | Low | 5 |
| 22 | Present | Low | 6 |
| 23 | Present | Low | 5 |
| 24 | Present | Low | 7 |
| 25 | Present | Mod | 15 |
| 26 | Present | Mod | 10 |
| 27 | Present | Mod | 8 |
| 28 | Present | Mod | 9 |
| 29 | Present | Mod | 7 |
| 30 | Present | Mod | 11 |
| 31 | Present | High | 15 |
| 32 | Present | High | 12 |
| 33 | Present | High | 15 |
| 34 | Present | High | 16 |
| 35 | Present | High | 12 |
| 36 | Present | High | 14 |

To run the two-way between-subjects analysis of variance, we can build upon our code from our one-way between-subjects analysis of variance. The code is similar, except now we add the other factor and the interaction term:

```
> sugars.aov <- aov(times~buffet+exposure+buffet:exposure,
data=sugars)

> summary(sugars.aov)
```

```
              Df Sum Sq Mean Sq F value    Pr(>F)
buffet         1      0       0     0.0   1.00000
exposure       2    150      75    15.0 3.05e-05 ***
buffet:exposure 2     54      27     5.4 0.00993 **
Residuals     30    150       5
---
Signif. codes:  0 '***' 0.001 '**' 0.01 '*' 0.05 '.' 0.1 ' ' 1
```

Our results converge with those we calculated by hand. There are other ways we can run this analysis in R. A shortcut is by using the asterisk symbol (*) to tell R what two factors to include in the analysis:

```
> sugars.aov2 <- aov(times ~ buffet*exposure, data=sugars)

> summary(sugars.aov2)

              Df Sum Sq Mean Sq F value    Pr(>F)
buffet         1      0       0     0.0   1.00000
exposure       2    150      75    15.0 3.05e-05 ***
buffet:exposure 2     54      27     5.4 0.00993 **
Residuals     30    150       5
---
Signif. codes:  0 '***' 0.001 '**' 0.01 '*' 0.05 '.' 0.1 ' ' 1
```

Notice that the results are the same as those from the sugars.aov analysis. In Section 12.8 R in Focus, we discussed two approaches to ANOVAs. We can also use the linear model function in R to run the analysis:

```
> model <- lm(times ~ buffet + exposure + buffet:exposure,
data=sugars)

> anova(model)

Analysis of Variance Table

Response: times
              Df Sum Sq Mean Sq F value     Pr(>F)
buffet         1      0       0     0.0   1.000000
exposure       2    150      75    15.0 3.052e-05 ***
buffet:exposure 2     54      27     5.4 0.009929 **
```

```
Residuals        30    150       5

---

Signif. codes: 0 '***' 0.001 '**' 0.01 '*' 0.05 '.' 0.1 ' ' 1
```

Again, the results are the same! Next, we can use a post hoc analysis to determine where the differences are:

```
> TukeyHSD(sugars.aov)
 Tukey multiple comparisons of means
  95% family-wise confidence level

Fit: aov(formula = times ~ buffet + exposure + buffet:exposure, data =
sugars)

$buffet
                 diff      lwr     upr p adj
Present-Absent      0 -1.52222 1.52222     1

$exposure
           diff        lwr        upr       p adj
Low-High   -5.0 -7.2504745 -2.7495255 0.0000177
Mod-High   -2.5 -4.7504745 -0.2495255 0.0269833
Mod-Low     2.5  0.2495255  4.7504745 0.0269833

$'buffet:exposure'
                                  diff          lwr          upr       p adj
Present:High-Absent:High  3.000000e+00  -0.9266813    6.9266813 0.2161771
Absent:Low-Absent:High   -2.000000e+00  -5.9266813    1.9266813 0.6365316
Present:Low-Absent:High  -5.000000e+00  -8.9266813   -1.0733187 0.0065166
Absent:Mod-Absent:High   -1.000000e+00  -4.9266813    2.9266813 0.9697515
Present:Mod-Absent:High  -1.000000e+00  -4.9266813    2.9266813 0.9697515
Absent:Low-Present:High  -5.000000e+00  -8.9266813   -1.0733187 0.0065166
Present:Low-Present:High -8.000000e+00 -11.9266813   -4.0733187 0.0000112
Absent:Mod-Present:High  -4.000000e+00  -7.9266813   -0.0733187 0.0439185
Present:Mod-Present:High -4.000000e+00  -7.9266813   -0.0733187 0.0439185
```

```
Present:Low-Absent:Low   -3.000000e+00  -6.9266813  0.9266813  0.2161771

Absent:Mod-Absent:Low     1.000000e+00  -2.9266813  4.9266813  0.9697515

Present:Mod-Absent:Low    1.000000e+00  -2.9266813  4.9266813  0.9697515

Absent:Mod-Present:Low    4.000000e+00   0.0733187  7.9266813  0.0439185

Present:Mod-Present:Low   4.000000e+00   0.0733187  7.9266813  0.0439185

Present:Mod-Absent:Mod   -1.776357e-15  -3.9266813  3.9266813  1.0000000
```

Visualization for ANOVAs is important. Figures help your reader understand your data. An interaction plot is a great tool for viewing data. We can re-create Figure 14.4 in R:

```
> interaction.plot(sugars$exposure, sugars$buffet, sugars$times)
```

**Figure 14.1**   Interaction Plot Done Incorrectly

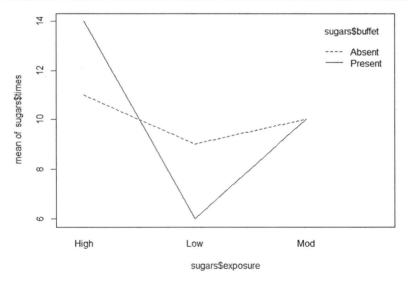

In addition to looking sloppy and unprofessional, this plot has problems with the *x*-axis. The exposure label is out of order and needs to be corrected.

In addition to being unprofessional, this plot is also incorrect. The sugar exposure conditions go from High to Low to Moderate. We need to change this order to *Low, Moderate, High*, which we can do with the factor() function:

```
>reorder <- factor(sugars$exposure, levels=levels(sugars$exposure)
[c(2,3,1)])
```

Once we have done this, we can use this reordering in the interaction.plot() function. We can also specify other arguments to relabel the *x*-axis and *y*-axis, to give the figure a title, and to change the *y*-axis limits:

```
> interaction.plot(reorder, sugars$buffet, sugars$times,
+ ylim=range(0,16),xlab="Exposure to Sugars",
+ ylab="Time to Complete Task (in seconds)",
+ col=c("red","blue"), main="Interaction Plot")
```

These are some quick, simple changes. Again, you can create many aesthetic plots in R using base R or other packages.

**Figure 14.2**   Interaction Plot With Corrections

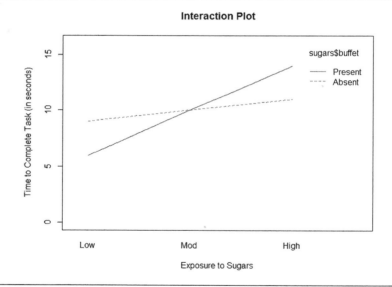

Compared to the plot in Figure 14.1, the plot in Figure 14.2 looks cleaner, and the *x*-axis labels have improved.

# 15.4 R IN FOCUS

## Pearson Correlation Coefficient

Privitera's *Statisics for the Behavioral Sciences,* Third Edition (p. 501)

In Example 15.1, we concluded that mood and eating were significantly correlated ($r = -.744$, $p < .05$) using the Pearson correlation coefficient. Let us confirm this conclusion using R by using the cor.test() function. The only argument we need for this analysis is the data. The defaults for this function are the Pearson method, a two-tailed test, and a .05 level of significance. We can specify them to see how the arguments could be changed, if we needed to:

```
> mood <- data.frame(Mood=c(6,4,7,4,2,5,3,1),
+ Eating=c(480,490,500,590,600,400,545,650))

> mood
  Mood Eating
1   6    480
2   4    490
3   7    500
4   4    590
5   2    600
6   5    400
7   3    545
8   1    650

> cor.test(mood$Mood,mood$Eating,method=c("pearson"),
+ alternative=c("two.sided"),conf.level=.95)

        Pearson's product-moment correlation

data: mood$Mood and mood$Eating
t = -2.7266, df = 6, p-value = 0.03434
alternative hypothesis: true correlation is not equal to 0
95 percent confidence interval:
 -0.9503792 -0.0824521
```

```
sample estimates:
      cor
-0.743903
```

The results converge with those we calculated by hand. In addition to getting the correlation value, R gives us the *t* value, the degrees of freedom, the *p* value, and the confidence intervals.

## 15.8 R IN FOCUS

### Spearman Correlation Coefficient

Privitera's *Statisics for the Behavioral Sciences,* Third Edition (p. 512)

In Example 15.2, we concluded that a significant correlation was evident between the order of ranks on each task ($r_s = .768$, $p < .05$) using the Spearman correlation coefficient. Let us confirm this conclusion using R. We will use the same cor.test() function as in Section 15.4 R in Focus, except we will change the method to Spearman:

```
> ranks <- data.frame(Food=c(1,1,3,4,5,6,7,8),
+ Water=c(1,3,2,6,4,7,8,5))

> ranks

Food Water

1  1     1

2  1     3

3  3     2

4  4     6

5  5     4

6  6     7

7  7     8

8  8     5

> cor.test(ranks$Food,ranks$Water,method=c("spearman"),
+ alternative=c("two.sided"),conf.level=.95) # ERROR!

        Spearman's rank correlation rho

data: ranks$Food and ranks$Water

S = 19.616, p-value = 0.02652

alternative hypothesis: true rho is not equal to 0

sample estimates:

      rho

0.7664808
```

```
Warning message:

In cor.test.default(ranks$Food, ranks$Water, method = c("spearman"), :
  Cannot compute exact p-value with ties
```

Note the warning. This is a warning to let you know that there are tied ranks, which the Spearman test does not always handle well. We can set the exact argument to FALSE, or there are other nonparametric tests that can be used, such as the Kendall tau rank correlation.

```
> cor.test(ranks$Food,ranks$Water,method=c("spearman"),
+ alternative=c("two.sided"),conf.level=.95,exact=F)
        Spearman's rank correlation rho
data: ranks$Food and ranks$Water
S = 19.616, p-value = 0.02652
alternative hypothesis: true rho is not equal to 0
sample estimates:
      rho
0.7664808

> cor.test(ranks$Food,ranks$Water,method=c("kendall"),
+ alternative=c("two.sided"),conf.level=.95)
        Kendall's rank correlation tau
data: ranks$Food and ranks$Water
z = 2.1195, p-value = 0.03405
alternative hypothesis: true tau is not equal to 0
sample estimates:
      tau
0.618284

Warning message:

In cor.test.default(ranks$Food, ranks$Water, method = c("kendall"), :
  Cannot compute exact p-value with ties
```

Note we again get the warning. Though the correlation (tau) value is not as strong, it is still significant. Again, it is important to consider your data and know the different types of analyses that can be used.

Regardless, the output from the Spearman method yielded similar results to those we computed by hand. The correlation value, rho, was .766 and the $p$ value was .027.

# 15.10 R IN FOCUS

## Point-Biserial Correlation Coefficient

Privitera's *Statisics for the Behavioral Sciences,* Third Edition (p. 517)

To compute a point-biserial correlation coefficient using R, we first code the dichotomous factor and then compute the Pearson correlation coefficient. The point-biserial correlation coefficient is derived mathematically from the Pearson correlation coefficient, so the value we obtain using R will be identical to that obtained for a point-biserial correlation using the cor.test() function.

In Example 15.3, we concluded that a correlation between sex and duration of laughter was not significant ($r_{pb} = -.163$, $p > .05$) using the point-biserial correlation coefficient. Let us confirm this conclusion using R.

First create the dataframe, and then use the cor.test() function to compute the correlation coefficient and $p$ value:

```
> comedy <- data.frame(sex=c(1,1,1,1,1,2,2,2,2,2,2,2),
+ laughter=c(23,9,12,12,29,32,10,8,20,12,24,34))
> comedy
   sex laughter
1    1       23
2    1        9
3    1       12
4    1       12
5    1       29
6    2       32
7    2       10
8    2        8
9    2       20
10   2       12
11   2       24
12   2       34
> cor.test(comedy$laughter, comedy$sex)

        Pearson's product-moment correlation
```

data: comedy$laughter and comedy$sex

t = 0.52346, df = 10, p-value = 0.6121

alternative hypothesis: true correlation is not equal to 0

95 percent confidence interval:

 -0.4530538 0.6740380

sample estimates:

      cor

0.1633097

# 15.12 R IN FOCUS

## Phi Correlation Coefficient

Privitera's *Statisics for the Behavioral Sciences*, Third Edition (p. 522)

To compute a phi correlation coefficient using R, we first code each dichotomous factor and compute a Pearson correlation coefficient. Because the phi correlation coefficient is derived mathematically from the Pearson correlation coefficient, the value we obtain using R will be identical to that obtained for a phi correlation.

In Example 15.4, we concluded that a correlation between employment and happiness was significant ($r_\Phi = .40$, $p < .05$) using the phi correlation coefficient. We can confirm this conclusion using R. First, we can code the variables as 1s and 0s (happy = 1, unhappy = 0, and employed = 1, unemployed = 0):

```
> emp <- data.frame(Emp=c(rep(0,20),rep(1,20)),

+ Happy=c(rep(0,14),rep(1,6),rep(0,6),rep(1,14)))

> emp

  Emp Happy

1   0     0

2   0     0

3   0     0

4   0     0

5   0     0

6   0     0

7   0     0

8   0     0

9   0     0

10  0     0

11  0     0

12  0     0

13  0     0

14  0     0

15  0     1
```

| | | |
|---|---|---|
| 16 | 0 | 1 |
| 17 | 0 | 1 |
| 18 | 0 | 1 |
| 19 | 0 | 1 |
| 20 | 0 | 1 |
| 21 | 1 | 0 |
| 22 | 1 | 0 |
| 23 | 1 | 0 |
| 24 | 1 | 0 |
| 25 | 1 | 0 |
| 26 | 1 | 0 |
| 27 | 1 | 1 |
| 28 | 1 | 1 |
| 29 | 1 | 1 |
| 30 | 1 | 1 |
| 31 | 1 | 1 |
| 32 | 1 | 1 |
| 33 | 1 | 1 |
| 34 | 1 | 1 |
| 35 | 1 | 1 |
| 36 | 1 | 1 |
| 37 | 1 | 1 |
| 38 | 1 | 1 |
| 39 | 1 | 1 |
| 40 | 1 | 1 |

We can use the table() function to make sure we have the correct number of subjects in each category:

```
> table(emp)
     Happy
Emp   0  1
  0  14  6
  1   6 14
```

Finally, we use the cor.test() function to calculate our correlation and $p$ value, which converge with those we calculated by hand:

```
> cor.test(emp$Emp,emp$Happy)

        Pearson's product-moment correlation
data: emp$Emp and emp$Happy
t = 2.6904, df = 38, p-value = 0.01055
alternative hypothesis: true correlation is not equal to 0
95 percent confidence interval:
 0.1010864 0.6326756
sample estimates:
cor
0.4
```

# 16.7 R IN FOCUS

## Analysis of Regression

Privitera's *Statisics for the Behavioral Sciences,* Third Edition (p. 551)

To illustrate how all of our calculations are completed in R, let us compute the data in Example 16.3 in R. The data for Example 16.3 are reproduced in Table 16.5 from data originally given in Figure 16.5. We will compare how our analysis computed by hand matches the analysis computed using R.

**Table 16.5**   A Table Showing the Number of Sessions Eight Patients ($n = 8$) Attended and the Number of Symptoms They Expressed

| Number of Sessions (X) | Number of Symptoms (Y) |
|:---:|:---:|
| 9 | 0 |
| 5 | 3 |
| 8 | 2 |
| 2 | 5 |
| 6 | 3 |
| 3 | 4 |
| 5 | 2 |
| 4 | 3 |

The lm() function can be used to run a regression in R. We can save the analysis and output as an object by assigning a name to it, such as symp. We need to tell R to regress the symptoms variable on the sessions variable, so we do that by using the ~ symbol. We also tell R where the data can be found (the symp dataframe). The function that reports the most informative information from the linear model is the summary() function:

```
> symp <-data.frame(Sessions=c(9,5,8,2,6,3,5,4),

+ Symptoms=c(0,3,2,5,3,4,2,3))

> symp
```

```
  Sessions Symptoms
1        9        0
2        5        3
3        8        2
4        2        5
5        6        3
6        3        4
7        5        2
8        4        3
> symp.model <- lm(Symptoms~Sessions, data=symp)
> symp.model
Call:
lm(formula = Symptoms ~ Sessions, data = symp)
Coefficients:
(Intercept)    Sessions
     5.7405     -0.5696
```

This output is not very informative, so we use the summary() function:

```
> summary(symp.model)

Call:
lm(formula = Symptoms ~ Sessions, data = symp)

Residuals:
     Min      1Q  Median      3Q     Max
-0.89241 -0.50000 0.03797 0.46835 0.81646

Coefficients:
            Estimate Std. Error t value Pr(>|t|)
(Intercept)   5.7405     0.6066   9.463 7.93e-05 ***
Sessions     -0.5696     0.1064  -5.353  0.00174 **
---
Signif. codes:  0 '***' 0.001 '**' 0.01 '*' 0.05 '.' 0.1 ' ' 1
```

```
Residual standard error: 0.6688 on 6 degrees of freedom

Multiple R-squared: 0.8269,    Adjusted R-squared: 0.798

F-statistic: 28.66 on 1 and 6 DF, p-value: 0.001739
```

The results of this regression are significant for the predictor (Sessions variable), because the $p$ value is less than .05 (it is .00174). The estimate for the Sessions variable is −0.5696. This means that for every one-unit increase in the independent variable, there is a 0.5696-unit decrease in the dependent variable. For our example, this means that an increase in one session is related to a decrease of 0.5696 reported symptoms, on average. Simply stated: Attending more sessions is related to fewer symptoms, on average. The $F$ statistic is 28.66, and the $R$-squared value is .8269. This is an important number because it is an indicator of how good our model is. The closer to 100% (or 1.00) the $R$-squared value is, the better our model is.

We can also calculate the correlation coefficient in R using the cor() function:

```
> cor(symp$Sessions,symp$Symptoms)

[1] -0.9093229
```

We can also use the cor.test() function to test for statistical significance of that correlation:

```
> cor.test(symp$Sessions,symp$Symptoms)

        Pearson's product-moment correlation

data: symp$Sessions and symp$Symptoms

t = -5.3531, df = 6, p-value = 0.001739

alternative hypothesis: true correlation is not equal to 0

95 percent confidence interval:

 -0.9836788 -0.5696989

sample estimates:

        cor

-0.9093229

> (-0.9093229)^2

[1] 0.8268681
```

Notice that if we square our correlation, we get the $R$-squared value. Thus, our results from the correlation and regression are converging, as they should.

Finally, R gives the standard error of estimate, which is labeled as the residual standard error. This will be discussed in the next section.

## Multiple Regression Analysis

Privitera's *Statisics for the Behavioral Sciences,* Third Edition (p. 566)

While the many levels of computation and the many coefficients computed to perform an analysis of multiple regression might seem overwhelming, it can help to see how these values are summarized in the R output. To illustrate how all of our calculations are computed in R, let us use R to compute the data in Example 16.4. The data for Example 16.4 are reproduced in Table 16.13 from data originally given in Table 16.8. We will compare how our analysis computed by hand matches the analysis reported in the R output for multiple regression.

**Table 16.13** Data for the Age, Education Level, and Sales Among Six Patrons

| Age (years) $X_1$ | Education (years) $X_2$ | Sales (dollars) y |
|:---:|:---:|:---:|
| 19 | 12 | 20 |
| 21 | 14 | 40 |
| 26 | 13 | 30 |
| 28 | 18 | 68 |
| 32 | 17 | 70 |
| 30 | 16 | 60 |

In R, multiple regression is similar to simple regression, except now we add a variable, or variables, to our lm() function using the + symbol:

```
> sales <-data.frame(age=c(19,21,26,28,32,30),
+ education=c(12,14,13,18,17,16),
+ sales=c(20,40,30,68,70,60))
> sales
  age education sales
1  19        12    20
2  21        14    40
3  26        13    30
4  28        18    68
```

```
5   32          17      70

6   30          16      60

> sales.model <- lm(sales~age+education,data=sales)

> summary(sales.model)

Call:

lm(formula = sales ~ age + education, data = sales)

Residuals:
        1        2        3        4        5        6
  -0.3892   3.3114  -3.2814  -3.6587   2.5389   1.4790

Coefficients:
              Estimate Std. Error t value Pr(>|t|)
(Intercept)  -82.9401    10.9574   -7.569  0.00478 **
age            0.7904     0.5538    1.427  0.24880
education      7.3593     1.1933    6.167  0.00858 **
---
Signif. codes: 0 '***' 0.001 '**' 0.01 '*' 0.05 '.' 0.1 ' ' 1

Residual standard error: 3.826 on 3 degrees of freedom

Multiple R-squared:  0.98,      Adjusted R-squared: 0.9667

        F-statistic: 73.66 on 2 and 3 DF, p-value: 0.002819
```

Our results give us the beta coefficients for age (0.7904) and education (7.3593). Age is not a significant predictor of sales; however, education is. For every 1-year increase in years of education, sales increase by 7.36 units, on average, holding age constant. Again, we also see the $F$ statistic, multiple $R$-squared, residual standard error, and the degrees of freedom.

One last thing we need to do is generate standardized beta coefficients, which can be helpful for interpreting and reporting results. This is simple in R. We need to use the lm.beta() function in the QuantPsyc package. Download and load this package, then run the lm.beta() function by supplying the linear model as the only argument:

```
> install.packages("QuantPsyc")

> library(QuantPsyc)
```

```
> lm.beta(sales.model)
       age education
  0.1921400 0.8302389
```

The results give us the standardized coefficients for both predictors.

# 17.3 R IN FOCUS

## The Chi-Square Goodness-of-Fit Test

Privitera's *Statisics for the Behavioral Sciences,* Third Edition (p. 586)

In Example 17.1, we concluded from the chi-square goodness-of-fit test that the frequency of dream recall during REM sleep was similar to what was expected, $\chi^2(2) = 3.06$, $p > .05$. Let us confirm this result using R.

First, we need to create a vector of our observations:

```
> recall<-c(58,12,10)
> recall
[1] 58 12 10
```

We can use the chisq.test() function for the chi-square goodness-of-fit test. The function takes two arguments. First, we give it the vector of our observations, then we give the expected observations:

```
> chisq.test(recall, p=c(.8,.1,.1))

        Chi-squared test for given probabilities

data: recall
X-squared = 3.0625, df = 2, p-value = 0.2163
```

Our results converge with those we calculated by hand. We fail to reject the null hypothesis and conclude that our observations are similar to what we expected.

# 17.9 R IN FOCUS

## The Chi-Square Test for Independence

Privitera's *Statisics for the Behavioral Sciences,* Third Edition (p. 601)

In Example 17.2, a 2 × 2 chi-square test for independence showed a significant relationship between type of counseling and outcome of counseling, $\chi^2(1) = 5.386$, $p < .05$. Let us confirm this conclusion using R. First, let us create a table of our data. To do this, we have to create a matrix of our data using the matrix() function, and then we can rename the columns and rows to look like the table in Example 17.2. We can supply the matrix() function with three arguments. First, we give it our data. Next, we tell the function how many columns we want our matrix to have with the ncol argument. Finally, we specify that our data should be entered into our matrix across the two columns, and then the data should circle back down to the next row:

```
> obs.matrix <- matrix(c(22,12,31,45),ncol=2,byrow=TRUE)
> obs.matrix
     [,1] [,2]
[1,]  22   12
[2,]  31   45
```

If we had specified the byrow argument as FALSE, our data would have been entered into our matrix down the first column (the column on the left), and then the data would have finished in the second column (the column on the right). See how this differs from the matrix we previously made:

```
> obs.matrix2 <- matrix(c(22,12,31,45),ncol=2,byrow=FALSE)
> obs.matrix2
     [,1] [,2]
[1,]  22   31
[2,]  12   45
```

The data should look like that in the first matrix, so let us continue with that. We need to rename the columns and rows. We can do that with the colnames() and rownames() functions:

```
> colnames(obs.matrix) <- c("Completion","Premature Termination")
> rownames(obs.matrix) <- c("Family","Individual")
```

Now, let us convert the matrix to a table and view our table:

```
> obs.table<- as.table(obs.matrix)

> obs.table

        Completion Premature Termination

Family          22                     12

Individual      31                     45
```

Finally, let us run the chi-square test with the chisq.test() function we used in the previous R in Focus example:

```
> chisq.test(obs.table)

        Pearson's Chi-squared test with Yates' continuity correction

data: obs.table

X-squared = 4.4665, df = 1, p-value = 0.03457
```

Notice that these results do not converge with those we computed by hand. This is because the default argument in R is to do a continuity correction for $2 \times 2$ tables. If we do not want that correction, we can set the correct argument to FALSE:

```
> chisq.test(obs.table,correct=F)

        Pearson's Chi-squared test

data: obs.table

X-squared = 5.3818, df = 1, p-value = 0.02035
```

Notice that our results now converge with those we computed by hand (with minor differences due to rounding).

# 18.3 R IN FOCUS

## The Related-Samples Sign Test

Privitera's *Statisics for the Behavioral Sciences,* Third Edition (p. 621)

Based on data given in Table 18.2 in Example 18.2, we concluded that outbursts were more common in a class taught by a substitute teacher compared to a class taught by a full-time teacher, $x = 9$, $p < .05$. We can confirm this conclusion in R using the SIGN.test() function in the BSDA package. First, we need to install this package and load the library:

```
> install.packages("BSDA")

> library(BSDA)
```

Next, we create our dataframe:

```
> outburst <- data.frame(sub=c(3,2,5,3,4,2,0,3,1,6,4),

+ full=c(2,0,4,3,2,0,2,1,0,4,3))

> outburst

   sub full

1    3    2

2    2    0

3    5    4

4    3    3

5    4    2

6    2    0

7    0    2

8    3    1

9    1    0

10   6    4

11   4    3
```

The SIGN.test() function takes two arguments, the before and the after data:

```
> SIGN.test(outburst$sub,outburst$full)

     Dependent-samples Sign-Test
```

```
data: outburst$sub and outburst$full

S = 9, p-value = 0.02148

alternative hypothesis: true median difference is not equal to 0

95 percent confidence interval:

 0.7127273 2.0000000

sample estimates:

median of x-y

          1
```

|  | Conf.Level | L.E.pt | U.E.pt |
|---|---|---|---|
| Lower Achieved CI | 0.9346 | 1.0000 | 2 |
| Interpolated CI | 0.9500 | 0.7127 | 2 |
| Upper Achieved CI | 0.9883 | 0.0000 | 2 |

Our results converge with those we calculated by hand.

# 18.5 R IN FOCUS

## The Wilcoxon Signed-Ranks *T* Test

Privitera's *Statisics for the Behavioral Sciences,* Third Edition (p. 626)

Based on data given in Table 18.5 in Example 18.3, we concluded that patients significantly reduced their cigarette use six months following diagnosis of heart disease, $z = -2.28$, $p < .05$. Let us confirm this conclusion using R.

First, let us create our data table:

```
> smoked <- data.frame(before=c(23,12,11,15,25,20,11,9,13,15,30,21),
+ following=c(20,16,10,0,5,8,0,15,8,13,12,0))
> smoked
   before following
1      23        20
2      12        16
3      11        10
4      15         0
5      25         5
6      20         8
7      11         0
8       9        15
9      13         8
10     15        13
11     30        12
12     21         0
```

For this test, we can use the wilcox.test() function. Because we set our data up to have the observations for each condition in two separate columns, our first two arguments will be the data for those two columns. Next, we need to specify that each row of observations is the same participant. We do this with the paired=TRUE argument, similar to what we did with the paired *t* test:

```
> wilcox.test(smoked$before,smoked$following, paired=TRUE)

        Wilcoxon signed rank test
```

```
data: smoked$before and smoked$following
```

```
V = 68, p-value = 0.021
```

```
alternative hypothesis: true location shift is not equal to 0
```

We can specify two more arguments to our function. First, we are using a normal distribution, which has a smooth curve. However, ranks can change—a participant could move from rank 1 to 2, which is *not* smooth. This is a discrete move. Thus, we can correct for this detail using the continuity correct by supplying the correct=TRUE argument. Second, the *p* value can be calculated differently. You can have R calculate an exact *p* value. However, if there are ties, the test will not work. Furthermore, the calculations can be slow if your sample size is large. To calculate exact *p* values, supply the exact=TRUE argument. For now, let us run the analysis with both correct=FALSE and exact=FALSE, because it is likely that a dataset you might encounter will be large or will have ties, or both. Together with these corrections, we get a *slightly* different *p* value:

```
> wilcox.test(smoked$before,smoked$following, paired=TRUE,
correct=F,exact=F)
```

```
        Wilcoxon signed rank test
```

```
data: smoked$before and smoked$following
```

```
V = 68, p-value = 0.02291
```

```
alternative hypothesis: true location shift is not equal to 0
```

# 18.7 R IN FOCUS

## The Mann-Whitney *U* Test

Privitera's *Statisics for the Behavioral Sciences,* Third Edition (p. 632)

Based on data given in Table 18.8 in Example 18.4, we concluded that job satisfaction was significantly greater among day-shift compared to night-shift employees, $U = 2$, $p < .05$. Let us confirm this conclusion using R.

First, create the data table:

```
> job.sat<-data.frame(day=c(88,72,93,67,62),
+ night=c(24,55,70,60,50))
> job.sat
  day night
1 88    24
2 72    55
3 93    70
4 67    60
5 62    50
```

The Mann-Whitney *U* test is similar to the Wilcoxon signed-rank *T* test in that they are both nonparametric *t* tests, except the former is for independent conditions and the latter is for related conditions. Thus, we can use the same wilcox.test() function as we did in Section 18.5 R in Focus, except now we will specify the paired=FALSE argument:

```
> wilcox.test(job.sat$day, job.sat$night, paired=FALSE)

        Wilcoxon rank sum test

data: job.sat$day and job.sat$night
W = 23, p-value = 0.03175
alternative hypothesis: true location shift is not equal to 0
```

# 18.9 R IN FOCUS

## The Kruskal-Wallis *H* Test

Privitera's *Statisics for the Behavioral Sciences,* Third Edition (p. 637)

Based on data given in Table 18.12 in Example 18.5, we concluded that rankings of three safe driving video clips were significantly different, $H = 7.28$, $p < .05$. Let us confirm this conclusion using R.

First, we can input our data and run the analysis with a simple kruskal.test() function:

```
> driving<-data.frame(ClipA=c(88,67,22,14,42),

+ ClipB=c(92,76,80,77,90),

+ ClipC=c(50,55,43,65,39))

> driving

  ClipA ClipB ClipC

1   88    92    50

2   67    76    55

3   22    80    43

4   14    77    65

5   42    90    39

> kruskal.test(driving)

        Kruskal-Wallis rank sum test

data: driving

Kruskal-Wallis chi-squared = 7.26, df = 2, p-value = 0.02652
```

Note our *p* value is less than .05, which means there is at least one difference between group means across the conditions. To find out where, we can run post hoc analyses. First, let us input our data differently and use different notation for the test to show another way we can do the same test and get the same results:

```
> driving2<-data.frame(Scores=c(88,67,22,14,42,92,76,80,77,90,

+ 50,55,43,65,39),

+ Condition=c(rep("A",5),rep("B",5),rep("C",5)))

> driving2
```

```
    Scores Condition
1      88        A
2      67        A
3      22        A
4      14        A
5      42        A
6      92        B
7      76        B
8      80        B
9      77        B
10     90        B
11     50        C
12     55        C
13     43        C
14     65        C
15     39        C
```

```
> kruskal.test(driving2$Scores~driving2$Condition)

        Kruskal-Wallis rank sum test

data: driving2$Scores by driving2$Condition
Kruskal-Wallis chi-squared = 7.26, df = 2, p-value = 0.02652
```

Let us use this setup for the post hoc analysis. To do this, we need another function in a package we have not yet used, so we need to install it first and load the library:

```
> install.packages("pgirmess")

> library(pgirmess)
```

In this package, we can use the kruskalmc() function to see where the differences are:

```
> kruskalmc(driving2$Scores~driving2$Condition)

Multiple comparison test after Kruskal-Wallis

p.value: 0.05
```

```
Comparisons

   obs.dif critical.dif difference

A-B   6.6      6.771197       FALSE

A-C   0.0      6.771197       FALSE

B-C   6.6      6.771197       FALSE
```

The last column is helpful; it explicitly states whether the differences between groups are significant or not. However, you can see that none of them are significant, yet our original analysis said that there were differences somewhere! How does this make sense? This sometimes happens because we are comparing each and every possible comparison. To help focus our analyses, we could specify to compare groups to only one group. For example, if, in this scenario, we had one group that was a control group, we could compare only that group to the others. We could do this by making sure the control group was the first group level listed (in this example, Clip A is first), and then specify another argument, cont="two-tailed":

```
> kruskalmc(driving2$Scores~driving2$Condition, cont="two-tailed")

Multiple comparison test after Kruskal-Wallis, treatments vs control
(two-tailed)

p.value: 0.05

Comparisons

   obs.dif critical.dif difference

A-B   6.6      6.339644        TRUE

A-C   0.0      6.339644       FALSE
```

Now we see that the analysis is only comparing Clip A to Clip B, and Clip A to Clip C, and we see the difference is between Clip A and Clip B.

# 18.11 R IN FOCUS

## The Friedman Test

Privitera's *Statisics for the Behavioral Sciences,* Third Edition (p. 641)

Based on data given in Table 18.15a in Example 18.6, we concluded that there are no significant differences in the number of office visits made by women in each trimester of their pregnancy, $\chi_R^2(2) = 2.658$, $p > .05$. Let us confirm this conclusion using R.

By now, you should be able to create a data table!

```
> trimester<-data.frame(trimester=c(rep("first",7),rep("second",7),
+ rep("third",7)),
+ scores=c(3,6,2,4,4,4,8,5,4,0,3,6,3,6,
+ 8,7,5,2,9,7,5))
> head(trimester)
  trimester scores
1     first      3
2     first      6
3     first      2
4     first      4
5     first      4
6     first      4
```

To run the analysis, we can use the friedman.test() function:

```
> friedman.test(trimester$scores~trimester$trimester)
Error in friedman.test.formula(trimester$scores ~ trimester$trimester) :
  incorrect specification for 'formula'
```

We have a problem! This function requires our data to be given in matrix format. First, let us make a new dataframe table, but this time let us make a column for scores for each condition. Then, we can convert the dataframe to a matrix by using the as.matrix() function and see what happens:

```
> trimester<-data.frame(first=c(3,6,2,4,4,4,8),
+ second=c(5,4,0,3,6,3,6),
```

```
+ third=c(8,7,5,2,9,7,5))
> trimester
 first second third
1    3        5        8
2    6        4        7
3    2        0        5
4    4        3        2
5    4        6        9
6    4        3        7
7    8        6        5
> trimester.matrix<-as.matrix(trimester)
> friedman.test(trimester.matrix)

        Friedman rank sum test

data: trimester.matrix
Friedman chi-squared = 2.5714, df = 2, p-value = 0.2765
```

There we go! Our results show there are no differences between groups. Therefore, we also do not need any post hoc analyses.

## General Instruction Guide

Most SPSS users use the point-and-click method to run analyses. However, R users generally type code. Therefore, to make it easier for you, we include a link to all the code used to run analyses and generate the output in the chapter examples. In this way, you can easily learn to run analyses or modify them by copying and pasting the code rather than typing it all out by hand, which can be tedious. To access the code, go to this link:

http://edge.sagepub.com/priviterastats3e/student-resources/general-instructions-guide

# PART II

# Analysis in Focus: SAS

# SAS in Focus

Sections for Privitera, *Statistics for the Behavioral Sciences,* Third Edition

Page numbers for corresponding sections in the third edition of Privitera's *Statistics for the Behavioral Sciences* are included in parentheses.

# To the Student—How to Use SAS With This Book

SAS (Statistical Analysis System) is a popular statistical software program. It is widely used in academia and industry, and has the ability to perform a wide range of analyses. Though there is a point-and-click user interface, we will learn the more advanced approach that involves coding and the SAS language. This requires more time and patience to learn how to use SAS in the beginning, but in the long run you will be able to do more and be more flexible with the analyses you run. You will also have a deeper understanding of SAS and statistical analyses.

To have and own the SAS software, you need to pay for it, or work for an organization that does. However, there is a free version of the software for students, the SAS University Edition. The interface and code are the same in both versions, so if you use the student edition and then transition to an organization that uses the paid version, you will be prepared and not have difficulty transitioning. Because many students and schools benefit from the free software, we will use the SAS University Edition in this tutorial. The screen shots and information provided in this tutorial are based on this SAS version. One thing to remind yourself is to be patient when learning SAS! There are a lot of commands and new terminology to learn, especially if you are not familiar with programming. Be patient! In addition to understanding how to compute a mean or plot a bar graph by hand, knowing how to enter, analyze, and interpret statistics using SAS is equally important for no other reason than you will need it. This is an essential complement to your readings in the textbook. By knowing how and why you compute certain statistics, you will better understand and interpret the output from SAS. So let us get started!

## Downloading and Installing SAS University Edition

To use the SAS University Edition, you need access to the Internet and a virtual machine. Though this edition is free and it includes the same base SAS and SAS/STAT as the paid SAS version, you do not physically download the software to your computer. Instead, you remotely access it over the Internet with the help of virtualization software, which can be downloaded freely. To download all of this software, go to this SAS University Edition website: http://www.sas.com/en_us/software/university-edition.html# and click on "Get free software." You can either download SAS or launch it via Amazon's web services. Before you download it, be sure to check the system requirements for your operating system (e.g., for Windows, you need Microsoft Windows 7, 8, 8.1, or 10). SAS is available for Windows, OS X, and Linux systems. Next, install the virtualization software, Oracle VirtualBox. Next, download the SAS University Edition vApp. You will have to create a profile and accept the licensing agreement. Once you do this, you will receive an email with more information, as well as some information on tutorials, which are much more in depth than the one we will do together. You can work through it, or at least use it as a resource if you need help in the future. Once you have successfully downloaded the software, it is important that you set up working folders that you will use to save your files. In the virtualization software, you need to make sure these folders are also added here. To properly do this, you will need to follow the instructions from Step 3, which can be found on the SAS University Edition website:

http://support.sas.com/software/products/university-edition/docs/en/SASUniversityEdition QuickStartVirtualBox.pdf

Once you have completed this step, you are ready to get started! These steps that you have completed, up until now, have to be completed only once for initial setup. From here on, to use SAS University Edition, you will need to do the following. First, start the virtualization software, Oracle VirtualBox. Click on Machine, Start, and Normal Start:

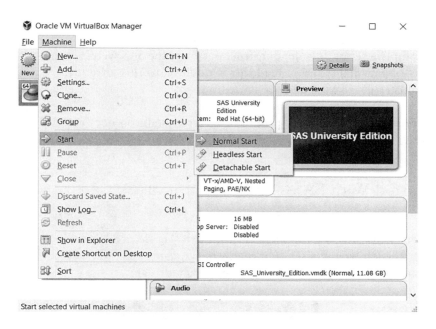

Be patient, but another window should appear. Once this window has finished loading, a URL will be given, which you can use to access SAS University Edition:

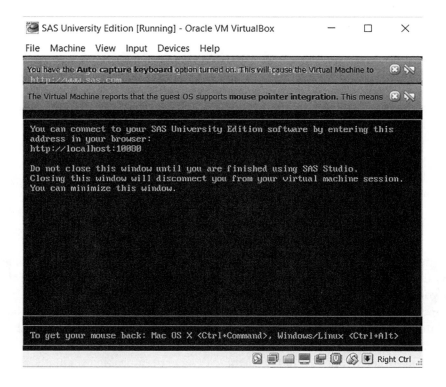

Using the URL, http://localhost:10080, type this into your browser and wait for the page to load, and click on "Start SAS Studio." Now you are ready to get started!

Again, a complete set of download instructions from the SAS website can be found here, and it is strongly recommended that you read this in addition to this introductory tutorial, as it will help you download the software and get started:

http://support.sas.com/software/products/university-edition/docs/en/SASUniversityEdition QuickStartVirtualBox.pdf

## Getting Started With SAS—A Brief Tutorial

Now that you have the program running, let us view the layout of SAS Studio and get started with some basics. On the left, you will see your files, which include .sas files, where you save your code. You can also save .csv files, such as Excel files that include data.

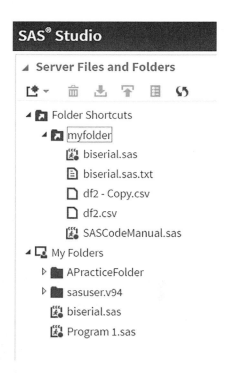

On the right, you will see an area where you can write and save your code. The title of the current .sas file is SASCodeManual.sas, which includes all the code you will use in this tutorial! At the top, you will see a person running. When you are ready to run your code, you can highlight your code and click that button. The Log tab, which is to the right of the Code tab, includes messages and information about your executed code. After you run your code, you should *always* check that section to see if there are any messages or errors. Sometimes, you will get output and assume everything went well, when in fact there may have been problems. Finally, the Results tab is where your output appears. After you run your code, there will also be an Output Data tab with more output. This tab will include tables and figures.

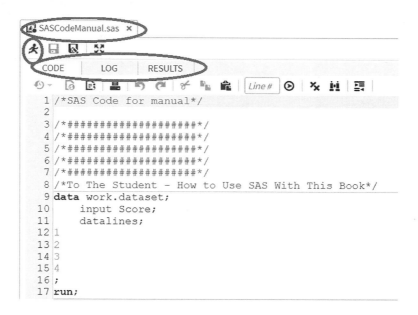

Now that we have our software running and we are becoming familiar with the layout, let us learn some basics. First, we need to make sure we have a Code tab opened so we can type and execute code. If you do not have a Code tab, click on the "New" icon on the left and select SAS Program (F4):

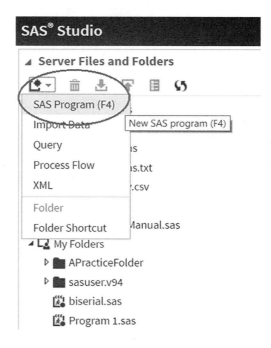

In SAS, DATA and PROC statements are needed to execute commands. DATA statements are used to obtain data or create datasets. PROC statements take our data and manipulate them for data management or analysis. SAS statements are not case sensitive, so there is no difference between these two statements:

```
 9 data work.dataset;
10     input Score;
11     datalines;
12 1
13 2
14 3
15 4
16 ;
17 run;
18
19 DATA work.dataset;
20     INPUT Score;
21     DATALINES;
22 1
23 2
24 3
25 4
26 ;
27 RUN;
```

Type this code—as it appears—into your Code tab. Highlight the first set of code and run it by clicking on the running person above the Code tab. Now, go to the Log tab and observe the Errors, Warnings, and Notes. There are no errors or warnings, so our code was executed without any problems. As stated before, check this after running your code to make sure there were no problems. Also, in case there were problems, you can read the error messages to find out what may have gone wrong.

SASCodeManual.sas ×

CODE | LOG | RESULTS | OUTPUT DATA

▲ Errors, Warnings, Notes
  ▷ ⊗ Errors
  ▷ ⚠ Warnings
  ▷ ① Notes (2)

```
1          OPTIONS NONOTES NOSTIMER NOSOURCE NOSYNTAXCHECK;
55
56         DATA work.dataset;
57         INPUT Score;
58         DATALINES;

NOTE: The data set WORK.DATASET has 4 observations and 1 variables.
NOTE: DATA statement used (Total process time):
      real time         0.01 seconds
      cpu time          0.01 seconds

63         ;

64         RUN;
65
66         OPTIONS NONOTES NOSTIMER NOSOURCE NOSYNTAXCHECK;
78
```

Next, click on the Output Data tab. Here, you will see the output from your code. A dataset was created with one column, titled "Score," which is filled with four scores from four subjects.

Try running the other set of code. You will notice the output is the same! Something you may have noticed is that after each line of code is a semicolon (;). This lets SAS know when one statement of code is separate from another. You can put these separate lines on one line as long as the semicolons are included. For example, this code will produce the same output as the other two sets of code:

```
29 DATA work.dataset; INPUT Score; DATALINES;
30 1
31 2
32 3
33 4
34 ;
35 RUN;
```

However, it is good practice to properly write your code to make it easier for others to follow, and even for yourself. This code is quite simple, but once you start adding more lines, it may get confusing. That is why it is good practice to start a new line for new code. Furthermore, take note of the actual data observations, Scores 1, 2, 3, and 4. Notice that they are all on separate lines. Try running this code. What does the output look like?

```
37 DATA work.dataset; INPUT Score; DATALINES;
38 1 2 3 4
39 ;
40 RUN;
```

Your output should be a dataset with one column, but only one row. This is because each new row of data needs to be entered on a new line, otherwise, SAS will not read it. The exception to this is if you use @@ after your variable titles. We will learn more about that later. One last thing to note is the Log tab for the code we just ran. If you look at it, you will notice there were no errors or warnings! Therefore, again, you need to be careful and always observe your Log tab and your data to make sure it makes sense. Clearly, this output does not make sense. This is why it is important to understand statistical analyses and not simply rely on software tools and programs. If you do, you may blindly accept output without realizing there are problems.

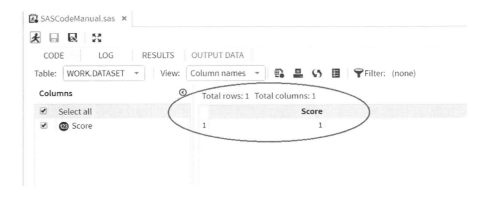

Let us also notice how we use the RUN statement at the end. This lets SAS know our code is complete and should be run once it is executed by clicking on the "Run" icon. Finally, you can use the forward slash and asterisk to let SAS know this code includes notes and should be ignored. The content between the forward slash and asterisk and the asterisk and forward slash are your notes. For example, we can write that this file of code is for our SAS Manual:

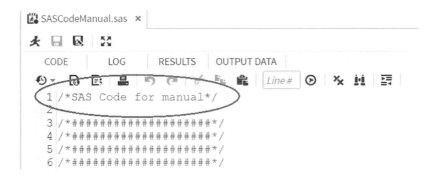

Let us save this .sas file. Click on the save icon, which is the icon to the right of the Run button. A window should appear. In the Name box, type "SASCodeManual." Save this file under the "Folder Shortcuts" and "myfolder" folders, then hit Save. From now on, when you start SAS Studio, this file should load. If not, you can open it and use it to type all your code and save it. This will be convenient if you have to start your work and need to save it for later.

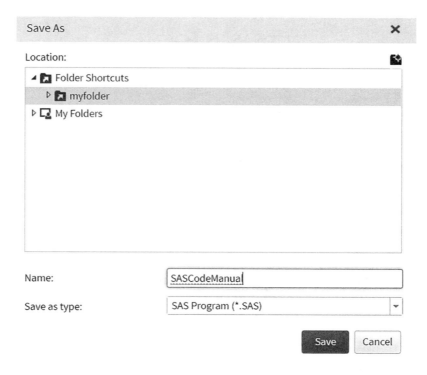

## Preview of SAS in Focus

This book is unique in that you will learn how to use SAS to perform statistical analyses as they are taught in this book. Most statistics textbooks for behavioral science omit such information, include it in an appendix separate from the main chapters in the book, include it at the end of chapters with no useful examples or context, or include it in ancillary materials that often are not included with course content. Instead, this book provides instructions for using SAS in each chapter as statistical concepts are taught using practical research examples and screenshots to support student learning. You will find this instruction in the SAS in Focus sections. These sections provide step-by-step instructions for how the concepts taught in each chapter can be applied to research problems using SAS.

The reason for this inclusion is simple: Most researchers use some kind of statistical software to analyze statistics, and in the social sciences, SAS is very popular. This textbook brings statistics in research to the 21st century, giving you both the theoretical and computational instruction needed to understand how, when, and why you perform certain statistical analyses under different conditions and the technical instruction you need to succeed in the modern era of data collection, data entry, data analysis, and statistical interpretation using SAS. This preface was written to familiarize you with this environment. Subsequent SAS in Focus sections will show you how to use SAS to perform the applications and statistics taught in this book.

# 1.7 SAS IN FOCUS

## Entering and Defining Variables

Privitera's *Statisics for the Behavioral Sciences,* Third Edition (p. 23)

Throughout this book, we present instructions for using the statistical software program SAS by showing you how this software can make all the work you do by hand much easier. Before you read this SAS section, please take the time to read the section titled "How to Use SAS With This Book" at the beginning of this book. That section provides an overview of the SAS program. This software is an innovative statistical computer program that can compute any statistic taught in this book.

In this chapter, we discuss how to enter data and define our variables. We will learn how to do this in two ways. The biggest challenge is making sure you enter the data correctly. Entering even a single value incorrectly can alter the data analyses that SAS computes. For this reason, always double-check the data to make sure the correct values have been entered.

We can use a simple example. Suppose you record the average GPA of students in one of three statistics classes. You record the following GPA scores for each class, given in Table 1.4.

**Table 1.4**  GPA Scores in Three Statistics Classes

| Class 1 | Class 2 | Class 3 |
|---------|---------|---------|
| 3.3 | 3.9 | 2.7 |
| 2.9 | 4.0 | 2.3 |
| 3.5 | 2.4 | 2.2 |
| 3.6 | 3.1 | 3.0 |
| 3.1 | 3.0 | 2.8 |

## Approach A

First, we can manually create this table in SAS using the DATA step:

```
49 /*Approach A*/
50 DATA myfirstdata;
51  INPUT Class_1 Class_2 Class_3;
52  Datalines;
53 3.3 3.9 2.7
54 2.9 4.0 2.3
55 3.5 2.4 2.2
56 3.6 3.1 3.0
57 3.1 3.0 2.8
58 ;
59 proc print;
60 RUN;
```

After the DATA statement, we define the name of our table, which we called "myfirstdata." The INPUT statement tells SAS what the column names are (Class_1, Class_2, and Class_3). Next, we need to enter our data by using the DATALINES statement. We tell SAS to start a new row to our table by starting the data on a new line. Finally, we use the PROC PRINT statement to create the table output, and end with the RUN statement. Remember to put the semicolon after each statement, but *not* at the end of each dataline. Also note that you can use the CARDS statement instead of DATALINES. Both produce the same output, which you will see in the OUTPUT DATA tab:

| Obs | Class_1 | Class_2 | Class_3 |
|-----|---------|---------|---------|
| 1 | 3.3 | 3.9 | 2.7 |
| 2 | 2.9 | 4.0 | 2.3 |
| 3 | 3.5 | 2.4 | 2.2 |
| 4 | 3.6 | 3.1 | 3.0 |
| 5 | 3.1 | 3.0 | 2.8 |

Something important to note is what type of variables we have. All of the variables in our table are numeric. However, we may want character data. For example, we may want to add a column for another class, which has letter grades. We can do this by creating a new table (which we can call "myseconddata") with a character column of data. We specify character data with the $ symbol:

```
62 /*Make a new data table with a character column*/
63 DATA myseconddata;
64   INPUT Class_1 Class_2 Class_3 Class_4 $;
65   Datalines;
66 3.3 3.9 2.7 A
67 2.9 4.0 2.3 C
68 3.5 2.4 2.2 B-
69 3.6 3.1 3.0 A
70 3.1 3.0 2.8 B+
71 ;
72 proc print;
73 RUN;
```

This is what our new data table looks like:

| Obs | Class_1 | Class_2 | Class_3 | Class_4 |
|-----|---------|---------|---------|---------|
| 1 | 3.3 | 3.9 | 2.7 | A |
| 2 | 2.9 | 4.0 | 2.3 | C |
| 3 | 3.5 | 2.4 | 2.2 | B- |
| 4 | 3.6 | 3.1 | 3.0 | A |
| 5 | 3.1 | 3.0 | 2.8 | B+ |

## Approach B

The second way we can enter our data into SAS is by creating an Excel file and uploading it. First, we need to enter our data into Excel. Enter the data in Table 1.4 into Excel, except do not enter the column names (Class 1, Class 2, and Class 3). Your Excel file should look like this:

|   | A | B | C | D |
|---|---|---|---|---|
| 1 | 3.3 | 3.9 | 2.7 | |
| 2 | 2.9 | 4 | 2.3 | |
| 3 | 3.5 | 2.4 | 2.2 | |
| 4 | 3.6 | 3.1 | 3 | |
| 5 | 3.1 | 3 | 2.8 | |
| 6 | | | | |

Now, let us save this file as a .csv (comma separated values) file. To do this, go to File, Save As, and save the file as GPA_Scores. Under the Save As Type, scroll through the options and select "CSV (Comma delimited)(*.csv)." What this means is that this file will be saved, but a *comma* will be used to indicate when a value is part of a new column. Thus, the data saved in this format will look like this:

```
3.3,3.9,2.7
2.9,4,2.3
3.5,2.4,2.2
3.6,3.1,3
3.1,3,2.8
```

If we look at the top row of the data above, 3.3 is in one column, then the comma means the next data value, 3.9, should be in a new column.

Now that we have these data saved in an appropriate format, we need to get them into SAS. To do this, let us create a new folder and call it "APracticeFolder." To do this, click on My Folder, and then the New option, which is circled in the screenshot below. A drop-down menu will appear. Click on Folder and save it as "APracticeFolder" in the menu that pops up and hit Save. Next, right-click on this new folder and select Upload Files. (For Mac users, press the control key followed by the track-pad.) A screen should pop up where you can select Choose Files. Do this and go to wherever you saved the GPA_Scores.csv file and select that file to upload. It should now be listed in your new folder.

Next, we need to create a temporary working data file from our .csv file. First, we create a path to tell SAS where to find our .csv file. Then we can use the DATA step to make a temporary dataset from the .csv file. Let us call this temporary dataset GPA. We use the INFILE statement to tell SAS which file to use and where to find it. Because we already set this path, we can use the &PATH code, then simply write the file name (GPA_Scores.csv). Put this in double quotes (""). The next part of the code (dlm=',') is telling SAS that a comma is what delimits, or defines, what separates each data observation. This makes sense because, as we learned earlier, the comma is what separates each data observation and puts the observations into separate columns. Finally, the INPUT statement tells SAS what to name the columns. Note there are no $ symbols after each of these column titles. When there are no $ symbols used, this means the column variables are formatted as numeric.

```
75 /*Approach B*/
76 %let path=/folders/myfolders/APracticeFolder;
77
78 data work.GPA;
79     infile "&path/GPA_Scores.csv" dlm=',';
80     input Class1  Class2  Class3;
81 run;
```

Next, we can get information about our new dataset with the PROC CONTENTS step:

```
83 proc contents data=work.GPA;
84 run;
```

From this step, we learn when the file was made, how many variables and observations there are, and many other bits of information. We also can confirm that our three variables are numeric.

| Alphabetic List of Variables and Attributes | | | |
|---|---|---|---|
| # | Variable | Type | Len |
| 1 | Class1 | Num | 8 |
| 2 | Class2 | Num | 8 |
| 3 | Class3 | Num | 8 |

Finally, we can use the PROC PRINT step to simply view our data:

```
86 proc print data=work.GPA;
87 run;
```

| Obs | Class1 | Class2 | Class3 |
|---|---|---|---|
| 1 | 3.3 | 3.9 | 2.7 |
| 2 | 2.9 | 4.0 | 2.3 |
| 3 | 3.5 | 2.4 | 2.2 |
| 4 | 3.6 | 3.1 | 3.0 |
| 5 | 3.1 | 3.0 | 2.8 |

Let us go over one more example that illustrates how to create new variables, rename variable observations, add output titles, and make new datasets that keep or drop specific variables. Based on what you learned in this section so far, create a .csv file in Excel named "Practice3" that has the following data observations for a class of students:

| | A | B | C | D | E | F |
|---|---|---|---|---|---|---|
| 1 | 1 | 18 | 1220 | M | B | 90 |
| 2 | 2 | 18 | 1400 | M | A- | 78 |
| 3 | 3 | 20 | 1020 | F | C | 67 |
| 4 | 4 | 19 | 1350 | F | A | 86 |
| 5 | 5 | 18 | 1520 | M | B+ | 93 |

As in most situations and datasets, each row represents one person and his or her data observations for different variables. The columns each represent a variable. In this example, when you upload your .csv file into SAS, title the columns with these names: ID, Age, SAT, Gender, Grade, and Exam. The first variable is an ID number for each subject. The second variable is Age, the third variable is SAT score, the fourth variable is Gender, the fifth variable is a Grade the students received on a paper, and the last variable is an Exam score. So far, your code and output should look like this:

```
89 /*Example 3*/
90 data work.Example3;
91     infile "&path/Practice3.csv" dlm=',';
92     input ID $ Age SAT Gender $ Grade $ Exam;
93 run;
94
95 proc print data=work.Example3;
96 run;
```

| Obs | ID | Age | SAT | Gender | Grade | Exam |
|---|---|---|---|---|---|---|
| 1 | 1 | 18 | 1220 | M | B | 90 |
| 2 | 2 | 18 | 1400 | M | A- | 78 |
| 3 | 3 | 20 | 1020 | F | C | 67 |
| 4 | 4 | 19 | 1350 | F | A | 86 |
| 5 | 5 | 18 | 1520 | M | B+ | 93 |

Now, let us learn how to change variable observations and add a title to our output. In the Gender column, we can change "M" to "Male" and "F" to "Female" with the PROC FORMAT step. We tell SAS that we want the Gender column to change to a new character variable, and we indicate that we want to change "F" to "Female" and "M" to "Male," and then RUN the code. Next, we use the TITLE1 statement to tell SAS that we want the first row to be titled "Class Information" and the second row (TITLE2 statement) to be titled "Created Mar 22 2016." Finally, in the PROC PRINT step, we tell SAS to use our new formatting for the Gender column. Together, we now have:

```
101 proc format;
102     value $Gender  "F"="Female"
103                    "M"="Male";
104 run;
105
106 title1 "Class Information";
107 title2 "Created Mar 22 2016";
108
109 proc print data=work.Example3;
110     format Gender $Gender.;
111 run;
```

**Class Information**
**Created Mar 22 2016**

| Obs | ID | Age | SAT | Gender | Grade | Exam |
|-----|----|-----|------|--------|-------|------|
| 1 | 1 | 18 | 1220 | Male | B | 90 |
| 2 | 2 | 18 | 1400 | Male | A- | 78 |
| 3 | 3 | 20 | 1020 | Female | C | 67 |
| 4 | 4 | 19 | 1350 | Female | A | 86 |
| 5 | 5 | 18 | 1520 | Male | B+ | 93 |

Now, let us learn how to create a new dataset from our work.Example3 dataset, where we select specific variables that meet certain criteria. Let us also create a new variable. In our example, assume we want to select individuals who are at least 18 years old *and* who are male. Assume we also want to create a new variable called "Curve," where we add a 5-point curve to the original exam score. In this new dataset, we want to include our new variable, Curve, and our original variables, but we no longer need the Age variable. Therefore, we can drop Age. Put together, our code should look like this:

```
113 data work.Subset;
114     set work.Example3;
115     where Age>=18 and Gender="M";
116     Curve=Exam+5;
117     Drop Age;
118 run;
```

We use the DATA step to create a new dataset called "Subset," and we tell SAS that this new dataset is based on our work.Example3 dataset. We specify that the new dataset should have subjects where their Age is at least 18 years, and they must be Males. We specify our new variable, Curve, which is equal to the Exam score plus 5 points. Finally, we use the DROP statement to tell SAS to get rid of the Age variable. Alternatively, we can use the KEEP statement, but we would have to list all the other variables. Therefore, using the DROP statement is less work, so we go with that. To see our new dataset, use the PROC PRINT statement:

```
120 proc print data=work.subset;
121 run;
```

| Obs | ID | SAT | Gender | Grade | Exam | Curve |
|---|---|---|---|---|---|---|
| 1 | 1 | 1220 | M | B | 90 | 95 |
| 2 | 2 | 1400 | M | A- | 78 | 83 |
| 3 | 5 | 1520 | M | B+ | 93 | 98 |

SAS does a lot more, too! For now, this is enough to get us started, and we will learn more as we go.

# 2.4 SAS IN FOCUS

## Frequency Distributions for Quantitative Data

Privitera's *Statisics for the Behavioral Sciences,* Third Edition (p. 46)

SAS can be used to construct frequency distributions. In this section, we will construct a frequency distribution table for the business safety data first listed in Table 2.3, which are reproduced here for reference.

Data reproduced from Table 2.3.

| 45 | 98 | 83 | 50 | 86 |
|----|-----|-----|-----|-----|
| 66 | 66 | 88 | 95 | 73 |
| 88 | 55 | 76 | 115 | 66 |
| 92 | 110 | 79 | 105 | 101 |
| 101 | 85 | 90 | 92 | 81 |
| 55 | 95 | 91 | 92 | |
| 78 | 66 | 73 | 58 | |
| 86 | 92 | 51 | 63 | |
| 91 | 77 | 88 | 86 | |
| 94 | 80 | 102 | 107 | |

First, we need to create a dataset in SAS (note that the data are cut off to save space):

```
182 data freqcomplaints;
183     input Complaints @@;
184     Datalines;
185 45 66 88 92 101 55 78 86 91 94 98 ͼ
186 ;
187 proc print;
188 run;
```

We learned this code in Section 1.7 SAS in Focus. However, we added the @@ symbol to tell SAS to fill in the data for variables until it reaches the end of the data observations. In this case, there is only one variable, Complaints, so SAS is simply taking each data observation and putting it in a new row. Remember, without the @@ symbol, SAS would normally read these data and see that they are all in one row (45 through 98 are listed on the same line), and would therefore assume all the data should be in one row. However, that is not how we want the data. We want each observation to be in its own row.

Next, we can use PROC FREQ to create a frequency distribution. We specify the dataset, freqcomplaints, and ask for a frequency table for the Complaints variable. Finally, we can add a title with the TITLE statement:

```
190 proc freq data=freqcomplaints;
191    tables Complaints;
192    title 'Complaints Frequencies';
193 run;
```

**Complaints Frequencies**

The FREQ Procedure

| Complaints | Frequency | Percent | Cumulative Frequency | Cumulative Percent |
|---|---|---|---|---|
| 45 | 1 | 2.22 | 1 | 2.22 |
| 50 | 1 | 2.22 | 2 | 4.44 |
| 51 | 1 | 2.22 | 3 | 6.67 |
| 55 | 2 | 4.44 | 5 | 11.11 |
| 58 | 1 | 2.22 | 6 | 13.33 |
| 63 | 1 | 2.22 | 7 | 15.56 |
| 66 | 4 | 8.89 | 11 | 24.44 |
| 73 | 2 | 4.44 | 13 | 28.89 |
| 76 | 1 | 2.22 | 14 | 31.11 |
| 77 | 1 | 2.22 | 15 | 33.33 |
| 78 | 1 | 2.22 | 16 | 35.56 |
| 79 | 1 | 2.22 | 17 | 37.78 |
| 80 | 1 | 2.22 | 18 | 40.00 |
| 81 | 1 | 2.22 | 19 | 42.22 |
| 83 | 1 | 2.22 | 20 | 44.44 |
| 85 | 1 | 2.22 | 21 | 46.67 |
| 86 | 3 | 6.67 | 24 | 53.33 |
| 88 | 3 | 6.67 | 27 | 60.00 |
| 90 | 1 | 2.22 | 28 | 62.22 |
| 91 | 2 | 4.44 | 30 | 66.67 |
| 92 | 4 | 8.89 | 34 | 75.56 |
| 94 | 1 | 2.22 | 35 | 77.78 |
| 95 | 2 | 4.44 | 37 | 82.22 |
| 98 | 1 | 2.22 | 38 | 84.44 |
| 101 | 2 | 4.44 | 40 | 88.89 |
| 102 | 1 | 2.22 | 41 | 91.11 |
| 105 | 1 | 2.22 | 42 | 93.33 |
| 107 | 1 | 2.22 | 43 | 95.56 |
| 110 | 1 | 2.22 | 44 | 97.78 |
| 115 | 1 | 2.22 | 45 | 100.00 |

# 2.7 SAS IN FOCUS

## Frequency Distributions for Categorical Data

Privitera's *Statisics for the Behavioral Sciences,* Third Edition (p. 51)

SAS can be used to summarize categorical data that are ungrouped. We can use SAS to create a frequency distribution for the following hypothetical example: A group of health practitioners wants to classify children in public schools as being lean, healthy, overweight, or obese; this type of classification is common (Centers for Disease Control and Prevention, 2013; Privitera, 2016). To do this, the researchers calculated the body mass index (BMI) score of 100 children. Based on the BMI scores, they classified 15 children as lean, 30 as healthy, 35 as overweight, and 20 as obese.

First, create the dataset use the DATA step and view the output:

```
197 data work.BMI;
198     input BMI $ Total@@;
199     datalines;
200 lean 15 healthy 30 overweight 35 obese 20
201 ;
202 proc print data=work.BMI;
203 run;
```

Similar to the previous section on frequency distributions for quantitative data, we can use the PROC FREQ step. Everything is the same, except we add a weight statement. This tells SAS the Total column in our dataset gives the counts for each classification type:

```
206 proc freq data=work.BMI;
207     tables BMI;
208     weight Total;
209     title 'BMI Frequencies';
210 run;
```

### BMI Frequencies

The FREQ Procedure

| BMI | Frequency | Percent | Cumulative Frequency | Cumulative Percent |
|---|---|---|---|---|
| healthy | 30 | 30.00 | 30 | 30.00 |
| lean | 15 | 15.00 | 45 | 45.00 |
| obese | 20 | 20.00 | 65 | 65.00 |
| overweig | 35 | 35.00 | 100 | 100.00 |

The output lists frequencies, cumulative frequencies, and cumulative percents. However, notice the BMI categories are listed alphabetically. One simple solution is to insert the letter "A" before lean, the letter "B" before healthy, and so on. There are other solutions, but they are beyond the scope of this chapter.

## 2.12 SAS IN FOCUS

### Histograms, Bar Charts, and Pie Charts

Privitera's *Statisics for the Behavioral Sciences,* Third Edition (p. 65)

To review, histograms are used for continuous or quantitative data, and bar charts and pie charts are used for discrete, categorical, or qualitative data. As an exercise to compare histograms, bar charts, and pie charts, we can construct these graphs for the same data by treating the data as a simple set of general values. Suppose we measure the data shown in Table 2.16.

**Table 2.16**   A Sample of 20 Values

| | | | |
|---|---|---|---|
| 1 | 4 | 5 | 7 |
| 2 | 3 | 6 | 8 |
| 3 | 6 | 7 | 9 |
| 2 | 6 | 5 | 4 |
| 4 | 5 | 8 | 5 |

First, create a dataset:

```
230 data work.numbers;
231     input Numbers@@;
232     datalines;
233 1 2 3 2 4 4 3 6 6 5 5 6 7 5 8 7 8 9 4 5
234 ;
235 proc print data=work.numbers;
236 run;
```

To save space, below are the first five observations from the PROC PRINT statement:

| Obs | Numbers |
|---|---|
| 1 | 1 |
| 2 | 2 |
| 3 | 3 |
| 4 | 2 |
| 5 | 4 |

116

To create a histogram, we can use the PROC UNIVARIATE statement and ask for a histogram:

```
238 proc univariate data=work.numbers;
239    histogram;
240 run;
```

You will notice this code produces a lot of output, in addition to the histogram:

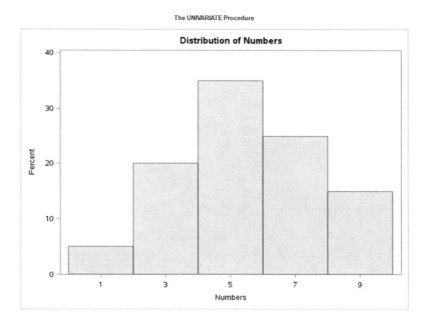

# 3.6 SAS IN FOCUS

## Mean, Median, and Mode

Privitera's *Statisics for the Behavioral Sciences,* Third Edition (p. 98)

SAS can be used to measure the mean, the median, and the mode for all sorts of data. In this section, we will work through a new example to compute each measure of central tendency. Suppose you want to study creativity using a paper clip, as has been used in prior studies on the topic (Chatterjea & Mitra, 1976; Piffer, 2012). You give students a paper clip, and the time (in seconds) it takes the students to list 10 uses for the paper clip is recorded. Faster times are presumed to reflect greater creativity. Using the data shown in Table 3.11, we can use SAS to compute the mean, the median, and the mode.

**Table 3.11** The Time (in seconds) That It Took 20 Participants to Write Down 10 Uses for a Paper Clip on a Creativity Test

| | |
|---|---|
| 41 | 80 |
| 65 | 80 |
| 123 | 64 |
| 46 | 59 |
| 48 | 51 |
| 87 | 36 |
| 38 | 80 |
| 90 | 143 |
| 132 | 122 |
| 115 | 100 |

First, we create our dataset. Next, we use the PROC UNIVARIATE statement we learned in the previous section to get the mean, median, and mode in the second table of the output:

```
249 data work.clips;
250     input Clips@@;
251     datalines;
252 41  65  123  46  48  87  38  90  132  115  80  80  64  59  51  36  80  143  122  100
253 ;
254 run;
255
256 proc print data=work.clips;
257 run;
258
259 proc univariate data=work.clips;
260 run;
```

| Basic Statistical Measures | | | |
|---|---|---|---|
| **Location** | | **Variability** | |
| Mean | 80.00000 | Std Deviation | 33.42234 |
| Median | 80.00000 | Variance | 1117 |
| Mode | 80.00000 | Range | 107.00000 |
| | | Interquartile Range | 58.00000 |

# 4.11 SAS IN FOCUS

## Range, Variance, and Standard Deviation

Privitera's *Statistics for the Behavioral Sciences,* Third Edition (p. 129)

In the SAS in Focus section of Chapter 3, we computed the mean, the median, and the mode for creativity, measured as the time (in seconds) it took participants to list 10 uses for a paper clip. The data for this example, originally given in Table 3.11, are reproduced here in Table 4.10. In this section, we will use these same data and the same code to compute the range, variance, and standard deviation.

**Table 4.10**   The Time (in seconds) That It Took a Group of 20 Participants to Write Down 10 Uses for a Paper Clip on a Creativity Test

| | |
|---|---|
| 41 | 80 |
| 65 | 80 |
| 123 | 64 |
| 46 | 59 |
| 48 | 51 |
| 87 | 36 |
| 38 | 80 |
| 90 | 143 |
| 132 | 122 |
| 115 | 100 |

```
249 data work.clips;
250     input Clips@@;
251     datalines;
252 41 65 123 46 48 87 38 90 132 115 80 80 64 59 51 36 80 143 122 100
253 ;
254 run;
255
256 proc print data=work.clips;
257 run;
258
259 proc univariate data=work.clips;
260 run;
```

| Basic Statistical Measures | | | |
|---|---|---|---|
| Location | | Variability | |
| Mean | 80.00000 | Std Deviation | 33.42234 |
| Median | 80.00000 | Variance | 1117 |
| Mode | 80.00000 | Range | 107.00000 |
| | | Interquartile Range | 58.00000 |

Additionally, we can look at the fourth table to get the minimum and maximum values. If we find the difference between these two values, we get the range:

| Quantiles (Definition 5) | |
|---|---|
| Level | Quantile |
| 100% Max | 143.0 |
| 99% | 143.0 |
| 95% | 137.5 |
| 90% | 127.5 |
| 75% Q3 | 107.5 |
| 50% Median | 80.0 |
| 25% Q1 | 49.5 |
| 10% | 39.5 |
| 5% | 37.0 |
| 1% | 36.0 |
| 0% Min | 36.0 |

Table 5.5 displayed a crosstabulation for the frequency of births based on the type of hospital (public versus private) and insurance status (insured versus uninsured) of mothers. We will use SAS to convert these data to a conditional probability table.

First, we can create Table 5.5:

```
290 data work.Hospital;
291     input Hospital $ Insurance $ Count;
292     datalines;
293 Private Uninsured  30
294 Private Insured   40
295 Public Uninsured   80
296 Public Insured 50
297 ;
```

The output looks like this:

Total rows: 4   Total columns: 3

|   | Hospital | Insurance | Count |
|---|----------|-----------|-------|
| 1 | Private | Uninsure | 30 |
| 2 | Private | Insured | 40 |
| 3 | Public | Uninsure | 80 |
| 4 | Public | Insured | 50 |

Notice that "Uninsured" is missing the d. This is because SAS cuts off letters or characters to save space, though you can manually override this.

Next, we can use the PROC FREQ statement to calculate the information we want. We can create one table that gives us frequencies (like those in the table above), overall percents for each category, conditional row and column probabilities, and row and column totals. We supply the data and use the TABLES statement to let SAS know we want a crosstabulation for the frequency of births based on the type of hospital (public versus private) and insurance status (insured versus uninsured). The WEIGHT statement states that the "Count" column has the total number of subjects for each condition. Finally, we can add a title:

```
299 proc freq data=work.Hospital;
300    tables Hospital*Insurance;
301    weight Count;
302    title 'Birth Frequency';
303 run;
```

The output gives us a key that lets us know what each row in each cell represents. For example, in the Private*Insured cell, 40 is the frequency, 20 is the overall percent ($40/200 = 20\%$), 57.14 is the conditional probability based on the row ($40/70 = 57.14\%$), and 44.44 is the conditional probability based on the column ($40/90 = 44.44\%$).

**Birth Frequency**

The FREQ Procedure

| Frequency Percent Row Pct Col Pct | | | |
|---|---|---|---|

| Table of Hospital by Insurance | | | |
|---|---|---|---|
| | Insurance | | |
| Hospital | Insured | Uninsure | Total |
| Private | 40 20.00 57.14 44.44 | 30 15.00 42.86 27.27 | 70 35.00 |
| Public | 50 25.00 38.46 55.56 | 80 40.00 61.54 72.73 | 130 65.00 |
| Total | 90 45.00 | 110 55.00 | 200 100.00 |

# 6.8 SAS IN FOCUS

## Converting Raw Scores to Standard *z* Scores

Privitera's *Statisics for the Behavioral Sciences,* Third Edition (p. 193)

SAS can be used to compute a *z* transformation for a given dataset. To demonstrate how SAS computes *z* scores, suppose you evaluate the effectiveness of an SAT remedial tutoring course with 16 students who plan to retake the standardized exam. Table 6.2 lists the number of points that each student gained on the exam after taking the remedial course. We will use SAS to convert these data into *z* scores using the PROC STANDARD statement. After creating our dataset, we tell SAS what dataset to use, and to set the mean to 0 and the standard deviation to 1. We can name this new dataset "zSAT" and print that output:

```
312 data work.SAT;
313     input SATScore@@;
314     datalines;
315 500 750 600 900 950 880 990 560 780 800 800 450 800 680 550 600
316 ;
317 run;
318
319 proc print data=work.SAT;
320 run;
321
322 PROC STANDARD data=work.SAT mean=0 STD=1 OUT=zSAT;
323 run;
324
325 proc print data=zSAT;
326 run;
```

| Obs | SAT Score |
|-----|-----------|
| 1 | -1.35157 |
| 2 | 0.15436 |
| 3 | -0.74920 |
| 4 | 1.05791 |
| 5 | 1.35910 |
| 6 | 0.93744 |
| 7 | 1.60005 |
| 8 | -0.99015 |
| 9 | 0.33507 |
| 10 | 0.45554 |
| 11 | 0.45554 |
| 12 | -1.65275 |
| 13 | 0.45554 |
| 14 | -0.26730 |
| 15 | -1.05038 |
| 16 | -0.74920 |

Researchers rarely know the value of the population standard deviation, which is in the numerator of the formula for standard error. It is more common to estimate the standard error by substituting the sample standard deviation in place of the population standard deviation in the formula for standard error. SAS makes this substitution to compute an estimate of standard error. The formula, which is discussed further in Chapter 9, is as follows:

$$s_M = \frac{s}{\sqrt{n}}.$$

We can use SAS to estimate the standard error using this formula. To illustrate, suppose we measure the individual reaction times (in seconds) for a team of 10 firefighters to respond to an emergency call. The reaction times are 93, 66, 30, 44, 20, 100, 35, 58, 70, and 81. To do this, we will use the PROC UNIVARIATE statement we previously used:

```
335 data work.ecall;
336     input Reaction@@;
337     datalines;
338 93 66 30 44 20 100 35 58 70 81
339 ;
340 run;
341
342 proc print data=work.ecall;
343 run;
344
345 proc univariate data=work.ecall;
346 run;
```

In the output, we see our data, as well as the Std Error Mean in the last row and column of the first table:

| Obs | Reaction |
|-----|----------|
| 1 | 93 |
| 2 | 66 |
| 3 | 30 |
| 4 | 44 |
| 5 | 20 |
| 6 | 100 |
| 7 | 35 |
| 8 | 58 |
| 9 | 70 |
| 10 | 81 |

The UNIVARIATE Procedure
Variable: Reaction

| Moments | | | |
|---------|---------|---------|---------|
| N | 10 | Sum Weights | 10 |
| Mean | 59.7 | Sum Observations | 597 |
| Std Deviation | 27.1827151 | Variance | 738.9 |
| Skewness | 0.03921025 | Kurtosis | -1.2287789 |
| Uncorrected SS | 42291 | Corrected SS | 6650.1 |
| Coeff Variation | 45.5321861 | Std Error Mean | 8.59592927 |

125

SAS can be used to compute the one-sample *t* test. To illustrate how to compute this test in SAS and how the output tables in SAS match with the data we computed by hand, let us compute this test using the same data given for Example 9.1 in Table 9.3. For reference, the social functioning scores in the sample of 18 relatives who care for patients with OCD were 20, 60, 48, 92, 50, 82, 48, 90, 30, 68, 43, 54, 60, 62, 94, 67, 63, and 85. We will compare these scores to the mean in the general healthy population ($\mu = 77.43$) using a .05 level of significance ($\alpha = .05$).

After we create our dataset, we can use the PROC TTEST statement. We give SAS our dataset, as well as the population mean and alpha level:

```
355 data work.OCD;
356     input Score@@;
357     datalines;
358 20 60 48 92 50 82 48 90 30 68 43 54 60 62 94 67 63 85
359 ;
360 run;
361
362 proc print data=work.OCD;
363 run;
364
365 proc ttest data=work.OCD h0=77.43 alpha=0.05;
366     var Score;
367 run;
```

SAS will give you a graph with the data distribution and confidence intervals. You will also see the sample size (*N*), the sample mean, the sample standard deviation, and the estimated standard error. The middle table gives the confidence intervals (confidence intervals will be described in Chapter 11), and the bottom table displays the obtained value for *t*, the degrees of freedom, and the *p* value.

### The TTEST Procedure
### Variable: Score

| N | Mean | Std Dev | Std Err | Minimum | Maximum |
|---|------|---------|---------|---------|---------|
| 18 | 62.0000 | 20.9425 | 4.9362 | 20.0000 | 94.0000 |

| Mean | 95% CL Mean | | Std Dev | 95% CL Std Dev | |
|------|------|------|---------|------|------|
| 62.0000 | 51.5855 | 72.4145 | 20.9425 | 15.7150 | 31.3958 |

| DF | t Value | Pr > \|t\| |
|----|---------|---------|
| 17 | -3.13 | 0.0062 |

## 9.9 SAS IN FOCUS

### Two-Independent-Sample *t* Test

Privitera's *Statisics for the Behavioral Sciences,* Third Edition (p. 297)

SAS can be used to compute the two-independent-sample *t* test. To illustrate how to compute this test in SAS and how the output tables in SAS match with the data we computed by hand, let us compute this test using the same data originally given for Example 9.2 in Table 9.7. For reference, Table 9.11 restates the original data for this example, which we will enter into SAS. We will compare these data between groups using a .05 level of significance ($\alpha = .05$).

**Table 9.11** The Number of Calories Consumed in a Meal Between Groups Asked to Eat Slowly or Fast

| Group Eating Slowly | Group Eating Fast |
|:---:|:---:|
| 700 | 450 |
| 450 | 800 |
| 850 | 750 |
| 600 | 700 |
| 450 | 550 |
| 550 | 650 |

After creating our dataset, we again use the PROC TTEST statement. We tell SAS what dataset to use, and use CLASS to specify that Speed is the variable that describes the different groups that are being compared. VAR tells SAS that the Calories column contains the data to be used for analysis.

```
371 data Calories;
372      input Speed $ Calories @@;
373      datalines;
374 Slow 700 Slow 450 Slow 850 Slow 600 Slow 450 Slow 550
375 Fast 450 Fast 800 Fast 750 Fast 700 Fast 550 Fast 650
376 ;
377 run;
378
379 proc print data=work.Calories;
380 run;
381
382 proc ttest data=work.Calories;
383      class Speed;
384      var Calories;
385 run;
```

Our output gives us a lot of information. For our example, we will assume equal variances between groups. The top table displays the sample size ($N = 6$), mean, standard deviation, and standard error for both groups. The second table displays the confidence intervals (see the Pooled Method output, −134.2 to 234.2; confidence intervals will be discussed in Chapter 11). The third table reports the degrees of freedom, the $t$ value, and the $p$ value (see Pooled method, Equal variances).

The TTEST Procedure
Variable: Calories

| Speed | N | Mean | Std Dev | Std Err | Minimum | Maximum |
|-------|---|------|---------|---------|---------|---------|
| Fast | 6 | 650.0 | 130.4 | 53.2291 | 450.0 | 800.0 |
| Slow | 6 | 600.0 | 154.9 | 63.2456 | 450.0 | 850.0 |
| Diff (1-2) | | 50.0000 | 143.2 | 82.6640 | | |

| Speed | Method | Mean | 95% CL Mean | | Std Dev | 95% CL Std Dev | |
|-------|--------|------|-------------|---|---------|----------------|---|
| Fast | | 650.0 | 513.2 | 786.8 | 130.4 | 81.3868 | 319.8 |
| Slow | | 600.0 | 437.4 | 762.6 | 154.9 | 96.7019 | 380.0 |
| Diff (1-2) | Pooled | 50.0000 | -134.2 | 234.2 | 143.2 | 100.0 | 251.3 |
| Diff (1-2) | Satterthwaite | 50.0000 | -134.9 | 234.9 | | | |

| Method | Variances | DF | t Value | Pr > \|t\| |
|--------|-----------|----|---------|-----------|
| Pooled | Equal | 10 | 0.60 | 0.5587 |
| Satterthwaite | Unequal | 9.7168 | 0.60 | 0.5591 |

| Equality of Variances | | | | |
|-------|---------|--------|---------|--------|
| Method | Num DF | Den DF | F Value | Pr > F |
| Folded F | 5 | 5 | 1.41 | 0.7144 |

The effect size is not given, although you can use the data given in the output tables to compute effect size. Also, notice that the top table gives the numerator and denominator for the $t$ test. If we substitute the values in the SAS output table (bottom row) into the formula, we will obtain the same values for the test statistic computed in Example 9.2:

$$t_{obt} = \frac{\text{Mean Difference}}{\text{Std. Error Difference}} = \frac{-50.00}{82.66} = -0.605.$$

# 10.4 SAS IN FOCUS

## The Related-Samples *t* Test

Privitera's *Statisics for the Behavioral Sciences,* Third Edition (p. 317)

In Example 10.1, we tested whether teacher supervision influences the time that elementary school children read. We used a two-tailed test at a .05 level of significance and decided to reject the null hypothesis. Thus, we concluded that elementary school children spent significantly more time reading in the presence of a teacher than when the teacher was absent, $t(7) = 2.804$, $p < .05$. We can confirm this result using SAS.

First, we need to make a dataset, as shown in Table 10.7. However, our dataset will look different from the one we did for the independent-sample *t* test. This time, we want it to look exactly as it appears in Table 10.7.

**Table 10.7** Data for the Related-Samples *t* Test

| present | absent |
|--------:|-------:|
| 220 | 210 |
| 245 | 220 |
| 215 | 195 |
| 260 | 265 |
| 300 | 275 |
| 280 | 290 |
| 250 | 220 |
| 310 | 285 |

```
394 data work.Supervision;
395     input Present Absent@@;
396     datalines;
397 220 210 245 220 215 195 260 265 300 275 280 290 250 220 310 285
398 ;
399 run;
400
401 proc print data=work.Supervision;
402 run;
```

129

| Obs | Present | Absent |
|-----|---------|--------|
| 1 | 220 | 210 |
| 2 | 245 | 220 |
| 3 | 215 | 195 |
| 4 | 260 | 265 |
| 5 | 300 | 275 |
| 6 | 280 | 290 |
| 7 | 250 | 220 |
| 8 | 310 | 285 |

Next, we use the PROC TTEST statement and the PAIRED statement to let SAS know which two columns have paired, or related, observations:

```
404 proc ttest data=work.Supervision;
405 paired Present*Absent;
406 run;
```

The TTEST Procedure
Difference: Present - Absent

| N | Mean | Std Dev | Std Err | Minimum | Maximum |
|---|------|---------|---------|---------|---------|
| 8 | 15.0000 | 15.1186 | 5.3452 | -10.0000 | 30.0000 |

| Mean | 95% CL Mean | | Std Dev | 95% CL Std Dev | |
|------|------|------|---------|------|------|
| 15.0000 | 2.3606 | 27.6394 | 15.1186 | 9.9960 | 30.7704 |

| DF | t Value | Pr > |t| |
|----|---------|---------|
| 7 | 2.81 | 0.0263 |

Notice that the calculations we made match the results displayed in the output tables.

# 11.5 SAS IN FOCUS

## Confidence Intervals for the One-Sample *t* Test

Privitera's *Statisics for the Behavioral Sciences,* Third Edition (p. 347)

In Chapter 9, we computed a one-sample *t* test using SAS for the data given in Example 11.2. The SAS output lists the 95% confidence interval for the outcome we observed. To change the confidence interval, we can choose any level of confidence in the ALPHA. In Chapter 9, we used a 95% confidence interval with the *t* test. Let us compare these results to those with a 90% confidence interval:

```
415 data work.OCD;
416     input Score@@;
417     datalines;
418 20  60  48  92  50  82  48  90  30  68  43  54  60  62  94  67  63  85
419 ;
420 run;
421
422 proc print data=work.OCD;
423 run;
424
425 proc ttest data=work.OCD h0=77.43 alpha=0.1;
426     var Score;
427 run;
```

The output in the tables on the left is for a 95% confidence interval, and the output in the tables on the right is for a 90% confidence interval.

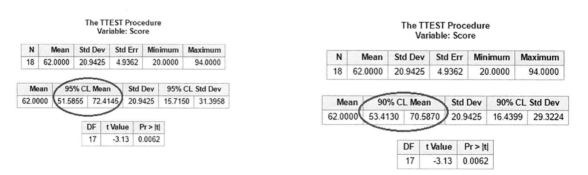

The TTEST Procedure
Variable: Score

| N | Mean | Std Dev | Std Err | Minimum | Maximum |
|---|---|---|---|---|---|
| 18 | 62.0000 | 20.9425 | 4.9362 | 20.0000 | 94.0000 |

| Mean | 95% CL Mean | | Std Dev | 95% CL Std Dev | |
|---|---|---|---|---|---|
| 62.0000 | 51.5855 | 72.4145 | 20.9425 | 15.7150 | 31.3958 |

| DF | t Value | Pr > \|t\| |
|---|---|---|
| 17 | -3.13 | 0.0062 |

The TTEST Procedure
Variable: Score

| N | Mean | Std Dev | Std Err | Minimum | Maximum |
|---|---|---|---|---|---|
| 18 | 62.0000 | 20.9425 | 4.9362 | 20.0000 | 94.0000 |

| Mean | 90% CL Mean | | Std Dev | 90% CL Std Dev | |
|---|---|---|---|---|---|
| 62.0000 | 53.4130 | 70.5870 | 20.9425 | 16.4399 | 29.3224 |

| DF | t Value | Pr > \|t\| |
|---|---|---|
| 17 | -3.13 | 0.0062 |

In this example, we see that our confidence interval is wider at the 95% level (table on the previous page):

95% confidence interval width:

$72.414 - 51.5855 = 20.829$

90% confidence interval width:

$70.5870 - 53.4130 = 17.174$

This makes sense, intuitively, because if we want to be more confident (95% versus 90%) that the actual population mean is between two values, we should make the range of possible values for the mean larger! Clearly, the difference in our 95% confidence level range is larger (20.83, rounded) than that of the 90% confidence level (17.17, rounded).

# 11.7 SAS IN FOCUS

## Confidence Intervals for the Two-Independent-Sample *t* Test

Privitera's *Statisics for the Behavioral Sciences,* Third Edition (p. 350)

In Chapter 9, we computed a two-independent-sample *t* test using SAS for the data given in Example 11.3. Note that in the PROC TTEST statement we do not have to specify the alpha level; the default is .05:

```
436 data Calories;
437      input Speed $ Calories @@;
438      datalines;
439 Slow 700 Slow 450 Slow 850 Slow 600 Slow 450 Slow 550
440 Fast 450 Fast 800 Fast 750 Fast 700 Fast 550 Fast 650
441 ;
442 run;
443
444 proc print data=work.Calories;
445 run;
446
447 proc ttest data=work.Calories;
448      class Speed;
449      var Calories;
450 run;
```

The SAS output lists the 95% confidence interval for the mean difference between the groups (circled):

The TTEST Procedure
Variable: Calories

| Speed | N | Mean | Std Dev | Std Err | Minimum | Maximum |
|-------|---|------|---------|---------|---------|---------|
| Fast | 6 | 650.0 | 130.4 | 53.2291 | 450.0 | 800.0 |
| Slow | 6 | 600.0 | 154.9 | 63.2456 | 450.0 | 850.0 |
| Diff (1-2) | | 50.0000 | 143.2 | 82.6640 | | |

| Speed | Method | Mean | 95% CL Mean | | Std Dev | 95% CL Std Dev | |
|-------|--------|------|------|------|---------|------|------|
| Fast | | 650.0 | 513.2 | 786.8 | 130.4 | 81.3868 | 319.8 |
| Slow | | 600.0 | 437.4 | 762.6 | 154.9 | 96.7019 | 380.0 |
| Diff (1-2) | Pooled | 50.0000 | -134.2 | 234.2 | 143.2 | 100.0 | 251.3 |
| Diff (1-2) | Satterthwaite | 50.0000 | -134.9 | 234.9 | | | |

| Method | Variances | DF | t Value | Pr > |t| |
|--------|-----------|-----|---------|---------|
| Pooled | Equal | 10 | 0.60 | 0.5587 |
| Satterthwaite | Unequal | 9.7168 | 0.60 | 0.5591 |

| Equality of Variances | | | | |
|--------|--------|--------|---------|-------|
| Method | Num DF | Den DF | F Value | Pr > F |
| Folded F | 5 | 5 | 1.41 | 0.7144 |

Using these 95% confidence limits, we conclude that it is likely that there is no difference in calories consumed between groups instructed to eat slowly or fast because zero falls within the interval (−134.2 to 234.2, rounded).

# 11.9 SAS IN FOCUS

## Confidence Intervals for the Related-Samples *t* Test

Privitera's *Statisics for the Behavioral Sciences,* Third Edition (p. 353)

In Chapter 10, we computed a related-samples *t* test using SAS for the data given in Example 11.4. The SAS output lists the 95% confidence interval for the mean difference in time spent talking:

```
459 data work.Supervision;
460     input Present Absent@@;
461     datalines;
462 220 210 245 220 215 195 260 265 300 275 280 290 250 220 310 285
463 ;
464 run;
465
466 proc print data=work.Supervision;
467 run;
468
469 proc ttest data=work.Supervision;
470 paired Present*Absent;
471 run;
```

### The TTEST Procedure
### Difference: Present - Absent

| N | Mean | Std Dev | Std Err | Minimum | Maximum |
|---|------|---------|---------|---------|---------|
| 8 | 15.0000 | 15.1186 | 5.3452 | -10.0000 | 30.0000 |

| Mean | 95% CL Mean | | Std Dev | 95% CL Std Dev | |
|------|-------------|--------|---------|----------------|--------|
| 15.0000 | 2.3606 | 27.6394 | 15.1186 | 9.9960 | 30.7704 |

| DF | t Value | Pr > \|t\| |
|----|---------|-----------|
| 7 | 2.81 | 0.0263 |

## 12.8 SAS IN FOCUS

### The One-Way Between-Subjects ANOVA

Privitera's *Statisics for the Behavioral Sciences,* Third Edition (p. 389)

Using the data given in Table 12.10, which is reproduced from data originally given in Table 12.4, we will analyze this dataset using the PROC ANOVA statement in SAS. First, we need to enter our data; however, our dataset will look different from that in Table 12.10.

Table 12.10    Data for Example 12.1

| Perceived Stress Level of Workplace | | |
|---|---|---|
| Low | Moderate | High |
| 3.4 | 3.5 | 2.9 |
| 3.2 | 3.6 | 3.0 |
| 3.0 | 2.7 | 2.6 |
| 3.0 | 3.5 | 3.3 |
| 3.5 | 3.8 | 3.7 |
| 3.8 | 2.9 | 2.7 |
| 3.6 | 3.4 | 2.4 |
| 4.0 | 3.2 | 2.5 |
| 3.9 | 3.3 | 3.3 |
| 2.9 | 3.1 | 3.4 |

```
480 data work.Stress;
481    input Stress $ Score@@;
482    datalines;
483 Low 3.4 Low 3.2 Low 3.0 Low 3.0 Low 3.5 Low 3.8 Low 3.6 Low 4.0 Low 3.9 Low 2.9
484 Moderate 3.5 Moderate 3.6 Moderate 2.7 Moderate 3.5 Moderate 3.8 Moderate 2.9
485 Moderate 3.4 Moderate 3.2 Moderate 3.3 Moderate 3.1
486 High 2.9 High 3.0 High 2.6 High 3.3 High 3.7 High 2.7 High 2.4 High 2.5 High 3.3 High 3.4
487 ;
488 run;
```

To run the ANOVA, we can use the PROC ANOVA statement. We specify our dataset first. Next, we need to tell SAS that the treatment factor is given in the Stress variable. This is done with the CLASS statement. Finally, we tell SAS the response data can be found in the Score variable:

```
493 proc anova data=work.Stress;
494     class Stress;
495     model Score = Stress;
496 run;
```

The ANOVA Procedure
Dependent Variable: Score

| Source | DF | Sum of Squares | Mean Square | F Value | Pr > F |
|---|---|---|---|---|---|
| Model | 2 | 1.07266667 | 0.53633333 | 3.52 | 0.0439 |
| Error | 27 | 4.11700000 | 0.15248148 | | |
| Corrected Total | 29 | 5.18966667 | | | |

| R-Square | Coeff Var | Root MSE | Score Mean |
|---|---|---|---|
| 0.206693 | 12.06453 | 0.390489 | 3.236667 |

| Source | DF | Anova SS | Mean Square | F Value | Pr > F |
|---|---|---|---|---|---|
| Stress | 2 | 1.07266667 | 0.53633333 | 3.52 | 0.0439 |

The output gives us a lot of information. In the bottom table, we see the degrees of freedom, ANOVA Sum of Squares, Mean Square, our $F$ statistic, and the $p$ value. Visually inspecting your data is always a great idea, which is one great thing about the SAS output. By default, you will get a distribution plot of the data for each treatment group:

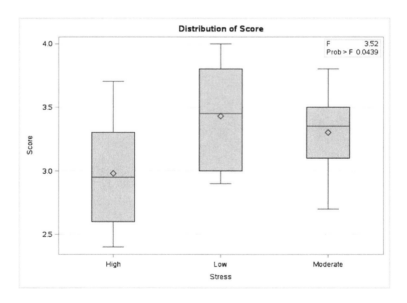

In this example, we see that $p$ is less than .05, so we can conclude that there is a statistically significant difference between the groups. However, where exactly are the differences? It is even a little difficult to see based on observing the plots. In order to find out which groups statistically differ from one another, we need post hoc analyses. There are several types, but we can illustrate a post hoc analysis with Tukey's HSD (Honestly Significant Difference). To do this, we add the MEANS statement to PROC ANOVA and specify we want the means for the Stress treatment groups to be compared. Finally, we specify Tukey for the post hoc analysis (note that there are several other post hoc analyses that you can specify):

```
498 proc anova data=work.Stress;
499     class Stress;
500     model Score = Stress;
501     means Stress / tukey;
502
503 run;
```

The ANOVA Procedure
Tukey's Studentized Range (HSD) Test for Score

Note: This test controls the Type I experimentwise error rate, but it generally has a higher Type II error rate than REGWQ.

| Alpha | 0.05 |
|---|---|
| Error Degrees of Freedom | 27 |
| Error Mean Square | 0.152481 |
| Critical Value of Studentized Range | 3.50633 |
| Minimum Significant Difference | 0.433 |

Means with the same letter are not significantly different.

| Tukey Grouping | | Mean | N | Stress |
|---|---|---|---|---|
| | A | 3.4300 | 10 | Low |
| | A | | | |
| B | A | 3.3000 | 10 | Moderate |
| B | | | | |
| B | | 2.9800 | 10 | High |

The bottom table shows the means for each Stress group. We can determine which groups are significantly different by looking at the letters (A, B) in the two columns on the left (Tukey Grouping). When two groups have the same letter, they are *not* significantly different. For example, the Low Stress group has the letter A. Also, the Moderate Stress group has the letter A. Therefore, these two groups are not significantly different. However, the Low Stress group only has the letter A, and the High Stress group only has the letter B; therefore, they do not share the same letter and the means of these two groups are significantly different. Finally, the Moderate and High Stress groups both share the letter B, which means they are not significantly different.

In Example 13.1, we concluded that ratings of effectiveness for the three advertisements significantly varied, $F(2, 12) = 17.38, p < .05$. A Bonferroni procedure showed that participants rated the effectiveness of an ad with smoking-related cues higher compared to an ad with no cues and compared to an ad with generic cues. We will use SAS to confirm the calculations we computed in Example 13.1.

First, we have to create our dataset. We will set it up to have each row represent a subject. The first row will specify the subject, and the next three columns will be the scores for each of the advertisement conditions (Cues, Generic, and Smoking):

```
512 data work.Adver;
513     input Subject Cues Generic Smoking;
514     datalines;
515 1 2 5 5
516 2 3 5 6
517 3 1 4 5
518 4 4 5 7
519 5 4 3 6
520 6 5 4 7
521 7 2 2 6
522 ;
523 run;
```

The data table should look like this:

Total rows: 7  Total columns: 4      Rows 1-7

|   | Subject | Cues | Generic | Smoking |
|---|---------|------|---------|---------|
| 1 | 1 | 2 | 5 | 5 |
| 2 | 2 | 3 | 5 | 6 |
| 3 | 3 | 1 | 4 | 5 |
| 4 | 4 | 4 | 5 | 7 |
| 5 | 5 | 4 | 3 | 6 |
| 6 | 6 | 5 | 4 | 7 |
| 7 | 7 | 2 | 2 | 6 |

To run the analysis, we can use the PROC ANOVA statement. We specify the dataset, which we titled Work.Ader. Our MODEL statement lets SAS know the three outcome variable scores are in the Cues, Generic, and Smoking columns. The NOUNI statement simply asks SAS to omit separate analyses for each of the variables. Finally, the REPEATED statement simply creates labels for our output:

```
525 proc ANOVA data=work.Adver;
526     model Cues Generic Smoking= /NOUNI;
527     repeated Time 3 (1 2 3);
528 run;
```

**The ANOVA Procedure**
**Repeated Measures Analysis of Variance**
**Univariate Tests of Hypotheses for Within Subject Effects**

| Source | DF | Anova SS | Mean Square | F Value | Pr > F | Adj Pr > F G - G | Adj Pr > F H - F |
|--------|----|----------|-------------|---------|--------|------------------|------------------|
| Time | 2 | 32.66666667 | 16.33333333 | 17.29 | 0.0003 | 0.0022 | 0.0011 |
| Error(Time) | 12 | 11.33333333 | 0.94444444 | | | | |

| Greenhouse-Geisser Epsilon | 0.6613 |
|----------------------------|--------|
| Huynh-Feldt Epsilon | 0.7759 |

Our results converge with those we calculated by hand. The *F* statistic is 17.29 and the *p* value is less than .05. Next, we need to find out which group means are different statistically. In other words, we want to compare the mean of the No Cues group to the mean of the Generic Cues group, and the mean of the No Cues group to the mean of the Smoking = Related Cues group, and so on. We can do this with a related *t* test. However, we cannot *just* do paired *t* tests because we are simultaneously calculating multiple comparisons. Therefore, we need to make an adjustment to our *p* value. We can do this by dividing our *p* value by the number of comparisons we are making. In this example, we are making three comparisons. This correction is called the Bonferroni correction. Let us calculate the related *t* tests in SAS:

```
530 proc ttest data=work.Adver;
531     paired Cues*Generic Cues*Smoking Generic*Smoking;
532 run;
```

**The TTEST Procedure**
**Difference: Cues - Generic**

| N | Mean | Std Dev | Std Err | Minimum | Maximum |
|---|------|---------|---------|---------|---------|
| 7 | -1.0000 | 1.7321 | 0.6547 | -3.0000 | 1.0000 |

| Mean | 95% CL Mean | | Std Dev | 95% CL Std Dev | |
|------|-------------|--|---------|----------------|--|
| -1.0000 | -2.6019 | 0.6019 | 1.7321 | 1.1161 | 3.8141 |

| DF | t Value | Pr > |t| |
|----|---------|---------|
| 6 | -1.53 | 0.1775 |

Difference: Cues - Smoking

| N | Mean | Std Dev | Std Err | Minimum | Maximum |
|---|---|---|---|---|---|
| 7 | -3.0000 | 0.8165 | 0.3086 | -4.0000 | -2.0000 |

| Mean | 95% CL Mean | | Std Dev | 95% CL Std Dev | |
|---|---|---|---|---|---|
| -3.0000 | -3.7551 | -2.2449 | 0.8165 | 0.5261 | 1.7980 |

| DF | t Value | Pr > |t| |
|---|---|---|
| 6 | -9.72 | <.0001 |

Difference: Generic - Smoking

| N | Mean | Std Dev | Std Err | Minimum | Maximum |
|---|---|---|---|---|---|
| 7 | -2.0000 | 1.4142 | 0.5345 | -4.0000 | 0 |

| Mean | 95% CL Mean | | Std Dev | 95% CL Std Dev | |
|---|---|---|---|---|---|
| -2.0000 | -3.3079 | -0.6921 | 1.4142 | 0.9113 | 3.1142 |

| DF | t Value | Pr > |t| |
|---|---|---|
| 6 | -3.74 | 0.0096 |

The SAS output gives us *p* values for the different group comparisons. Dividing those *p* values by three gives us the Bonferroni correction we want. Our results converge with those we calculated by hand. We find that the means of the Generic and No Cues groups are not statistically different from one another; however, the means of the Generic versus Smoking-Related Cues groups are statistically different from one another, as are the means of the Smoking-Related and No Cues groups.

# 14.8 SAS IN FOCUS

## The Two-Way Between-Subjects ANOVA

Privitera's *Statisics for the Behavioral Sciences,* Third Edition (p. 474)

In Example 14.1, we tested whether levels of exposure to sugars interfered with the time it took participants to complete a computer task in the presence or absence of a buffet of sugary foods. We concluded that participants with more exposure to sugars took longer to complete the computer task when the buffet of sugary foods was present. Using the same data as in Example 14.1, we will use SAS to confirm the calculations that we computed for these data.

First, enter the data:

```
541 data work.Sugars;
542    input Buffet $ Exposure $ Times@@;
543    datalines;
544 Absent Low 8 Absent Low 7 Absent Low 9 Absent Low 10 Absent Low 12 Absent Low 8
545 Absent Mod 10 Absent Mod 12 Absent Mod 15 Absent Mod 8 Absent Mod 6 Absent Mod 9
546 Absent High 13 Absent High 9 Absent High 11 Absent High 8 Absent High 13 Absent High 12
547 Present Low 5 Present Low 8 Present Low 5 Present Low 6 Present Low 5 Present Low 7
548 Present Mod 15 Present Mod 10 Present Mod 8 Present Mod 9 Present Mod 7 Present Mod 11
549 Present High 15 Present High 12 Present High 15 Present High 16 Present High 12 Present High 14
550 ;
551 run;
```

Next, we can use the PROC ANOVA statement to run the ANOVA. We provide our data, then use the CLASS statement to let SAS know what our treatment groups are. The MODEL statement defines the response variable (Times) and then lets SAS know there are two main effects (Buffet and Exposure) and an interaction (Buffet*Exposure). The MEANS statement asks SAS to report post hoc tests:

```
556 proc anova data=work.Sugars;
557    class Buffet Exposure;
558    model Times = Buffet Exposure Buffet*Exposure;
559    means Buffet Exposure / tukey;
560    means Buffet Exposure Buffet*Exposure / tukey;
561 run;
```

SAS provides a lot of output. First, we see there is a significant Exposure main effect. Also, there is a significant Buffet*Exposure interaction:

The ANOVA Procedure
Dependent Variable: Times

| Source | DF | Sum of Squares | Mean Square | F Value | Pr > F |
|---|---|---|---|---|---|
| Model | 5 | 204.0000000 | 40.8000000 | 8.16 | <.0001 |
| Error | 30 | 150.0000000 | 5.0000000 | | |
| Corrected Total | 35 | 354.0000000 | | | |

| R-Square | Coeff Var | Root MSE | Times Mean |
|---|---|---|---|
| 0.576271 | 22.36068 | 2.236068 | 10.00000 |

| Source | DF | Anova SS | Mean Square | F Value | Pr > F |
|---|---|---|---|---|---|
| Buffet | 1 | 0.0000000 | 0.0000000 | 0.00 | 1.0000 |
| Exposure | 2 | 150.0000000 | 75.0000000 | 15.00 | <.0001 |
| Buffet*Exposure | 2 | 54.0000000 | 27.0000000 | 5.40 | 0.0099 |

141

Next, the Buffet plot shows there is most likely no Buffet main effect, which our analyses revealed in the main output (just discussed) and the table below the Buffet plot:

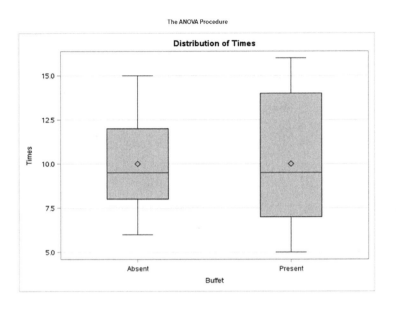

The ANOVA Procedure

**Distribution of Times**

The ANOVA Procedure
Tukey's Studentized Range (HSD) Test for Times

**Note:** This test controls the Type I experimentwise error rate, but it generally has a higher Type II error rate than REGWQ.

| Alpha | 0.05 |
|---|---|
| Error Degrees of Freedom | 30 |
| Error Mean Square | 5 |
| Critical Value of Studentized Range | 2.88818 |
| Minimum Significant Difference | 1.5222 |

Means with the same letter are not significantly different.

| Tukey Grouping | Mean | N | Buffet |
|---|---|---|---|
| A | 10.0000 | 18 | Absent |
| A | | | |
| A | 10.0000 | 18 | Present |

Next, we see that all Exposure groups are significantly different from one another, given the bottom table in the Exposure output shows that no two groups share a letter:

**The ANOVA Procedure**
**Tukey's Studentized Range (HSD) Test for Times**

**Note:** This test controls the Type I experimentwise error rate, but it generally has a higher Type II error rate than REGWQ.

| | |
|---|---|
| Alpha | 0.05 |
| Error Degrees of Freedom | 30 |
| Error Mean Square | 5 |
| Critical Value of Studentized Range | 3.48640 |
| Minimum Significant Difference | 2.2505 |

Means with the same letter are not significantly different.

| Tukey Grouping | Mean | N | Exposure |
|---|---|---|---|
| A | 12.5000 | 12 | High |
| B | 10.0000 | 12 | Mod |
| C | 7.5000 | 12 | Low |

Finally, the interaction plot shows clear differences between groups:

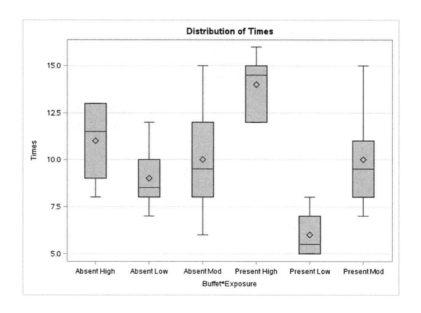

## Pearson Correlation Coefficient

Privitera's *Statisics for the Behavioral Sciences,* Third Edition (p. 501)

In Example 15.1, we concluded that mood and eating were significantly correlated ($r = -.744$, $p < .05$) using the Pearson correlation coefficient. Let us confirm this conclusion in SAS using the PROC CORR statement. We only need to specify the dataset and the two variables being correlated:

```
577 data work.Mood;
578     input Mood Eating@@;
579     datalines;
580 6 480 4 490 7 500 4 590 2 600 5 400 3 545 1 650
581 ;
582 run;
583
584 proc corr data=work.Mood;
585    var  Mood Eating;
586 run;
```

The output in the bottom table tells us the correlation ($-.74390$) and the $p$ value ($.0343$):

The CORR Procedure

| 2 Variables: | Mood Eating |
|---|---|

| Simple Statistics | | | | | | |
|---|---|---|---|---|---|---|
| Variable | N | Mean | Std Dev | Sum | Minimum | Maximum |
| Mood | 8 | 4.00000 | 2.00000 | 32.00000 | 1.00000 | 7.00000 |
| Eating | 8 | 531.87500 | 80.17559 | 4255 | 400.00000 | 650.00000 |

| Pearson Correlation Coefficients, N = 8 Prob > \|r\| under H0: Rho=0 | | |
|---|---|---|
|  | Mood | Eating |
| Mood | 1.00000 | -0.74390 0.0343 |
| Eating | -0.74390 0.0343 | 1.00000 |

# 15.8 SAS IN FOCUS

## Spearman Correlation Coefficient

Privitera's *Statisics for the Behavioral Sciences,* Third Edition (p. 512)

In Example 15.2, we concluded that a significant correlation was evident between the order of ranks on each task ($r_s = .768$, $p < .05$) using the Spearman correlation coefficient. Let us confirm this conclusion using SAS and the PROC CORR statement. We specify the dataset, let SAS know we are using the Spearman test, and specify the variables to be used in the VAR statement:

```
590 data work.Ranks;
591     input Food Water@@;
592     datalines;
593 1 1 1 3 3 2 4 6 5 4 6 7 7 8 8 5
594 ;
595 run;
596
597 proc corr data=work.Ranks Spearman;
598     var Food Water;
599 run;
```

The output in the bottom table gives us the correlation (.76648) and the *p* value (.0265).

The CORR Procedure

| 2 Variables: | Food Water |
|---|---|

| Simple Statistics | | | | | | |
|---|---|---|---|---|---|---|
| Variable | N | Mean | Std Dev | Median | Minimum | Maximum |
| Food | 8 | 4.37500 | 2.61520 | 4.50000 | 1.00000 | 8.00000 |
| Water | 8 | 4.50000 | 2.44949 | 4.50000 | 1.00000 | 8.00000 |

| Spearman Correlation Coefficients, N = 8 Prob > \|r\| under H0: Rho=0 | | |
|---|---|---|
| | Food | Water |
| Food | 1.00000 | 0.76648 0.0265 |
| Water | 0.76648 0.0265 | 1.00000 |

# 15.10 SAS IN FOCUS

## Point-Biserial Correlation Coefficient

Privitera's *Statisics for the Behavioral Sciences,* Third Edition (p. 517)

There is no command in SAS to compute a point-biserial correlation coefficient, so in order to do so, we need a macro definition. This just means there is no command in our base SAS program for this analysis. Instead, we need to get written code to calculate a point-biserial correlation. We can obtain that code by downloading a macro definition and saving it to our computer to run the analysis. We will save it to wherever we have been saving our .csv and SAS files. First, let us enter the data into SAS. In Example 15.3, we concluded that a correlation between sex and duration of laughter was not significant ($r_{pb} = -.163$, $p > .05$) using the point-biserial correlation coefficient.

```
603 data work.Comedy;
604     input Sex Laughter@@;
605     datalines;
606 1 23 1 9 1 12 1 12 1 29 2 32 2 10 2 8 2 20 2 12 2 24 2 34
607 ;
608 run;
```

The complete set of instructions and information about this macro can be found here: http://support.sas.com/kb/24/991.html. Go to the "Downloads" tab. You will see a blue link that says, "Download and save biserial.sas." Right-click on it and save it to where you have your .sas and .csv files saved. It should be in a folder called "myfolder," which should be saved in the "SASUniversityEdition" folder.

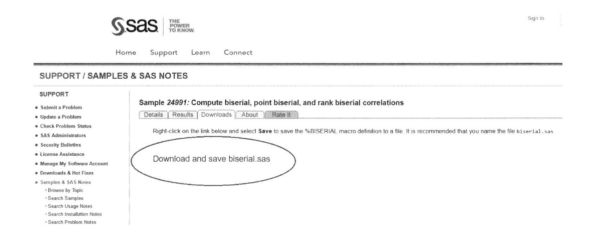

Now that we have the macro definition saved, we can run the analysis and create output:

```
610  /* Define the BISERIAL macro */
611 %let path=/folders/myfolders;
612
613
614 %biserial(data=work.Comedy, contin=Laughter, binary=Sex, out=out1);
615
616 proc print data=out1 label noobs;
617     title 'Point Biserial, Biserial and Rank Biserial Correlations';
618 run;
```

First, we need to define the path where the macro is saved. This is the "path=" code. Next, we specify that the data come from the work.Comedy dataset that we created. We also specify that "Laughter" is our continuous variable, and the binary variable is "Sex." The output from the analysis will be saved as "out1." Next, we use the PROC PRINT command to print our output, "out1." We can also add a TITLE to it:

### Point Biserial, Biserial and Rank Biserial Correlations

| Point Biserial Corr | Biserial Corr | Rank Biserial Corr |
|---|---|---|
| 0.16331 | . | 0.14286 |

The output results converge with those we calculated by hand. If your code did not run, you can copy and paste the macro definition code into your .sas file and run it *first*, and then run Proc Print function. The code can be found here:

http://support.sas.com/kb/24/addl/fusion24991_1_biserial.sas.txt

To compute a phi correlation coefficient using SAS, we first code each dichotomous factor and compute a Pearson correlation coefficient. Because the phi correlation coefficient is derived mathematically from the Pearson correlation coefficient, the value we obtain using SAS will be identical to that obtained for a phi correlation.

In Example 15.4, we concluded that a correlation between employment and happiness was significant ($r_\phi = .40$, $p < .05$) using the phi correlation coefficient. We can confirm this conclusion using SAS. First, we can code the variables as 1s and 0s (happy = 1, unhappy = 0, and employed = 1, unemployed = 0):

```
711 data work.Emp;
712     input Emp Happy@@;
713     datalines;
714 0 0 0 0 0 0 0 0 0 0 0 0 0 0 0 0 0 0 0 0 0 0 0 0 0 0 0 0 0 0
715 0 1 0 1 0 1 0 1 0 1 0 1 1 0 1 0 1 0 1 0 1 0 1 0 1 0
716 1 1 1 1 1 1 1 1 1 1 1 1 1 1 1 1 1 1 1 1 1 1 1 1 1 1 1 1
717 ;
718 run;
```

We use the PROC CORR statement to calculate the phi correlation, which converges with the one we calculated by hand:

```
720 proc corr data=work.Emp;
721     var  Emp Happy;
722 run;
```

The CORR Procedure

| 2 Variables: | Emp Happy |
|---|---|

| Simple Statistics | | | | | | |
|---|---|---|---|---|---|---|
| Variable | N | Mean | Std Dev | Sum | Minimum | Maximum |
| Emp | 40 | 0.50000 | 0.50637 | 20.00000 | 0 | 1.00000 |
| Happy | 40 | 0.50000 | 0.50637 | 20.00000 | 0 | 1.00000 |

| Pearson Correlation Coefficients, N = 40 Prob > \|r\| under H0: Rho=0 | | |
|---|---|---|
| | Emp | Happy |
| Emp | 1.00000 | 0.40000 0.0105 |
| Happy | 0.40000 0.0105 | 1.00000 |

# 16.7 SAS IN FOCUS

## Analysis of Regression

Privitera's *Statisics for the Behavioral Sciences,* Third Edition (p. 551)

To illustrate how all of our calculations are completed in SAS, let us compute the data in Example 16.3 in SAS. The data for Example 16.3 are reproduced in Table 16.5 from data originally given in Figure 16.5. We will compare how our analysis computed by hand matches the analysis computed using SAS.

**Table 16.5**  A Table Showing the Number of Sessions Eight Patients ($n = 8$) Attended and the Number of Symptoms They Expressed

| Number of Sessions (X) | Number of Symptoms (Y) |
|:---:|:---:|
| 9 | 0 |
| 5 | 3 |
| 8 | 2 |
| 2 | 5 |
| 6 | 3 |
| 3 | 4 |
| 5 | 2 |
| 4 | 3 |

An analysis of regression is easy in SAS! First, we enter our data, and then we use the PROC REG statement. We simply tell SAS which dataset to use, then we specify the dependent variable and the independent variable in the MODEL statement. Just like in a regression equation, the dependent variable goes on the left side of the equal sign, and the independent variable goes on the right side of the equal sign:

```
731 data work.Symp;
732     input Sessions Symptoms@@;
733     datalines;
734 9 0 5 3 8 2 2 5 6 3 3 4 5 2 4 3
735 ;
736 run;
737
738 proc reg data=work.Symp;
739     model Symptoms=Sessions;
740 run;
```

The REG Procedure
Model: MODEL1
Dependent Variable: Symptoms

| Number of Observations Read | 8 |
|---|---|
| Number of Observations Used | 8 |

**Analysis of Variance**

| Source | DF | Sum of Squares | Mean Square | F Value | Pr > F |
|---|---|---|---|---|---|
| Model | 1 | 12.81646 | 12.81646 | 28.66 | 0.0017 |
| Error | 6 | 2.68354 | 0.44726 | | |
| Corrected Total | 7 | 15.50000 | | | |

| Root MSE | 0.66877 | R-Square | 0.8269 |
|---|---|---|---|
| Dependent Mean | 2.75000 | Adj R-Sq | 0.7980 |
| Coeff Var | 24.31902 | | |

**Parameter Estimates**

| Variable | DF | Parameter Estimate | Standard Error | t Value | Pr > \|t\| |
|---|---|---|---|---|---|
| Intercept | 1 | 5.74051 | 0.60663 | 9.46 | <.0001 |
| Sessions | 1 | -0.56962 | 0.10641 | -5.35 | 0.0017 |

The results of this regression are significant for the predictor (Sessions variable) because the $p$ value is less than .05 (it is 0.0017). The estimate for the Sessions variable is $-0.56962$. This means that for every one-unit increase in the independent variable, there is a 0.56962-unit decrease in the dependent variable. For our example, this means that an increase in one session is related to a decrease of 0.56962 reported symptoms, on average. Simply put: Attending more sessions is related to fewer symptoms, on average. The $F$ statistic is 28.66, and the $R$-squared value is .8269. This is an important number because it is an indicator of how good our model is. The closer to 100% (or 1.00) the $R$-squared value is, the better our model is.

# 16.13 SAS IN FOCUS

## Multiple Regression Analysis

Privitera's *Statisics for the Behavioral Sciences,* Third Edition (p. 566)

While the many levels of computation and the many coefficients computed to perform an analysis of multiple regression might seem overwhelming, it can help to see how these values are summarized in the SAS output. To illustrate how all of our calculations are computed in SAS, let us use SAS to compute the data in Example 16.4. The data for Example 16.4 are reproduced in Table 16.13 from data originally given in Table 16.8. We will compare how our analysis computed by hand matches the analysis reported in the SAS output for multiple regression.

**Table 16.13** Data for the Age, Education Level, and Sales Among Six Patrons

| Age (years) $X_1$ | Education (years) $X_2$ | Sales (dollars) y |
|:---:|:---:|:---:|
| 19 | 12 | 20 |
| 21 | 14 | 40 |
| 26 | 13 | 30 |
| 28 | 18 | 68 |
| 32 | 17 | 70 |
| 30 | 16 | 60 |

In SAS, multiple regression is similar to simple regression, except now we add a variable, or variables, to our PROC REG and MODEL statements:

```
744 data work.Sales;
745     input Age Education Sales@@;
746     datalines;
747 19 12 20 21 14 40 26 13 30 28 18 68 32 17 70 30 16 60
748 ;
749 run;
750
751 proc reg data=work.Sales;
752     model Sales=Age Education;
753 run;
```

The REG Procedure
Model: MODEL1
Dependent Variable: Sales

| Number of Observations Read | 6 |
|---|---|
| Number of Observations Used | 6 |

| Analysis of Variance | | | | | |
|---|---|---|---|---|---|
| Source | DF | Sum of Squares | Mean Square | F Value | Pr > F |
| Model | 2 | 2156.09581 | 1078.04790 | 73.66 | 0.0028 |
| Error | 3 | 43.90419 | 14.63473 | | |
| Corrected Total | 5 | 2200.00000 | | | |

| Root MSE | 3.82554 | R-Square | 0.9800 |
|---|---|---|---|
| Dependent Mean | 48.00000 | Adj R-Sq | 0.9667 |
| Coeff Var | 7.96987 | | |

| Parameter Estimates | | | | | |
|---|---|---|---|---|---|
| Variable | DF | Parameter Estimate | Standard Error | t Value | Pr > \|t\| |
| Intercept | 1 | -82.94012 | 10.95740 | -7.57 | 0.0048 |
| Age | 1 | 0.79042 | 0.55382 | 1.43 | 0.2488 |
| Education | 1 | 7.35928 | 1.19333 | 6.17 | 0.0086 |

Our results give us the beta coefficients for age (0.79042) and education (7.35928). Age is not a significant predictor of sales; however, education is. For every 1-year increase in years of education, sales increase by 7.36 units, on average, holding age constant. Again, we also see the $F$ statistic, multiple $R$-squared, residual standard error, and the degrees of freedom.

One last thing we need to do is generate standardized beta coefficients, which can be helpful for interpreting and reporting results. This is simple in SAS. We simply add "stb" to the MODEL statement:

```
756 proc reg data=work.Sales;
757    model Sales=Age Education / stb;
758 run;
```

The results give us the standardized coefficients for both predictors:

The REG Procedure
Model: MODEL1
Dependent Variable: Sales

| Number of Observations Read | 6 |
|---|---|
| Number of Observations Used | 6 |

| Analysis of Variance | | | | | |
|---|---|---|---|---|---|
| Source | DF | Sum of Squares | Mean Square | F Value | Pr > F |
| Model | 2 | 2156.09581 | 1078.04790 | 73.66 | 0.0028 |
| Error | 3 | 43.90419 | 14.63473 | | |
| Corrected Total | 5 | 2200.00000 | | | |

| Root MSE | 3.82554 | R-Square | 0.9800 |
|---|---|---|---|
| Dependent Mean | 48.00000 | Adj R-Sq | 0.9667 |
| Coeff Var | 7.96987 | | |

| Parameter Estimates | | | | | | |
|---|---|---|---|---|---|---|
| Variable | DF | Parameter Estimate | Standard Error | t Value | Pr > \|t\| | Standardized Estimate |
| Intercept | 1 | -82.94012 | 10.95740 | -7.57 | 0.0048 | 0 |
| Age | 1 | 0.79042 | 0.55382 | 1.43 | 0.2488 | 0.19214 |
| Education | 1 | 7.35928 | 1.19333 | 6.17 | 0.0086 | 0.83024 |

# 17.3 SAS IN FOCUS

## The Chi-Square Goodness-of-Fit Test

Privitera's *Statisics for the Behavioral Sciences,* Third Edition (p. 586)

In Example 17.1, we concluded from the chi-square goodness-of-fit test that the frequency of dream recall during REM sleep was similar to what was expected, $\chi^2(2) = 3.06$, $p > .05$. Let us confirm this result using SAS.

First, we need to enter our data:

```
767  data work.Recall;
768      input Recall $ Count;
769      datalines;
770  Did 58
771  DidNot 12
772  Unsure 10
773  ;
774  run;
```

Total rows: 3  Total columns: 2

|   | Recall | Count |
|---|--------|-------|
| 1 | Did    | 58    |
| 2 | DidNot | 12    |
| 3 | Unsure | 10    |

We can use the PROC FREQ statement for the chi-square goodness-of-fit test. We specify our dataset, and then we use the CHISQ TESTP statement to specify our expected values. Finally, we tell SAS our observed values are in the Count column of our dataset:

```
776  proc freq data = work.Recall;
777     tables Recall / chisq testp=(80 10 10);
778     weight Count;
779  run;
```

The FREQ Procedure

| Recall | Frequency | Percent | Test Percent | Cumulative Frequency | Cumulative Percent |
|--------|-----------|---------|--------------|----------------------|--------------------|
| Did | 58 | 72.50 | 80.00 | 58 | 72.50 |
| DidNot | 12 | 15.00 | 10.00 | 70 | 87.50 |
| Unsure | 10 | 12.50 | 10.00 | 80 | 100.00 |

| Chi-Square Test for Specified Proportions | |
|-------------------------------------------|--------|
| Chi-Square | 3.0625 |
| DF | 2 |
| Pr > ChiSq | 0.2163 |

Our results converge with those we calculated by hand. We fail to reject the null hypothesis and conclude that our observations are similar to what we expected.

# 17.9 SAS IN FOCUS

## The Chi-Square Test for Independence

Privitera's *Statisics for the Behavioral Sciences,* Third Edition (p. 601)

In Example 17.2, a 2 × 2 chi-square test for independence showed a significant relationship between type of counseling and outcome of counseling, $\chi^2(1) = 5.386$, $p < .05$. Let us confirm this conclusion using SAS. First, let us create a table of our data:

```
783 data work.Counsel;
784     input Counsel $ Completion $ Count;
785     datalines;
786 Family Complete 22
787 Family Termination 12
788 Ind Complete 31
789 Ind Termination 45
790 ;
791 run;
```

Here is what the output looks like:

Total rows: 4   Total columns: 3

| | Counsel | Completion | Count |
|---|---|---|---|
| 1 | Family | Complete | 22 |
| 2 | Family | Terminat | 12 |
| 3 | Ind | Complete | 31 |
| 4 | Ind | Terminat | 45 |

Finally, let us run the chi-square test with the PROC FREQ statement. We supply the data, and we let SAS know we want to look at the "Counsel" and "Completion" variables (Counsel*Completion), we want a "chisq" (chi-square) test, and we want to use the number of observations in the "Count" column:

```
793 proc freq data=work.Counsel;
794     tables Counsel*Completion / chisq;
795     weight Count;
796 run;
```

The FREQ Procedure

| Frequency Percent Row Pct Col Pct | Table of Counsel by Completion | | |
|---|---|---|---|
| | | Completion | |
| Counsel | Complete | Terminat | Total |
| Family | 22 20.00 64.71 41.51 | 12 10.91 35.29 21.05 | 34 30.91 |
| Ind | 31 28.18 40.79 58.49 | 45 40.91 59.21 78.95 | 76 69.09 |
| Total | 53 48.18 | 57 51.82 | 110 100.00 |

Statistics for Table of Counsel by Completion

| Statistic | DF | Value | Prob |
|---|---|---|---|
| Chi-Square | 1 | 5.3818 | 0.0203 |
| Likelihood Ratio Chi-Square | 1 | 5.4334 | 0.0198 |
| Continuity Adj. Chi-Square | 1 | 4.4665 | 0.0346 |
| Mantel-Haenszel Chi-Square | 1 | 5.3329 | 0.0209 |
| Phi Coefficient | | 0.2212 | |
| Contingency Coefficient | | 0.2160 | |
| Cramer's V | | 0.2212 | |

SAS provides many different outputs for different tests. We want the output from the Chi-Square test in the bottom table. Notice that our results now converge with those we computed by hand.

### The Related-Samples Sign Test

Privitera's *Statisics for the Behavioral Sciences,* Third Edition (p. 621)

Based on data given in Table 18.2 in Example 18.2, we concluded that outbursts were more common in a class taught by a substitute teacher compared to a class taught by a full-time teacher, $x = 9$, $p < .05$. We can confirm this conclusion in SAS.

First, we create the dataset. We also need to create a new variable that calculates the difference in outbursts when the substitute teacher is present compared to when the full-time teacher is present. We can call this dataset work.Outburst2. We let SAS know we are building off the Work.Outburst dataset with the SET statement, and we can call the new variable "diff":

```
805 data work.Outburst;
806     input Sub Full@@;
807     datalines;
808 3 2 2 0 5 4 3 3 4 2 2 0 0 2 3 1 1 0 6 4 4 3
809 ;
810 run;
811
812 data work.Outburst2;
813     set work.Outburst;
814     diff=Sub-Full;
815 run;
```

To run the analysis, we use the PROC UNIVARIATE statement. We let SAS know the difference variable is in the "diff" column:

```
817 proc univariate data=work.Outburst2;
818     var diff;
819 run;
```

The results from the analysis are in the "Tests for Location Mu0=0" table. Analyses from three tests are produced, but we are interested in the Sign output. We see our results converge with those we computed by hand:

| Tests for Location: Mu0=0 | | | | |
|---|---|---|---|---|
| **Test** | | **Statistic** | **p Value** | |
| Student's t | t | 2.963189 | Pr > \|t\| | 0.0142 |
| Sign | M | 4 | Pr >= \|M\| | 0.0215 |
| Signed Rank | S | 20 | Pr >= \|S\| | 0.0410 |

# 18.5 SAS IN FOCUS

## The Wilcoxon Signed-Ranks *T* Test

Privitera's *Statisics for the Behavioral Sciences,* Third Edition (p. 626)

Based on the data given in Table 18.5 in Example 18.3, we concluded that patients significantly reduced their cigarette use six months following diagnosis of heart disease, $z = -2.28, p < .05$. Let us confirm this conclusion using SAS.

First, let us create our data table. We also need to create a new variable that gives us the difference between the before and following scores. We can call that "diff":

```
823 data work.Smoked;
824     input Before Following@@;
825     datalines;
826 23 20 12 16 11 10 15 0 25 5 20 8 11 0 9 15 13 8 15 13 30 12 21 0
827 ;
828 run;
829
830 data work.Smoked2;
831     set Smoked;
832     diff= Before-Following;
833 run;
```

The output should look like this:

Total rows: 12   Total columns: 3

|    | Before | Following | diff |
|----|--------|-----------|------|
| 1  | 23     | 20        | 3    |
| 2  | 12     | 16        | -4   |
| 3  | 11     | 10        | 1    |
| 4  | 15     | 0         | 15   |
| 5  | 25     | 5         | 20   |
| 6  | 20     | 8         | 12   |
| 7  | 11     | 0         | 11   |
| 8  | 9      | 15        | -6   |
| 9  | 13     | 8         | 5    |
| 10 | 15     | 13        | 2    |
| 11 | 30     | 12        | 18   |
| 12 | 21     | 0         | 21   |

For this test, we can use the PROC UNIVARIATE statement. We simply supply the dataset and let SAS know the difference variable is in the "diff" column:

```
835 proc univariate data=work.Smoked2;
836     var diff;
837 run;
```

Our results, which are in the bottom row of the bottom table, converge with those we calculated by hand:

### The UNIVARIATE Procedure
### Variable: diff

| Moments | | | |
|---|---|---|---|
| N | 12 | Sum Weights | 12 |
| Mean | 8.16666667 | Sum Observations | 98 |
| Std Deviation | 9.27198452 | Variance | 85.969697 |
| Skewness | -0.0406316 | Kurtosis | -1.3548248 |
| Uncorrected SS | 1746 | Corrected SS | 945.666667 |
| Coeff Variation | 113.534504 | Std Error Mean | 2.67659138 |

| Basic Statistical Measures | | | |
|---|---|---|---|
| Location | | Variability | |
| Mean | 8.166667 | Std Deviation | 9.27198 |
| Median | 8.000000 | Variance | 85.96970 |
| Mode | . | Range | 27.00000 |
| | | Interquartile Range | 15.00000 |

| Tests for Location: Mu0=0 | | | | |
|---|---|---|---|---|
| Test | | Statistic | p Value | |
| Student's t | t | 3.051144 | Pr > \|t\| | 0.0110 |
| Sign | M | 4 | Pr >= \|M\| | 0.0386 |
| Signed Rank | S | 29 | Pr >= \|S\| | 0.0210 |

# 18.7 SAS IN FOCUS

## The Mann-Whitney *U* Test

Privitera's *Statisics for the Behavioral Sciences,* Third Edition (p. 632)

Based on data given in Table 18.8 in Example 18.4, we concluded that job satisfaction was significantly greater among day-shift compared to night-shift employees, $U = 2$, $p < .05$. Let us confirm this conclusion using SAS.

First, create the data table. We use the PROC NPAR1WAY statement and specify the dataset as well as the Wilcoxon test. This may be confusing, but this is because the Mann-Whitney *U* Test can also be referred to as the Mann-Whitney-Wilcoxon test. We specify that the categorical independent variable (class) is found in the "Shift" column, and the outcome variable (var) is in the "Score" column. We ask for the exact Wilcoxon calculation:

```
841 data work.JobSat;
842     input Shift $ Score@@;
843     datalines;
844 Day 88 Day 72 Day 93 Day 67 Day 62
845 Night 24 Night 55 Night 70 Night 60 Night 50
846 ;
847 run;
848
849 proc npar1way data=work.JobSat wilcoxon;
850     class Shift;
851     var Score;
852     exact wilcoxon;
853 run;
```

Our results converge with those we calculated by hand:

The NPAR1WAY Procedure

| Wilcoxon Scores (Rank Sums) for Variable Score Classified by Variable Shift | | | | | |
|---|---|---|---|---|---|
| Shift | N | Sum of Scores | Expected Under H0 | Std Dev Under H0 | Mean Score |
| Day | 5 | 38.0 | 27.50 | 4.787136 | 7.60 |
| Night | 5 | 17.0 | 27.50 | 4.787136 | 3.40 |

| Wilcoxon Two-Sample Test | |
|---|---|
| Statistic (S) | 38.0000 |
| | |
| Normal Approximation | |
| Z | 2.0889 |
| One-Sided Pr > Z | 0.0184 |
| Two-Sided Pr > |Z| | 0.0367 |
| | |
| t Approximation | |
| One-Sided Pr > Z | 0.0331 |
| Two-Sided Pr > |Z| | 0.0663 |
| | |
| Exact Test | |
| One-Sided Pr >= S | 0.0159 |
| Two-Sided Pr >= |S - Mean| | 0.0317 |
| Z includes a continuity correction of 0.5. | |

| Kruskal-Wallis Test | |
|---|---|
| Chi-Square | 4.8109 |
| DF | 1 |
| Pr > Chi-Square | 0.0283 |

# 18.9 SAS IN FOCUS

## The Kruskal-Wallis *H* Test

Privitera's *Statisics for the Behavioral Sciences,* Third Edition (p. 637)

Based on data given in Table 18.12 in Example 18.5, we concluded that rankings of three safe driving video clips were significantly different, $H = 7.28$, $p < .05$. Let us confirm this conclusion using SAS.

First, we enter the data, and then we can use the PROC NPAR1WAY statement. We supply the data and let SAS know our class variable is in the "Clip" column, and the continuous variable is in the "Score" column. Notice we specify the Wilcoxon test, which may seem odd! This is because the test we want to use—the Kruskal-Wallis test—reduces to the Wilcoxon test when there are two samples.

```
857 data work.Driving;
858     input Clip $ Score@@;
859     datalines;
860 A 88 A 67 A 22 A 14 A 42 B 92 B 76 B 80 B 77 B 90 C 50 C 55 C 43 C 65 C 39
861 ;
862 run;
863
864 proc nparlway data=work.Driving wilcoxon;
865     class Clip;
866     var Score;
867 run;
```

### The NPAR1WAY Procedure

| Wilcoxon Scores (Rank Sums) for Variable Score Classified by Variable Clip | | | | | |
|---|---|---|---|---|---|
| Clip | N | Sum of Scores | Expected Under H0 | Std Dev Under H0 | Mean Score |
| A | 5 | 29.0 | 40.0 | 8.164966 | 5.80 |
| B | 5 | 62.0 | 40.0 | 8.164966 | 12.40 |
| C | 5 | 29.0 | 40.0 | 8.164966 | 5.80 |

| Kruskal-Wallis Test | |
|---|---|
| Chi-Square | 7.2600 |
| DF | 2 |
| Pr > Chi-Square | 0.0265 |

Our results converge with those we calculated by hand.

# 18.11 SAS IN FOCUS

## The Friedman Test

Privitera's *Statisics for the Behavioral Sciences,* Third Edition (p. 641)

Based on data given in Table 18.15a in Example 18.6, we concluded that there are no significant differences in the number of office visits made by women in each trimester of their pregnancy, $\chi_R^2(2) = 2.658$, $p > .05$. Let us confirm this conclusion using SAS.

For this dataframe, we need three columns. We need a column to specify the trimester, another one to specify the number of visits, and another column to specify the subject:

```
872 data work.Trimester;
873     input Subject Trimester $ Number@@;
874     datalines;
875 1 First 3 2 First 6 3 First 2 4 First 4 5 First 4 6 First 4 7 First 8
876 1 Second 5 2 Second 4 3 Second 0 4 Second 3 5 Second 6 6 Second 3 7 Second 6
877 1 Third 8 2 Third 7 3 Third 5 4 Third 2 5 Third 9 6 Third 7 7 Third 5
878 ;
879 run;
```

For the analysis, we use the PROC FREQ statement. We use the TABLE statement to specify the three variables we need (Subject, Trimester, and Number). The Friedman test is called with the cmh2 statement, and the "scores=rank" lets SAS know we are using rank scores:

```
881 proc freq data=work.Trimester;
882     tables Subject*Trimester*Number/
883             cmh2 scores=rank noprint;
884 run;
```

The FREQ Procedure

Summary Statistics for Trimester by Number
Controlling for Subject

| Cochran-Mantel-Haenszel Statistics (Based on Rank Scores) | | | | |
|---|---|---|---|---|
| Statistic | Alternative Hypothesis | DF | Value | Prob |
| 1 | Nonzero Correlation | 1 | 0.6429 | 0.4227 |
| 2 | Row Mean Scores Differ | 2 | 2.5714 | 0.2765 |

Total Sample Size = 21

There we go! Our results show there are no differences between groups ($p > .05$). Therefore, we also do not need any post hoc analyses.

## General Instruction Guide

Most SPSS users use the point-and-click method to run analyses. However, SAS users generally type code. Therefore, to make it easier for you, we include a link to all the code used to run analyses and generate the output in the chapter examples. In this way, you can easily learn to run analyses or modify them by copying and pasting the code rather than typing it all out by hand, which can be tedious. To access the code, go to this link:

http://edge.sagepub.com/priviterastats3e/student-resources/general-instructions-guide

# PART III

# Analysis in Focus: Stata

# Stata in Focus

## Sections for Privitera, *Statistics for the Behavioral Sciences,* Third Edition

Page numbers for corresponding sections in the third edition of Privitera's *Statistics for the Behavioral Sciences* are included in parentheses.

# To the Student—How to Use Stata With This Book

Stata is one of the major statistical software packages that is widely used in social science research. It is very powerful and can conduct a variety of analyses. Compared to other similar mainstream software, Stata has several advantages:

1. It is easier to access because it is relatively inexpensive. A perpetual license of the student version costs only $89. (The $89 version is called Small Stata. It has complete functionality and can support up to 99 distinctive variables/columns.)

2. It has a less steep learning curve because of its friendly, well-designed graphical user interface that supports pointing and clicking—just like using a spreadsheet-like application (e.g., Excel).

3. More importantly, in addition to pointing and clicking, Stata also supports the command line control.

The commands/codes used in Stata are simple and intuitive to learn. As you read through this chapter, you may gradually find the command line feature very productive, especially when you need to repeat certain analyses but with different variables. Stata also has a well-established support community where users can not only get help but also find and install user-created applications that are not originally embedded in Stata—similar to installing add-ons in Excel. In this chapter, we take a little different approach to help you start using Stata. Rather than solely focusing on pointing and clicking, or only on using the command line, we show you how to use both—thanks to Stata's powerful functionality.

This preface provides an overview to familiarize you with some features of Stata, including some basic interfaces and functions. Understanding this software is especially important for those interested in research careers because it is the most widely used statistical program in the social and behavioral sciences. That is not to minimize the importance of understanding how to compute a mean or plot a bar graph by hand—but knowing how to enter, analyze, and interpret statistics using Stata is equally important for no other reason than you will need it. This is an essential complement to your readings in this book. By knowing how and why you compute certain statistics, you will better understand and interpret the output from Stata software.

Please note, the screenshots in this book show Stata 14 for the PC. Still, even if you use a Mac or a different PC version, the figures and instructions should provide a rather effective guide for helping you use this software.

## Overview of Stata: What Are You Looking At?

When you open Stata, you will see the main interface. The interface is divided into five different "windows": Review, Results, Command, Variables, and Properties (see Figure P.1).

In case you do not see these five windows, or if you wish to add more windows to the main interface, go to the menu at the top of the interface and click on the Windows tab. You will see a list of windows that you can add to the current main interface.

### The Review Window

This window displays the history of commands that we have entered. A good feature of the review window is that the successful commands (i.e., the commands entered correctly) will be displayed in black, while the unsuccessful commands are highlighted in red, along with their error codes.

**Figure P.1** Stata Main Interface and Five Windows

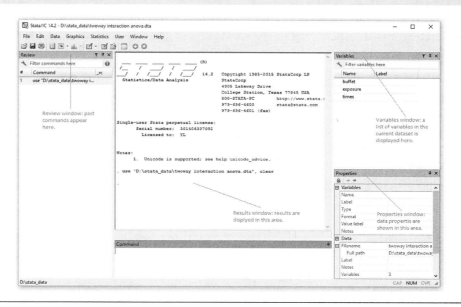

Furthermore, if we click on the command in the Review window, this command will copy to the Command window. With this feature, in case we want to conduct the same analysis but with different variables, we can easily manipulate and modify the command without entering it or going through the whole pointing and clicking process again. All the commands in the Review window can be exported and saved to a "Do-file," which is a program used to store the commands (see Figure P.2). When we right-click on the command (or highlight a set of commands, then right-click), there is an option called "Send selected to Do-file editor." The biggest benefit of this feature is that we can reproduce the results easily in the future, without redoing the analyses that have already been conducted.

**Figure P.2** An Example of a Do-File

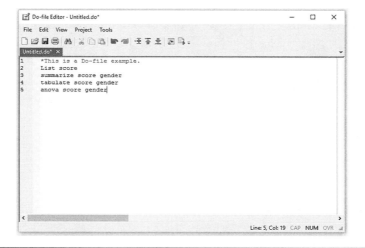

## The Results Window

All the results are shown in the Results window. If there is too much information in the window, we can easily clear it by right-clicking in the window and selecting Clear results. Please note that this action is not undoable.

## The Command Window

We input our codes in this window. By pressing *Enter*, we submit our complete commands to Stata. These commands will also appear under the command history in the Review window. As we previously noted, all of the successful commands are displayed in black, while the unsuccessful ones are highlighted in red.

## The Variables Window

The Variables window displays a list of variables in the current dataset, as well as the variables' properties. We can utilize this window to transfer the variable to the Command window by clicking on the variable we need.

## The Properties Window

This window shows the properties of the dataset and variables. We can also do some editing on our variables such as changing variable names and types or managing the variable label. One thing you should note is that by default, changes are not allowed. In order to modify the variable information, you need to first click on the lock icon 🔒 to unlock the area.

## The Toolbar

The toolbar, as displayed in Figure P.3, is similar to the toolbar in Excel or Word. It consists of some buttons/icons that provide quick access to some common features. If you need to know what a button does, move the mouse pointer to an icon and wait a second for a description to appear.

**Figure P.3**  The Toolbar in Stata

*Do-File Editor*

When we click on the icon 📝▾, the Do-file editor (as shown in Figure P.3) will open up.

*Data Editor (Edit)*

The Data Editor (Edit) window will open up when clicking on the icon 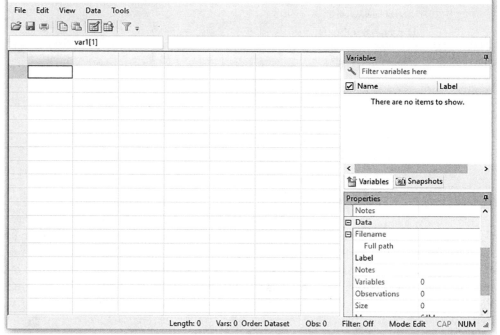, as shown in Figure P.4. This spreadsheet-like window allows us to enter, manage, and edit the data—just like we use Excel. We can input the new data, change the variable name, and manage the variable value label. Even better, we can directly copy and paste the data from Excel into Stata. On the right side, we can also find the Variables window and the Properties window, which display the variable names and the properties information. The Data Editor (Edit) window is one of the major windows with which we constantly interact.

**Figure P.4**  Data Editor (Edit) Window

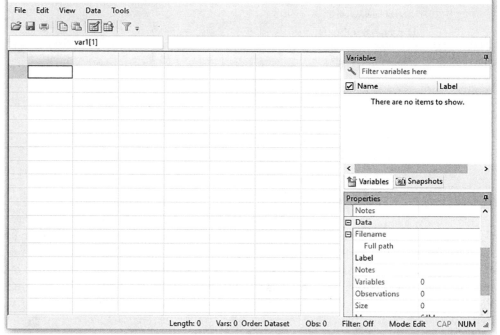

As a comparison, a similar icon, with a magnifier over the table, to the right of the Data Editor (Edit) icon is the Data Editor (Browse) icon. As its name indicates, this will change the Data Editor to the browse mode, where we can safely view the data without accidentally altering the original information.

Now, let us take a look at how to create a new variable and enter data in the Data Editor (Edit) window. Still in this window, click on the Data tab, then Create or change data → Create new variable, to open up the variable generation dialog box, as displayed in Figure P.5.

**Figure P.5**   Data Generation Dialog Box

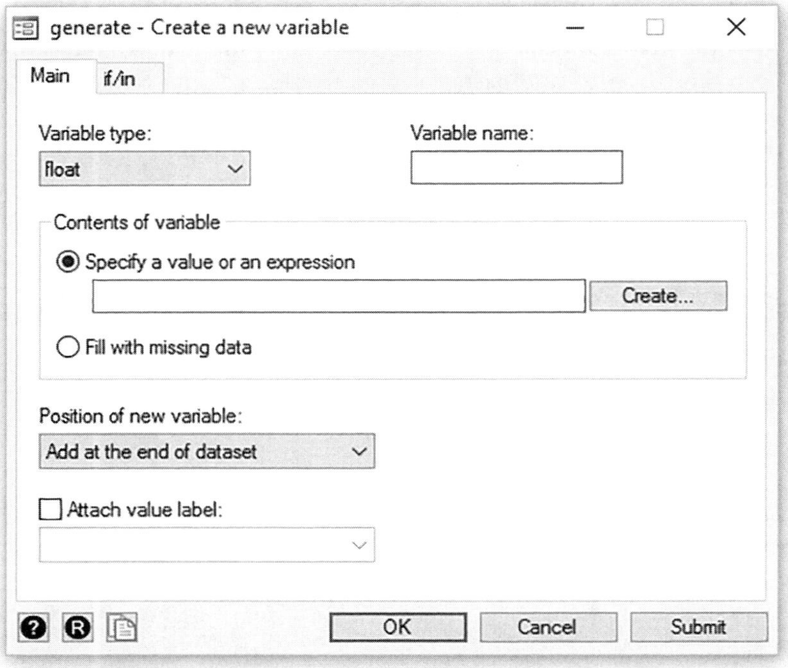

Below is some brief information on what some boxes in this window mean.

*Variable name.* We input the variable name in the Variable name box. When choosing a variable name, there are two things you need to pay attention to. First, always use lower-case letters. The variable name in Stata is case sensitive, which means the variable *scores* is different from the variable *Scores*. Second, spaces are not allowed when creating names. For example, we can use *class_scores* as the variable name, but a name such as *class scores* is not permitted.

*Variable type.* Usually, using "float" can do the work. However, if we want to be more accurate, we may also use other data types. For example, if we are certain that all the data are integers, then we can use "int" (stands for integers) as the data type. Another example is that if we have string variables (e.g., texts), then we can use the "str" data type.

*Contents of variable.* There are two options. For Specify a value or an expression, we usually use this option for complex manipulations of the variable, such as when we want to create a variable based on certain conditions. For Fill with missing data, when we select this option, we temporarily leave the values of the data empty, but we will input the data in the Data Editor (Edit) window after we close the variable generation dialog box.

After we input the variable name and specify the variable and contents, we can click OK to close the variable generation box, and return to the Data Editor (Edit) window. If we want to create another variable, click Submit instead of OK, so we can still remain in the same dialog box. One thing you should note is that after entering the information for the last variable, click OK, instead of Submit, to close the window. If you click Submit first, then close the dialog box directly without clicking OK, because the last variable has already been created the moment you click Submit. Otherwise, an error message will appear and warn you that the same variable has been created.

Now you can start to enter data just like using Excel!

## Preview of Stata in Focus

This book is unique in that you will learn how to use Stata to perform statistical analyses as they are taught in this book. Most statistics textbooks for behavioral science omit such information, include it in an appendix separate from the main chapters in the book, include it at the end of chapters with no useful examples or context, or include it in ancillary materials that often are not included with course content. Instead, this book provides instructions for using Stata in each chapter as statistical concepts are taught using practical research examples and screenshots to support student learning. You will find this instruction in the Stata in Focus sections. These sections provide step-by-step instructions for how the concepts taught in each chapter can be applied to research problems using Stata.

The reason for this inclusion is simple: Most researchers use some kind of statistical software to analyze statistics, and in behavioral science, the most common statistical software used by researchers is Stata. This textbook brings statistics in research to the 21st century, giving you both the theoretical and computational instruction needed to understand how, when, and why you perform certain statistical analyses under different conditions and the technical instruction you need to succeed in the modern era of data collection, data entry, data analysis, and statistical interpretation using Stata statistical software. This preface was written to familiarize you with this software. Subsequent Stata in Focus sections will show you how to use Stata to perform the applications and statistics taught in this book.

# 1.7 STATA IN FOCUS

## Entering and Defining Variables

Privitera's *Statisics for the Behavioral Sciences*, Third Edition (p. 23)

Throughout this book, we present instructions for using the statistical software program Stata by showing you how this software can make all the work you do by hand as simple as point and click, or using simple command lines. Before you read this Stata section, please take the time to read the section titled "How to Use Stata With This Book" at the beginning of this chapter. That section provides an overview of the different views and features in Stata. This software is an innovative statistical computer program that can compute any statistic taught in this book.

In this chapter, we discussed how variables are defined, coded, and measured. Let us see how Stata makes this simple. When entering data, make sure that all values or scores are entered in each cell of the Data Editor (Edit) window. The biggest challenge is making sure you enter the data correctly. Entering even a single value incorrectly can alter the data analyses that Stata computes. For this reason, always double-check the data to make sure the correct values have been entered.

We can use a simple example. Suppose you record the average GPA of students in one of three statistics classes. You record the following GPA scores for each class, given in Table 1.4.

Table 1.4 GPA Scores in Three Statistics Classes

| Class 1 | Class 2 | Class 3 |
|---------|---------|---------|
| 3.3 | 3.9 | 2.7 |
| 2.9 | 4.0 | 2.3 |
| 3.5 | 2.4 | 2.2 |
| 3.6 | 3.1 | 3.0 |
| 3.1 | 3.0 | 2.8 |

There are two ways you can enter these data: by column or by row. To enter data by *column*:

1. Click on the Data Editor (Edit) icon ✍ and bring up the Data Editor (Edit) window. Click on the Data tab and select Create or change data → Create new variable. Enter *class1* in the Variable name box. In the Variable type box, select "float" from the drop-down list. Under Contents of variable, select Fill with missing value and click OK. Under Contents of variable, select Fill with missing value and click Submit.

2. Repeat Step 1 to create *class2* and *class3*. Click OK instead of Submit after entering the information for the *class3* variable (or, if you click Submit again, close the dialog box directly).

3. Return to the Data Editor (Edit) window. Notice that the first three columns are now labeled with the group names, as shown in Figure 1.7. Enter the data, given in Table 1.4, for each class in the appropriate column. The data for each group are now listed down each column.

**Figure 1.7**   Data Entry in Data Editor (Edit) Window for Entering Data by Column

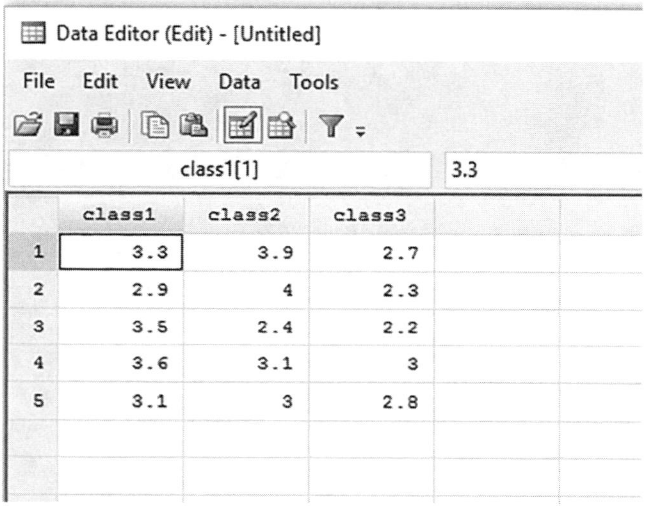

There is another way to enter these data in Stata: You can enter data by *row*, which requires coding the data. To begin, open a new Stata data file and follow the instructions given here:

1. Click on the Data Editor (Edit) icon and bring up the Data Editor (Edit) window. Click on the Data tab and select Create or change data → Create new variable. Enter *classes* in the Variable name box. In the Variable type box select "int" from the drop-down list. Under Contents of variable, select Fill with missing value and click Submit. Repeat this procedure and create the *GPA* variable, but using "float" as the variable type.

2. To code *classes*, still in the Data Editor (Edit) window, click on the Data tab and select Variable Manager to bring up the Variable Manager dialog box. Select the *classes* variable and, in the right panel, under Variable properties, locate the Variable label box and click on the Manage button. This will open up the Manage value labels dialog box, shown in Figure 1.8. Click on Create label and bring up the Create label dialog box. Enter *class_num* in Label Name box, then enter 1 in the value cell and *class 1* in the label cell, and then click Add; enter 2 in the value cell and *class 2* in the label cell, and then click Add; enter 3 in the value cell and *class 3* in the label cell, as displayed in Figure 1.9. Select OK.

**Figure 1.8**   Top: Variable Manager Dialog Box; Bottom: Manage Value Labels Dialog Box

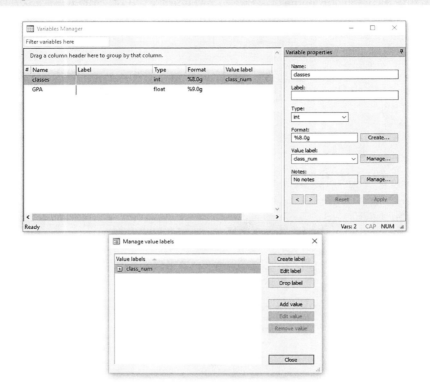

**Figure 1.9**   Create Label Dialog Box

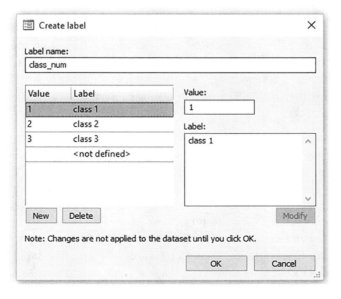

3. Close the Manage value labels dialog box, and you should be at the Variable Manager dialog box now (Figure 1.8, top). With the *classes* variable selected, again in the right panel, click on the drop-down list in the Value label box and select *class_num*, which we just created. Click Apply and close the Variable Manager dialog box. Stata will now recognize 1 as *class 1*, 2 as *class 2*, and so on.

4. In the Data Editor (Edit) window, in the first column, enter 1 five times, 2 five times, and 3 five times, as shown in Figure 1.10. This tells Stata that there are five students in each class. In the second column, enter the GPA scores for each class by row, as shown in Figure 1.10. The data are now entered by row.

**Figure 1.10**   Data Editor (Edit) Window for Entering Data by Row

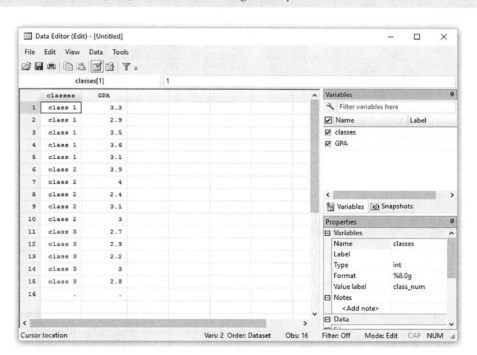

The data for all the variables are labeled, coded, and entered. If you do this correctly, Stata will make summarizing, computing, and analyzing any statistic taught in this book fast and simple.

## Frequency Distributions for Quantitative Data

Privitera's *Statisics for the Behavioral Sciences,* Third Edition (p. 46)

Stata can be used to construct frequency distributions. In this section, we will construct a frequency distribution table for the business safety data first listed in Table 2.3, which are reproduced here for reference.

Data reproduced from Table 2.3.

| | | | | |
|---|---|---|---|---|
| 45 | 98 | 83 | 50 | 86 |
| 66 | 66 | 88 | 95 | 73 |
| 88 | 55 | 76 | 115 | 66 |
| 92 | 110 | 79 | 105 | 101 |
| 101 | 85 | 90 | 92 | 81 |
| 55 | 95 | 91 | 92 | |
| 78 | 66 | 73 | 58 | |
| 86 | 92 | 51 | 63 | |
| 91 | 77 | 88 | 86 | |
| 94 | 80 | 102 | 107 | |

1. Click on the Data Editor (Edit) icon and bring up the Data Editor (Edit) window. Click on the Data tab and select Create or change data → Create new variable. Enter *complaints* in the Variable name box. Because we are measuring the number of complaints, we will enter whole numbers, so go to the Variable type box and select "int" from the drop-down list. Under Contents of variable, select Fill with missing value and click OK.

2. In the Data Editor (Edit) window, start to enter the 45 values from Table 2.3 in the column labeled *complaints.* You can enter the data in any order you wish, but make sure all the data are entered correctly. When you finish, close the Data Editor (Edit) window.

3. Go to the menu bar and click Statistics, then select Summaries, tables, and tests → Frequency tables → One-way table to bring up the dialog box shown in Figure 2.2.

**Figure 2.2**   One-Way Table Dialog Box

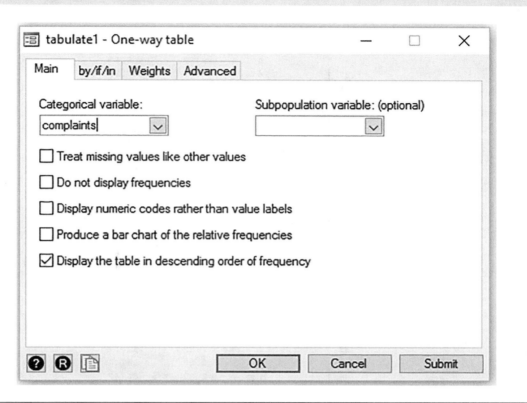

4. In the Categorical variable box, select the "complaints" variable from the drop-down list. Check the option Display the table in descending order of frequency. By selecting this option, we can easily examine which business filed the most and least complaints.

5. Select OK. The results should be displayed in the results window.

Alternatively, for Steps 3 and 4, we can also use the following command line to conduct the analysis:

```
tabulate complaints, sort
```

Figure 2.3 shows the Stata results table. Stata did not distribute these data into intervals as we did. Instead, every value in the original dataset is listed and sorted by frequencies. Relative percents (the third column, with title "Percent") and cumulative percents are also given for each value.

**Figure 2.3**   Stata Results Table

| complaints | Freq. | Percent | Cum. |
|---|---|---|---|
| 66 | 4 | 8.89 | 8.89 |
| 92 | 4 | 8.89 | 17.78 |
| 86 | 3 | 6.67 | 24.44 |
| 88 | 3 | 6.67 | 31.11 |
| 55 | 2 | 4.44 | 35.56 |
| 73 | 2 | 4.44 | 40.00 |
| 91 | 2 | 4.44 | 44.44 |
| 95 | 2 | 4.44 | 48.89 |
| 101 | 2 | 4.44 | 53.33 |
| 45 | 1 | 2.22 | 55.56 |
| 50 | 1 | 2.22 | 57.78 |
| 51 | 1 | 2.22 | 60.00 |
| 58 | 1 | 2.22 | 62.22 |
| 63 | 1 | 2.22 | 64.44 |
| 76 | 1 | 2.22 | 66.67 |
| 77 | 1 | 2.22 | 68.89 |
| 78 | 1 | 2.22 | 71.11 |
| 79 | 1 | 2.22 | 73.33 |
| 80 | 1 | 2.22 | 75.56 |
| 81 | 1 | 2.22 | 77.78 |
| 83 | 1 | 2.22 | 80.00 |
| 85 | 1 | 2.22 | 82.22 |
| 90 | 1 | 2.22 | 84.44 |
| 94 | 1 | 2.22 | 86.67 |
| 98 | 1 | 2.22 | 88.89 |
| 102 | 1 | 2.22 | 91.11 |
| 105 | 1 | 2.22 | 93.33 |
| 107 | 1 | 2.22 | 95.56 |
| 110 | 1 | 2.22 | 97.78 |
| 115 | 1 | 2.22 | 100.00 |
| Total | 45 | 100.00 | |

# 2.7 STATA IN FOCUS

## Frequency Distributions for Categorical Data

Privitera's *Statisics for the Behavioral Sciences,* Third Edition (p. 51)

Stata can be used to summarize categorical data that are ungrouped. We can use Stata to create a frequency distribution for the following hypothetical example: A group of health practitioners wants to classify children in public schools as being lean, healthy, overweight, or obese; this type of classification is common (Centers for Disease Control and Prevention, 2013; Privitera, 2016). To do this, the researchers calculated the body mass index (BMI) score of 100 children. Based on the BMI scores, they classified 15 children as lean, 30 as healthy, 35 as overweight, and 20 as obese.

1. Click on the Data Editor (Edit) icon and bring up the Data Editor (Edit) window. Click on the Data tab and select Create or change data → Create new variable. Enter *categories* in the Variable name box. We will enter whole numbers, so go to the Variable type box and select "int" from the drop-down list. Under Contents of variable, select Fill with missing value and click Submit. Repeat this procedure and create the *frequencies* variable, but click OK instead of Submit this time (or, if you click Submit again, close the Create new variable dialog box directly).

2. In the Data Editor (Edit) window, enter 1, 2, 3, and 4 in the categories column. In the frequencies column, enter 15, 30, 35, and 20 next to the corresponding numeric codes.

3. Next, we need to code the data for the categorical variable so that we can better understand what each category value (i.e., 1, 2, 3, and 4) represents. Still in the Data Editor (Edit) window, click on the Data tab and select Variable Manager to bring up the Variable Manager dialog box. Select the *categories* variable and, in the right panel, under Variable properties, locate the Variable label box and click on the Manage button. This will open up the Manage value labels dialog box. Click on Create label and bring up the Create label dialog box. Enter *health_condition* in Label name box, then enter 1 in the Value box, lean in the Label box, and click Add. Repeat these steps by entering 2 for healthy, 3 for overweight, and 4 for obese, and then select OK. Now each level of the categorical variable is coded.

4. Close the Manage value labels dialog box, and you should be at the Variables Manager dialog box now. With the *categories* variable selected, again in the right panel, click on the drop-down list in the Value label box and select *health_condition*, which we just created. Click Apply and close the Variable Manager dialog box. Now we can see that the original categorical values are replaced by the corresponding health conditions. Close the Data Editor (Edit) window.

5. Go to the menu bar and click Statistics, then select Summaries, tables, and tests → Frequency tables → One-way table. In the Categorical variable box, select *categories* from the drop-down list. Still in this One-way table window, from the menu bar, click on the Weights tab and select Frequency weights as the Weight type. In the Frequency weight box,

select *frequencies* from the drop-down list. Now each frequency is matched to each level of the variable.

6. Select OK. Our results should be displayed in the Results window.

Alternatively, we can use the following command line to accomplish Steps 5 and 6:

```
tabulate categories [fweight = frequencies]
```

**Figure 2.5**  Stata Results Table

| categories | Freq. | Percent | Cum. |
|---|---|---|---|
| lean | 15 | 15.00 | 15.00 |
| healthy | 30 | 30.00 | 45.00 |
| overweight | 35 | 35.00 | 80.00 |
| obese | 20 | 20.00 | 100.00 |
| Total | 100 | 100.00 | |

Notice that Stata does not list the values as 1, 2, 3, and 4 in the output table shown in Figure 2.5, although you entered these values in the categories column. Instead, Stata lists the data as you labeled them in Step 3. This format makes it much easier to read the results. Also, every category in the original dataset is listed with frequencies, relative percents, and cumulative percents given.

# 2.12 STATA IN FOCUS

## Histograms, Bar Charts, and Pie Charts

Privitera's *Statisics for the Behavioral Sciences,* Third Edition (p. 65)

To review, histograms are used for continuous or quantitative data, and bar charts and pie charts are used for discrete, categorical, or qualitative data. As an exercise to compare histograms, bar charts, and pie charts, we can construct these graphs for the same data by treating the data as a simple set of general values. Suppose we measure the data shown in Table 2.16.

**Table 2.16** A Sample of 20 Values

| | | | |
|---|---|---|---|
| 1 | 4 | 5 | 7 |
| 2 | 3 | 6 | 8 |
| 3 | 6 | 7 | 9 |
| 2 | 6 | 5 | 4 |
| 4 | 5 | 8 | 5 |

Because we are not defining these values, we can just call the variable "numbers." Here are the steps:

1. Click on the Data Editor (Edit) icon and bring up the Data Editor (Edit) window. Click on the Data tab and select Create or change data → Create new variable. Enter *numbers* in the Variable name box. In the Variable type box, select "int" from the drop-down list. Under Contents of variable, select Fill with missing value and click OK.

2. In the Data Editor (Edit) window, enter the 20 values in the column you labeled numbers. You can enter the data in any order you wish, but make sure all the data are entered correctly.

3. Go to the menu bar and click Graphics, then select Histogram to bring up the histogram box.

4. In the dialog box, under the Main tab, in the Variable box, select the *numbers* variable from the drop-down list. To the right of the Variable box, select Data are discrete (you are also encourage to test Data are continuous by yourself and see the difference).

5. For Bins options, you may select how many bars you want the histogram to display, or the width of each bar. Check the Width of bins option and change the value to 0.5.

6. Please note: You can change the number of bins only when Data are continuous is selected. If Data are discrete is selected, the Number of bins options will be greyed out. In a similar vein, you can change the width of bins only when Data are discrete option is selected.

7. For the *y*-axis, select Frequency.

8. Click OK. A new graph window with histogram should display.

Alternatively, for Steps 3 to 6, we can use the following command line to generate the histogram:

```
histogram numbers, discrete width(0.5) frequency
```

**Figure 2.12**  A Sample Histogram

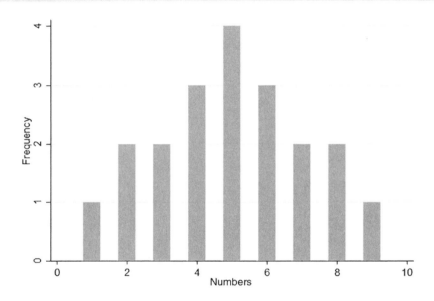

As you may notice, there are many options when creating graphs (e.g., modify the title, modify the color of the background or the bar, create a legend, etc.). Stata graph functions offer powerful tools for customization and can produce high-quality pictures.

# 3.6 STATA IN FOCUS

## Mean, Median, and Mode

Privitera's *Statisics for the Behavioral Sciences,* Third Edition (p. 98)

Stata can be used to measure the mean, the median, and the mode for all sorts of data. In this section, we will work through a new example to compute each measure of central tendency. Suppose you want to study creativity using a paper clip, as has been used in prior studies on the topic (Chatterjea & Mitra, 1976; Piffer, 2012). You give students a paper clip, and the time (in seconds) it takes the students to list 10 uses for the paper clip is recorded. Faster times are presumed to reflect greater creativity. Using the data shown in Table 3.11, we can use Stata to compute the mean, the median, and the mode. We first focus on computing mean and median using the graphical interface, then we use the command to compute the mode.

**Table 3.11**   The Time (in seconds) That It Took 20 Participants to Write Down 10 Uses for a Paper Clip on a Creativity Test

| | |
|---|---|
| 41 | 80 |
| 65 | 80 |
| 123 | 64 |
| 46 | 59 |
| 48 | 51 |
| 87 | 36 |
| 38 | 80 |
| 90 | 143 |
| 132 | 122 |
| 115 | 100 |

We start with the mean and the median:

1. Click on the Data Editor (Edit) icon and bring up the Data Editor (Edit) window. Click on the Data tab and select Create or change data → Create new variable. Enter *creativity* in the Variable name box. In the Variable type box, select "int" from the drop-down list. Under Contents of variable, select Fill with missing value and click OK.

2. In the Data Editor (Edit) window, enter the 20 values in the column labeled *creativity*.

3. Go to the menu bar and click Statistics, then Summaries, tables, and tests → Summary and descriptive statistics → Summary statistics to open the summary statistics dialog box.

4. In the dialog box, select the *creativity* variable from the drop-down list in the Variables box. Then select the option Display additional statistics under Options, as displayed in Figure 3.1.

5. Click OK. The results should be displayed in the Results window.

Alternatively, we can use the following command line to find the mean and median values:

```
summarize creativity, detail
```

**Figure 3.1**  Dialog Box for Step 4

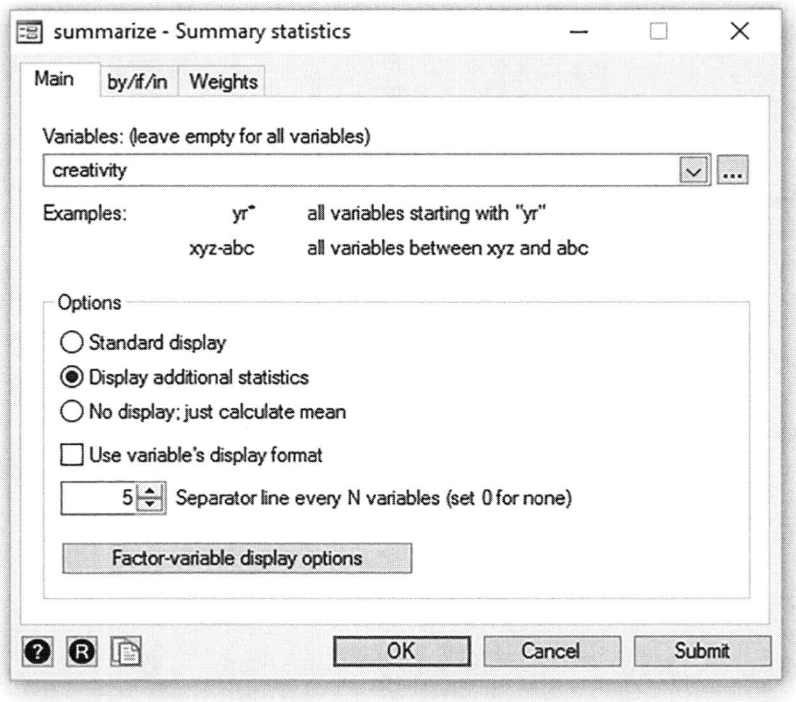

As shown in Table 3.12, the mean value (Mean = 80) is displayed on the right side of the table. The median value can be found easily by searching for the 50th percentile, which is also 80 in the current example.

**Table 3.12**  Stata Results Table Showing the Mean and the Median

creativity

|  | Percentiles | Smallest |  |  |
|---|---|---|---|---|
| 1% | 36 | 36 |  |  |
| 5% | 37 | 38 |  |  |
| 10% | 39.5 | 41 | Obs | 20 |
| 25% | 49.5 | 46 | Sum of Wgt. | 20 |
|  |  |  |  |  |
| 50% | 80 |  | Mean | 80 |
|  |  | Largest | Std. Dev. | 33.42234 |
| 75% | 107.5 | 122 |  |  |
| 90% | 127.5 | 123 | Variance | 1117.053 |
| 95% | 137.5 | 132 | Skewness | .3828264 |
| 99% | 143 | 143 | Kurtosis | 1.946648 |

Next, we will use the command to computer mode. As you may see, in Stata, mode is not directly calculated by any functions. Here, we use egen to create a new mode variable:

```
egen creativity_mode = mode (creativity)
```

Egen stands for "Extensions to generate." Users can enrich the contents of the data by using this command when creating new variables. Egen can also be used to organize and modify the data, offering even more flexibility.

Here, we use egen to create a new variable called *creativity_mode*, and then we take the mode of the original variable *creativity*. Table 3.13 shows the newly created *creativity_mode* variable and its value—the mode value of the original variable *creativity*. As we can see, the mode value is 80.

When multiple modes exist, we need to indicate in the command line whether we want the higher or the lower value. If we want the lower mode value, we should input

```
egen creativity_mode = mode(creativity), minmode,
```

or

```
egen creativity_mode = mode(creativity), maxmode
```

if we want the higher mode value.

**Table 3.13**   Mode Value for the Variable Creativity

| | creativity | creativity~e | |
|---|---|---|---|
| 1 | 41 | 80 | |
| 2 | 65 | 80 | |
| 3 | 123 | 80 | |
| 4 | 46 | 80 | |
| 5 | 48 | 80 | |
| 6 | 87 | 80 | |
| 7 | 38 | 80 | |
| 8 | 90 | 80 | |
| 9 | 132 | 80 | |
| 10 | 115 | 80 | |
| 11 | 80 | 80 | |
| 12 | 80 | 80 | |
| 13 | 64 | 80 | |
| 14 | 59 | 80 | |
| 15 | 51 | 80 | |
| 16 | 36 | 80 | |
| 17 | 80 | 80 | |
| 18 | 143 | 80 | |
| 19 | 122 | 80 | |
| 20 | 100 | 80 | |

# 4.11 STATA IN FOCUS

## Range, Variance, and Standard Deviation

Privitera's *Statisics for the Behavioral Sciences,* Third Edition (p. 129)

In the Stata in Focus section of Chapter 3, we computed the mean, the median, and the mode for creativity, measured as the time (in seconds) it took participants to list 10 uses for a paper clip. The data for this example, originally given in Table 3.11, are reproduced here in Table 4.10. In this section, we will use these same data to compute the range, variance, and standard deviation.

**Table 4.10**  The Time (in seconds) That It Took a Group of 20 Participants to Write Down 10 Uses for a Paper Clip on a Creativity Test

| | |
|---|---|
| 41 | 80 |
| 65 | 80 |
| 123 | 64 |
| 46 | 59 |
| 48 | 51 |
| 87 | 36 |

1. Click on the Data Editor (Edit) icon and bring up the Data Editor (Edit) window. Click on the Data tab and select Create or change data → Create new variable. Enter *creativity* in the Variable name box. In the Variable type box, select "int" from the drop-down list. Under Contents of variable, select Fill with missing value and click OK.

2. In the Data Editor (Edit) window, enter the 20 values in the *creativity* column.

3. Go to the menu bar and click Statistics, then select Summaries, tables, and tests → Summary and descriptive statistics → Summary statistics to open up a dialog box.

4. In the dialog box, select *creativity* from the drop-down list in the Variables cell. Under Options, select Display additional statistics.

5. Click OK. The results should be displayed in the Results window.

Alternatively, for Steps 3 and 4, we can use the following command line to conduct the descriptive analysis:

```
summarize creativity, details
```

The Stata results table shows the descriptive statistics (see Table 4.11). In this results table, the range is not calculated directly; rather, it is given by the minimum value (1%, 36) and the maximum value (99%, 123).

**Table 4.11**   Stata Results Table Displaying the Range, the Variance, and the Standard Deviation for the Creativity Data

|  |  |  |  |  |
|---|---|---|---|---|
|  |  | creativity |  |  |
|  | Percentiles | Smallest |  |  |
| 1% | 36 | 36 |  |  |
| 5% | 36 | 41 |  |  |
| 10% | 41 | 46 | Obs | 12 |
| 25% | 47 | 48 | Sum of Wgt. | 12 |
| 50% | 61.5 |  | Mean | 65 |
|  |  | Largest | Std. Dev. | 24.49119 |
| 75% | 80 | 80 |  |  |
| 90% | 87 | 80 | Variance | 599.8182 |
| 95% | 123 | 87 | Skewness | 1.031352 |
| 99% | 123 | 123 | Kurtosis | 3.568172 |

Table 5.5 displayed a crosstabulation for the frequency of births based on the type of hospital (public versus private) and insurance status (insured versus uninsured) of mothers. We will use Stata to convert these data to a conditional probability table.

## Construct a Probability Table

1. Click on the Data Editor (Edit) icon and bring up the Data Editor (Edit) window. Click on the Data tab and select Create or change data → Create new variable. Enter *hospital* in the Variable name box. In the Variable type box, select "int" from the drop-down list. Under Contents of variable, select Fill with missing value and click Submit. Repeat this procedure to create *insurance* and *frequencies* variables.

2. Coding hospital: To code *hospital,* click the small gray box with three dots in the Values column to display a dialog box. In the dialog box, enter 1 in the value cell and *public* in the label cell, and then click Add. Then enter 2 in the value cell and *private* in the label cell, and click Add.

3. Continue coding hospital: To code *hospital*, still in the Data Editor (Edit) window, click on the Data tab and select Variable Manager to bring up the Variable Manager dialog box. Select the *hospital* variable and, in the right panel, under Variable properties, locate the Variable label box and click on the Manage button. This will open up the Manage value labels dialog box. Click on Create label and bring up the Create label dialog box. Enter *hospital_type* in the Label Name box, then enter 1 in the value cell and *public* in the label cell, and then click Add; enter 2 in the value cell and *private* in the label cell, and then click Add. Select OK.

4. Close the Manage value labels dialog box, and you should be at the Variable Manager dialog box now. With the *hospital* variable selected, again in the right panel, click on the drop-down list in the Value label box and select *hospital_type*, which we just created. Click Apply and close the Variable Manager dialog box.

5. Repeat Steps 3 and 4 to code *insurance*. Use *insure_status* as the label name, and enter 1 for *insured* and 2 for *uninsured*.

6. In the Data Editor (Edit) window, enter 1, 1, 2, 2 down the first column. Then enter 1, 2, 1, 2 down the second column. In the *frequencies* column, list the frequencies for each coded cell: Enter 50, 80, 40, 30 down the third column.

7. Go to the menu bar and click Statistics, then Summaries, tables, and tests → Frequency tables → Two-way table with measures of association to display the Two-way table dialog box.

8. In the dialog box, under the Row variable box, select the *hospital* variable from the drop-down list in the cell. Next, under the Column variable, select the *insurance* variable into the cell.

9. Click on the Weights tab on the top of the Two-way table dialog box, select Frequency weights as the weight type, then select *frequencies* from the drop-down list in the Frequency weights cell, as shown in Figure 5.2.

10. Click OK. The results should be displayed in the Results window.

Alternatively, for Steps 7 to 9, we can use the following command line to construct the probability table:

```
tabulate hospital insurance [fweight = frequencies]
```

**Figure 5.2**   The Dialog Box for Step 9

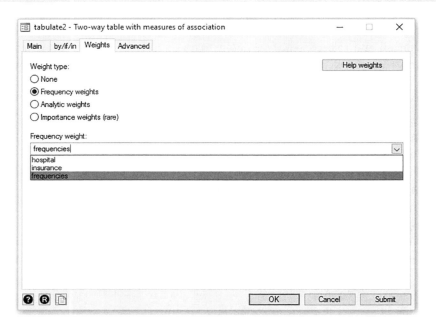

Stata converts the coded data into the probability table shown in Table 5.6. The Stata results table gives a probability display identical to that given in Table 5.5.

**Table 5.6**   Stata Results of the Crosstabulation Shown in Table 5.5

|  | insurance | | |
| --- | --- | --- | --- |
| hospital | insured | uninsured | Total |
| public | 50 | 80 | 130 |
| private | 40 | 30 | 70 |
| Total | 90 | 110 | 200 |

## Construct a Conditional Probability Table

We can also construct a conditional probability table with these same data. Having Stata compute conditional probabilities listed directly in a table is easier than having to compute these by hand using the probabilities displayed in Table 5.6.

1. Follow Steps 7 to 9 for constructing a probability table.

2. Under the Main tab at the top of the Two-way table dialog box, check the following two options for Cell contents, as shown in Figure 5.3:

   - Within-column relative frequencies
   - Within-row relative frequencies

3. Click OK. The results should be displayed in the Results window.

Alternatively, we can use the following command line to construct the conditional probability table:

```
tabulate hospital insurance [fweight = frequencies], column row
```

**Figure 5.3**   The Dialog Box Showing the Appropriate Selections to Make in Step 2 of Constructing a Conditional Probability Table

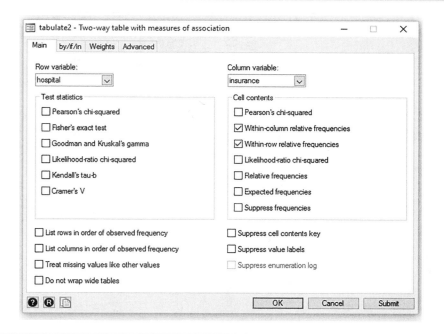

The Stata results table shown in Table 5.7 lists many probability values for the contingency between type of hospital and type of insurance. We computed by hand that the conditional probability is 62% for selecting a mother who is uninsured, given that she gave birth

in a public hospital. This conditional probability is circled in the table (61.5% rounds to 62%) and confirms our computation.

**Table 5.7**   Stata Results Table of the Conditional and Independent (total column) Probabilities for the Original Data in Table 5.5

| Key |
| --- |
| frequency |
| row percentage |
| column percentage |

| hospital | insurance insured | uninsured | Total |
|---|---|---|---|
| public | 50 | 80 | 130 |
|  | 38.46 | 61.54 | 100.00 |
|  | 55.56 | 72.73 | 65.00 |
| private | 40 | 30 | 70 |
|  | 57.14 | 42.86 | 100.00 |
|  | 44.44 | 27.27 | 35.00 |
| Total | 90 | 110 | 200 |
|  | 45.00 | 55.00 | 100.00 |
|  | 100.00 | 100.00 | 100.00 |

# 6.8 STATA IN FOCUS

## Converting Raw Scores to Standard *z* Scores

Privitera's *Statisics for the Behavioral Sciences,* Third Edition (p. 193)

Stata can be used to compute a *z* transformation for a given dataset. To demonstrate how Stata computes *z* scores, suppose you evaluate the effectiveness of an SAT remedial tutoring course with 16 students who plan to retake the standardized exam. Table 6.2 lists the number of points that each student gained on the exam after taking the remedial course. We will use Stata to convert these data into *z* scores.

**Table 6.2**  The Number of Points Gained on the SAT Exam After Taking a Remedial Course (for 16 students)

| | | | |
|---|---|---|---|
| +500 | +950 | +780 | +800 |
| +750 | +880 | +800 | +680 |
| +600 | +990 | +800 | +550 |
| +900 | +560 | +450 | +600 |

1.  Click on the Data Editor (Edit) icon and bring up the Data Editor (Edit) window. Click on the Data tab and select Create or change data → Create new variable. Enter *SAT* in the Variable name box. In the Variable type box, select "int" from the drop-down list. Under Contents of variable, select Fill with missing value and click OK.

2.  In the Data Editor (Edit) window, enter the 16 values in the column labeled *SAT.*

3.  Still in the Data Editor (Edit) window, click on the Data tab and select Create or change data → Create new variable (extended) to open up the Extensions to generate dialog box. Type *ZSAT* in the Generate variable cell, and select Standardized values from a list of functions under Egen function. Type *SAT* in the Expression cell. This step is also shown in Figure 6.13.

4.  Click OK. The *z* scores variable, with the name *ZSAT,* is created and displayed in the Data Editor window, as shown in Table 6.3.

Alternatively, we can use the following command line to generate *z* scores:

```
egen ZSAT = std(SAT), mean(0) std(1)
```

**Table 6.3**    Stata Results Table

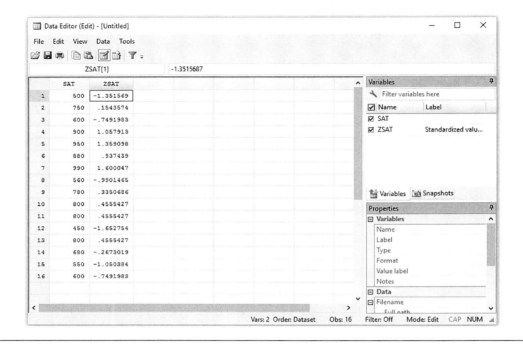

**Figure 6.13**    The Dialog Box for Step 3—Generate *z* Scores Using Menu

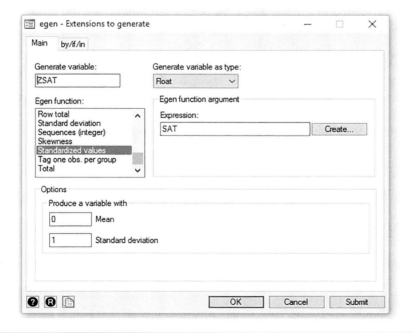

# 7.7 STATA IN FOCUS

## Estimating the Standard Error of the Mean

Privitera's *Statisics for the Behavioral Sciences,* Third Edition (p. 227)

Researchers rarely know the value of the population standard deviation, which is in the numerator of the formula for standard error. It is more common to estimate the standard error by substituting the sample standard deviation in place of the population standard deviation in the formula for standard error. The formula, which is discussed further in Chapter 9, is as follows:

$$s_M = \frac{s}{\sqrt{n}}.$$

To illustrate, suppose we measure the individual reaction times (in seconds) for a team of 10 firefighters to respond to an emergency call. The reaction times are 93, 66, 30, 44, 20, 100, 35, 58, 70, and 81. Let us use Stata to estimate the standard error of these data:

1. Click on the Data Editor (Edit) icon and bring up the Data Editor (Edit) window. Click on the Data tab and select Create or change data → Create new variable. Enter *reaction* in the Variable name box. In the Variable type box, select "int" from the drop-down list. Under Contents of variable, select Fill with missing value and click OK.

2. In the Data Editor (Edit) window, enter the 10 values in the column labeled *reaction*.

3. Go to the menu bar and click Statistics, then select Summaries, tables, and tests → Summary and descriptive statistics → Means to open up the Estimate means dialog box.

4. In the dialog box, select *reaction* from the drop-down list in the Variables cell.

5. Click OK.

Alternatively, we can use the following command line to find the standard error:

```
mean reaction
```

The Stata results table, shown in Table 7.5, gives the value for the standard error as 8.596. If we want to double-check that the value of the standard error is correct, we can use the value of the sample size, which is already in the Stata results table. We can also obtain the sample standard deviation by using the command line

```
summarize reaction
```

and find out the standard deviation, as shown in Table 7.6. When we enter these values into the formula for standard error, we obtain the same result:

$$\text{Standard error} = \frac{s}{\sqrt{n}} = \frac{27.183}{\sqrt{10}} \approx 8.596.$$

197

**Table 7.5**  Stata Results Table for the Value of Standard Error

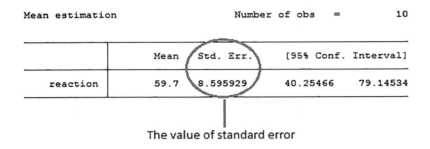

Mean estimation                    Number of obs   =        10

|          | Mean | Std. Err. | [95% Conf. Interval] |          |
|----------|------|-----------|----------------------|----------|
| reaction | 59.7 | 8.595929  | 40.25466             | 79.14534 |

The value of standard error

**Table 7.6**  Stata Results Table for the Descriptive Statistics

| Variable | Obs | Mean | Std. Dev. | Min | Max |
|----------|-----|------|-----------|-----|-----|
| reaction | 10  | 59.7 | 27.18272  | 20  | 100 |

# 9.6 STATA IN FOCUS

## One-Sample *t* Test

Privitera's *Statisics for the Behavioral Sciences,* Third Edition (p. 286)

Stata can be used to compute the one-sample *t* test. To illustrate how to compute this test in Stata and how the results tables in Stata match with the data we computed by hand, let us compute this test using the same data given for Example 9.1 in Table 9.3. For reference, the social functioning scores in the sample of 18 relatives who care for patients with OCD were 20, 60, 48, 92, 50, 82, 48, 90, 30, 68, 43, 54, 60, 62, 94, 67, 63, and 85. We will compare these scores to the mean in the general healthy population ($\mu = 77.43$) using a .05 level of significance ($\alpha = .05$).

1. Click on the Data Editor (Edit) icon and bring up the Data Editor (Edit) window. Click on the Data tab and select Create or change data → Create new variable. Enter *health* in the Variable name box. In the Variable type box, select "int" from the drop-down list. Under Contents of variable, select Fill with missing value and click OK.

2. In the Data Editor (Edit) window, enter the 18 values in the column labeled *health*.

3. Go to the menu bar and click Statistics, then select Summaries, tables, and tests → Classical tests of hypotheses → *t* test (mean comparison test) to open up the *t* tests dialog box.

4. Under *t* tests, keep the default selection One-sample, since we have only one sample here. Select *health* from the drop-down list in the Variable name box. Type the value 77.43 in the Hypothesized mean box. Select *95* from the drop-down list in the Confidence level box (by default, the value is 95).

5. Click OK. The results should be displayed in the Results window.

Alternatively, for Steps 3 and 4, we can use the following command line to conduct the one-sample *t* test:

```
ttest health == 77.43
```

Please note: Here, we need the double equal sign because we are testing the equality (whether the sample mean equals the population mean).

**Figure 9.4** Stata Dialog Box for Steps 3 and 4

In Table 9.5, the top part of the results table displays the sample size, the sample mean, the estimated standard error, the sample standard deviation, and the confidence intervals (confidence intervals will be described in Chapter 11). The bottom part of the results table displays the obtained value for *t*, the degrees of freedom, and the *p* value (Pr > (|T| > |t|) = 0.0062).

Please note: It looks like we have three sets of *p* values here. For the current null hypothesis, the *p* value we need is the one in the middle: H$_a$: mean != 77.43; Pr > (|T| > |t|) = 0.0062. In Stata, the sign "!=" means not equal to (≠). And based on this result, we confirm that the sample mean is not equal to the population mean.

**Table 9.5**  Stata Results Table for the One-Sample *t* Test

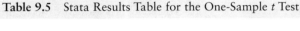
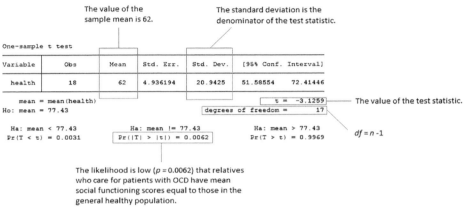

Although Stata does not compute effect size for the *t* test, notice that the results table provides almost all the information needed to compute effect size, except for the Mean Difference, which can be easily calculated by subtracting the population mean from the sample mean:

$$\text{Mean Difference} = \mu_{sample} - \mu_{population}$$

$$\text{Mean Difference} = 65 - 77.43$$

$$= -15.43$$

The formulas are restated here with the names of the headings in the Stata results table, where you will find the values needed to compute each estimate:

$$\text{Estimated Cohen's } d = \frac{\text{Mean Difference}}{\text{Std. Deviation}}.$$

$$\text{Proportion of variance } \eta^2 = \frac{(t)^2}{(t)^2 + df}.$$

$$\omega^2 = \frac{(t)^2 - 1}{(t)^2 + df}.$$

# 9.9 STATA IN FOCUS

## Two-Independent-Sample *t* Test

Privitera's *Statisics for the Behavioral Sciences,* Third Edition (p. 297)

Stata can be used to compute the two-independent-sample *t* test. To illustrate how to compute this test in Stata and how the output tables in Stata match with the data we computed by hand, let us compute this test using the same data originally given for Example 9.2 in Table 9.7. For reference, Table 9.11 restates the original data for this example, which we will enter into Stata. We will compare these data between groups using a .05 level of significance ($\alpha = .05$).

**Table 9.11**  The Number of Calories Consumed in a Meal Between Groups Asked to Eat Slowly or Fast

| Group Eating Slowly | Group Eating Fast |
|:---:|:---:|
| 700 | 450 |
| 450 | 800 |
| 850 | 750 |
| 600 | 700 |
| 450 | 550 |
| 550 | 650 |

1. Click on the Data Editor (Edit) icon and bring up the Data Editor (Edit) window. Click on the Data tab and select Create or change data → Create new variable. Enter *groups* in the Variable name box. In the Variable type box, select "int" from the drop-down list. Under Contents of variable, select Fill with missing value and click Submit. Repeat this procedure and create the *intake* variable this time.

2. To label the *groups* variable, still in the Data Editor (Edit) window, click on the Data tab and select Variable Manager to bring up the Variable Manager dialog box. Select the *groups* variable and, in the right panel, under Variable properties, locate the Variable label box and click on the Manage button. This will open up the Manage value labels dialog box. Click on Create label and bring up the Create label dialog box. Enter *consumption_speed* in the Label Name box, then enter 1 in the value cell and *Slowly* in the label cell, and then click Add. Then enter 2 in the value cell and *Fast* in the label cell, and click Add. Select OK.

3. Close the Manage value labels dialog box, and you should be at the Variable Manager dialog box now. With the *groups* variable selected, again in the right panel, click on the

201

drop-down list in the Value label box and select *consumption_speed*, which we just created. Click Apply and close the Variable Manager dialog box.

4. In the Data Editor (Edit) window, in the *groups* column, enter 1 in the first six cells, then 2 in the next six cells. In the *intake* column, enter the calorie intakes for each group in the cells that correspond with the codes for each group listed in the first column.

5. Go to the menu bar and click Statistics, then select Summaries, tables, and tests → Classical tests of hypotheses → t-tests (mean comparison test) to open up the t-tests dialog box, as shown in Figure 9.7.

6. Under t-tests, select Two-sample using groups. Select *intake* from the drop-down list in the Variable name box, and *groups* in the Group variable name box. Select 95 from the drop-down list in the Confidence level box (by default, the value is 95). Because we are assuming equal variances, we do not check the Unequal variances option.

7. Click OK. The results should be displayed in the Results window.

**Figure 9.7**   Stata Dialog Box for Steps 5 and 6

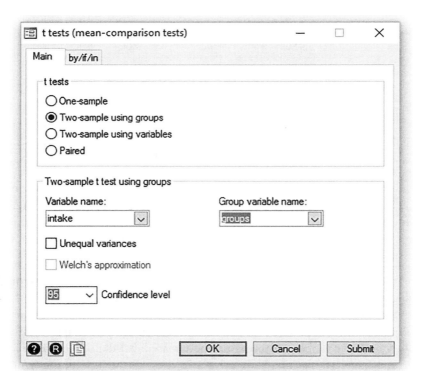

Alternatively, for Steps 5 and 6, we can use the following command line to conduct the two-sample *t* test:

```
ttest intake, by(groups)
```

Table 9.12 shows the output. The top part of the results table displays the sample size, mean, standard error, and standard deviation for both groups. The bottom part of the results table displays a summary for the *t* test. Also, notice that the bottom table gives the numerator and denominator for the *t* test. If we substitute the values in the Stata output table into the formula, we will obtain the same values for the test statistic computed in Example 9.2:

$$t_{obt} = \frac{\text{Mean Difference}}{\text{Std. Error Difference}} = \frac{-50.00}{82.66} = -0.605.$$

It is also worth noting that for the two-sample *t* test, Stata can produce Cohen's *d* effect size by using the command line:

```
esize twosample intake, by(groups) cohensd
```

The results for Cohen's *d* effect are shown in Table 9.13.

**Table 9.12**   Stata Results Table for the Two-Independent-Sample *t* Test

```
Two-sample t test with equal variances

  Group |     Obs        Mean    Std. Err.   Std. Dev.   [95% Conf. Interval]
---------+--------------------------------------------------------------------
   Fast |       6         600    63.24555    154.9193    437.4221    762.5779
 Slowly |       6         650    53.22906    130.384     513.1703    786.8297
---------+--------------------------------------------------------------------
combined |      12         625    40.12292    138.9899    536.6901    713.3099
---------+--------------------------------------------------------------------
   diff |                 -50    82.66398                -234.1868   134.1868

    diff = mean(Fast) - mean(Slowly)                      t =  -0.6049
Ho: diff = 0                             degrees of freedom =       10

  Ha: diff < 0                Ha: diff != 0                Ha: diff > 0
Pr(T < t) = 0.2794      Pr(|T| > |t|) = 0.5587      Pr(T > t) = 0.7206
```

**Table 9.13**   Stata Results Table for the Cohen's *d* Effect Size

```
Effect size based on mean comparison

                                 Obs per group:
                                       Fast =           6
                                     Slowly =           6

       Effect Size  |   Estimate    [95% Conf. Interval]
-------------------+-----------------------------------------
          Cohen's d |  -.3492151    -1.482379    .8008618
```

# 10.4 STATA IN FOCUS

## The Related-Samples *t* Test

Privitera's *Statisics for the Behavioral Sciences,* Third Edition (p. 317)

In Example 10.1, we tested whether teacher supervision influences the time that elementary school children read. We used a two-tailed test at a .05 level of significance and decided to reject the null hypothesis. Thus, we concluded that elementary school children spent significantly more time reading in the presence of a teacher than when the teacher was absent, $t(7) = 2.804$, $p < .05$. We can confirm this result using Stata.

1. Click on the Data Editor (Edit) icon and bring up the Data Editor (Edit) window. Click on the Data tab and select Create or change data → Create new variable. Enter *present* in the Variable name box. In the Variable type box, select "int" from the drop-down list. Under Contents of variable, select Fill with missing value and click Submit. Repeat this procedure and create *absent* variable this time.

2. In the Data Editor (Edit) window, enter the data in each column as shown in Table 10.7.

**Table 10.7**  Data Entered in Stata for Step 2

| present | absent |
|---|---|
| 220 | 210 |
| 245 | 220 |
| 215 | 195 |
| 260 | 265 |
| 300 | 275 |
| 280 | 290 |
| 250 | 220 |
| 310 | 285 |

3. Go to the menu bar and click Statistics, then select Summaries, tables, and tests → Classical tests of hypotheses → *t* tests (mean comparison test) to open up the *t* tests dialog box, as shown in Figure 10.4.

4. Under *t* tests, select Paired. Select *present* from the drop-down list in the First variable box, and *absent* in the Second variable box. Select 95 from the drop-down list in the Confidence level box (by default, the value is 95).

5. Click OK. The results should be displayed in the Results window.

**Figure 10.4**   Stata Dialog Box for Steps 3 and 4

Alternatively, for Steps 5 and 6, we can use the following command line to conduct the two-sample *t* test:

```
ttest present == absent
```

Please note: Here, we need the double equal sign because we are testing the equality.

Notice that the calculations we made match the results displayed in the results table shown in Table 10.8. These same step-by-step directions for using Stata can be used to compute the repeated-measures design (shown in this section) and the matched-pairs design. Finally, note that Stata gives the confidence intervals for this test in the output table (confidence intervals are described in Chapter 11).

**Table 10.8**    The Stata Results Table for the Related-Samples *t* Test

```
Paired t test
```

| Variable | Obs | Mean | Std. Err. | Std. Dev. | [95% Conf. Interval] | |
|---|---|---|---|---|---|---|
| present | 8 | 260 | 12.28385 | 34.74396 | 230.9533 | 289.0467 |
| absent | 8 | 245 | 13.29608 | 37.60699 | 213.5598 | 276.4402 |
| diff | 8 | 15 | 5.345225 | 15.11858 | 2.360552 | 27.63945 |

```
      mean(diff) = mean(present - absent)                         t =    2.8062
Ho: mean(diff) = 0                              degrees of freedom =         7

Ha: mean(diff) < 0              Ha: mean(diff) != 0              Ha: mean(diff) > 0
Pr(T < t) = 0.9869            Pr(|T| > |t|) = 0.0263            Pr(T > t) = 0.0131
```

# 11.5 STATA IN FOCUS

## Confidence Intervals for the One-Sample *t* Test

Privitera's *Statisics for the Behavioral Sciences,* Third Edition (p. 347)

In Chapter 9, we computed a one-sample *t* test using Stata for the data given in Example 11.2. Table 11.6 shows the Stata output table for that test, which was originally given in Table 9.5 in Chapter 9. The table lists the 95% confidence interval for the outcome we observed. To change the confidence interval, follow the steps for computing the one-sample *t* test given in Chapter 9, and select Options in the dialog box in Steps 3 to 5. This action will display an additional dialog box, shown in Figure 11.9, that allows you to choose any level of confidence. By default, Stata gives a 95% confidence interval with the *t* test.

If we want to use the command line to adjust the level of confidence interval, simply add an option to adjust the confidence level. For example, if we want to set the confidence level at 90%, we can use the following command line:

```
ttest health == 77.43, level(90)
```

**Table 11.6** Stata Results Table for Example 11.2

One-sample t test

| Variable | Obs | Mean | Std. Err. | Std. Dev. | [95% Conf. Interval] | |
|---|---|---|---|---|---|---|
| health | 18 | 62 | 4.936194 | 20.9425 | 51.58554 | 72.41446 |

```
    mean = mean(health)                                    t =  -3.1259
Ho: mean = 77.43                       degrees of freedom =       17
```

**Figure 11.9** The Stata Dialog Box to Select Any Level of Confidence Using Estimation as an Alternative to the One-Sample *t* Test

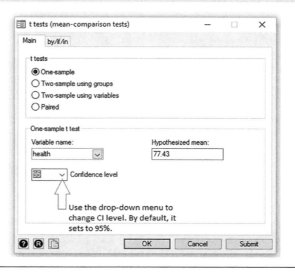

# 11.7 STATA IN FOCUS

## Confidence Intervals for the Two-Independent-Sample *t* Test

Privitera's *Statisics for the Behavioral Sciences,* Third Edition (p. 350)

In Chapter 9, we computed a two-independent-sample *t* test using Stata for the data given in Example 11.3. Table 11.7 shows the Stata output table for that test, which was originally given in Table 9.12 in Chapter 9. The table lists the 95% confidence interval for the mean difference between the groups. To change the confidence interval, follow the steps for computing the two-independent-sample *t* test given in Chapter 9, and select Options in the dialog box in Steps 4 to 6. This action will display an additional dialog box, shown in Figure 11.11, that allows you to choose any level of confidence. By default, Stata gives a 95% confidence interval with the *t* test.

**Table 11.7**   Stata Results Table for Example 11.3

```
Two-sample t test with equal variances

   Group |     Obs        Mean    Std. Err.   Std. Dev.   [95% Conf. Interval]

    Fast |       6         600    63.24555    154.9193    437.4221    762.5779
  Slowly |       6         650    53.22906     130.384    513.1703    786.8297

combined |      12         625    40.12292    138.9899    536.6901    713.3099

    diff |                 -50    82.66398               -234.1868    134.1868

    diff = mean(Fast) - mean(Slowly)                              t =  -0.6049
Ho: diff = 0                                   degrees of freedom =       10

    Ha: diff < 0                    Ha: diff != 0                   Ha: diff > 0
  Pr(T < t) = 0.2794         Pr(|T| > |t|) = 0.5587          Pr(T > t) = 0.7206
```

**Figure 11.11**   The Stata Dialog Box to Select Any Level of Confidence Using Estimation as an Alternative to the Two-Independent-Sample *t* Test

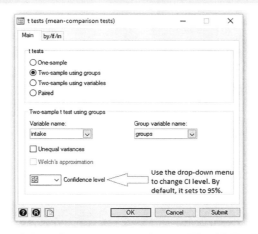

Similar to the previous example, if we want to use the command line to adjust the confidence level, we can add an option. For example, if we want to set the confidence interval at 90%, we can use the following command line:

```
ttest intake, by(groups) level(90)
```

The confidence limits are given in the Stata results table. The lower and upper confidence limits (shown in the square in Table 11.7) in the Stata results table match those we already computed, give or take rounding. Using these 95% confidence limits, we conclude that it is likely that there is no difference in calories consumed between groups instructed to eat slowly or fast because zero falls within the interval.

# 11.9 STATA IN FOCUS

## Confidence Intervals for the Related-Samples *t* Test

Privitera's *Statisics for the Behavioral Sciences,* Third Edition (p. 353)

In Chapter 10, we computed a related-samples *t* test using Stata for the data given in Example 11.4. Table 11.8 shows the Stata results table for that test, which was originally given in Table 10.8 in Chapter 10. The table lists the 95% confidence interval for the mean difference in time spent talking. To change the confidence interval, follow the steps for computing the related-samples *t* test given in Chapter 10, and select Options in the dialog box in Steps 3 to 4. This action will display an additional dialog box, shown in Figure 11.13, that allows you to choose any level of confidence. By default, Stata gives a 95% confidence interval with the *t* test.

**Table 11.8**   Stata Results Table for Example 11.4

```
Paired t test

Variable      Obs        Mean     Std. Err.    Std. Dev.    [95% Conf. Interval]

 present        8         260     12.28385     34.74396     230.9533    289.0467
  absent        8         245     13.29608     37.60699     213.5598    276.4402

    diff        8          15     5.345225     15.11858     2.360552    27.63945

      mean(diff) = mean(present - absent)                        t =     2.8062
Ho: mean(diff) = 0                              degrees of freedom =          7

Ha: mean(diff) < 0              Ha: mean(diff) != 0              Ha: mean(diff) > 0
Pr(T < t) = 0.9869           Pr(|T| > |t|) = 0.0263           Pr(T > t) = 0.0131
```

**Figure 11.13**   The Stata Dialog Box to Select Any Level of Confidence Using Estimation as an Alternative to the Related-Samples *t* Test

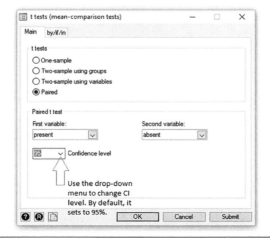

Similarly, if we want to use the command line to adjust the confidence level, we can add an option. For example, if we want to set the confidence interval at 90%, we can use the following command line:

```
ttest present == absent, level(90)
```

We can determine the effect size of the confidence interval using the confidence limits given in the Stata results table. The lower and upper confidence limits (in the square in Table 11.8) in the Stata results table match those we already computed, give or take rounding.

# 12.8 STATA IN FOCUS

## The One-Way Between-Subjects ANOVA

Privitera's *Statisics for the Behavioral Sciences,* Third Edition (p. 389)

There are two commands for computing a one-way between-subjects ANOVA using Stata—"One-Way ANOVA" and "Analysis of variance and covariance." Both of these commands can be found by clicking on the Statistics tab and selecting Linear models and related → ANOVA/MANOVA. In this section, we will use the "Analysis of variance and covariance" command to analyze Example 12.1. Please note that both commands yield the same results (e.g., $p$ value for the $F$ test), however, if further post hoc analysis is needed to distinguish the group difference, the "Analysis of variance and covariance" command can perform the postestimation analysis using Fisher's LSD and Tukey's HSD methods. (Some user-created applications also perform the post hoc analysis using these two methods. You can always use the findit command to search other ways of conducting the analysis.)

Using the data given in Table 12.10, which is reproduced from data originally given in Table 12.4, we will confirm our conclusion using the "Analysis of variance and covariance" command:

**Table 12.10**  Data for Example 12.1

| Perceived Stress Level of Workplace | | |
|---|---|---|
| Low | Moderate | High |
| 3.4 | 3.5 | 2.9 |
| 3.2 | 3.6 | 3.0 |
| 3.0 | 2.7 | 2.6 |
| 3.0 | 3.5 | 3.3 |
| 3.5 | 3.8 | 3.7 |
| 3.8 | 2.9 | 2.7 |
| 3.6 | 3.4 | 2.4 |
| 4.0 | 3.2 | 2.5 |
| 3.9 | 3.3 | 3.3 |
| 2.9 | 3.1 | 3.4 |

1. Click on the Data Editor (Edit) icon and bring up the Data Editor (Edit) window. Click on the Data tab and select Create or change data → Create new variable. Enter *groups* in the Variable name box. In the Variable type box, select "int" from the drop-down list. Under Contents of variable, select Fill with missing value and click Submit. Repeat this procedure and create the *length* variable, but this time select "float" as the variable type.

2. To code the *groups* variable, still in the Data Editor (Edit) window, click on the Data tab and select Variable Manager to bring up the Variable Manager dialog box. Select the *groups* variable and, in the right panel, under Variable properties, locate the Variable label box and click on the Manage button. This will open up the Manage value labels dialog box. Click on Create label and bring up the Create label dialog box. Enter *stress_level* in the Label Name box, then enter 1 in the value cell and *Low* in the label cell, and then click Add; enter 2 in the value cell and *Moderate* in the label cell, and then click Add; enter 3 in the value cell and *High* in the label cell, and then click Add. Select OK.

3. Close the Manage value labels dialog box, and you should be at the Variable Manager dialog box now. With the *groups* variable selected, again in the right panel, click on the drop-down list in the Value label box and select *stress_level*, which we just created. Click Apply and close the Variable Manager dialog box.

4. In the Data Editor (Edit) window, in the *groups* column, enter 1 in the first 10 cells, 2 in the next 10 cells, and 3 in the next 10 cells. These values (1, 2, and 3) are the codes for each group. In the *length* column, enter the length data in the cells that correspond with the codes for each group listed in the first column.

5. Go to the menu bar and click Statistics, then select Linear models and related → ANOVA/ MANOVA → Analysis of variance and covariance to display the ANOVA dialog box.

6. In the Dependent variable box, click on the drop-down list and select *length*. Next, in the Model box, click on the drop-down list and select *group*, as shown in Figure 12.8. (Please note: As you may notice, the Model box is, in fact, asking which variable is the factor variable. You can also click on Examples to display a complete list of what and how to input into the Model box if you have more than one factor variable.)

7. Click OK. The results should be displayed in the Results window.

**Figure 12.8**   Stata Dialog Box for Steps 5 and 6

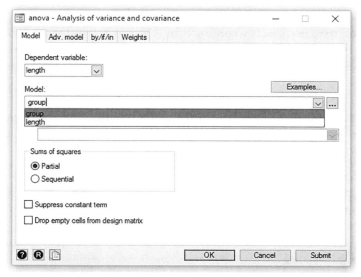

Alternatively, for Steps 5 and 6, we can use the following command line to conduct the ANOVA analysis:

```
anova length group
```

Note that to correctly use the anova command, the dependent variable (in this example, the *length* variable) should always be input first.

Notice that the ANOVA table, shown in Table 12.11, is similar to the one we computed for Example 12.1. In addition, Stata gives us the exact $p$ value for this test in the last column (Prob > F = 0.0439).

**Table 12.11**   The Stata Results Table Using the One-Way ANOVA Results for Example 12.1

| | | | | | |
|---|---|---|---|---|---|
| | Number of obs = | 30 | R-squared | = | 0.2067 |
| | Root MSE    = | .390489 | Adj R-squared = | | 0.1479 |
| Source | Partial SS | df | MS | F | Prob>F |
| Model | 1.0726666 | 2 | .53633332 | 3.52 | 0.0439 |
| groups | 1.0726666 | 2 | .53633332 | 3.52 | 0.0439 |
| Residual | 4.1169997 | 27 | .15248147 | | |
| Total | 5.1896664 | 29 | .17895401 | | |

Up until now, we have used Stata to produce the ANOVA results for our model, and the results indicate that there are significant differences among groups. However, we are also interested in where the difference lies within, so we need to conduct a post hoc analysis to identify the exact difference.

8. To conduct the post hoc analysis, go to the menu bar and click Statistics, then select Postestimation. In Stata 14, the Postestimation option is located second from the bottom of the list.

9. In the Postestimation dialog box, click on the "+" sign in front of the option Test, contrasts, and comparisons of parameter estimates to expand the menu. From the list, select Pairwise comparisons, then click Launch, as displayed in Figure 12.9.

Note that the Pairwise comparisons option will show up only *after* conducting the ANOVA analysis first, using the Analysis of variance and covariance command.

**Figure 12.9**   Stata Dialog Box for Step 9

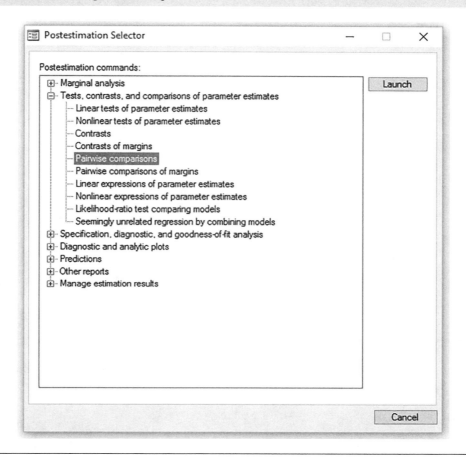

10. In the Pairwise comparisons dialog box, click on the drop-down list under the Factor terms to compute pairwise comparisons for box and select *groups*. Next, under Options, we can choose the method used to conduct the multiple comparisons from the drop-down list. Because Stata allows only one method each time, let us use the Fisher's LSD method first. The default choice under the Multiple comparisons box is Do not adjust for multiple comparisons. This is, in fact, the Fisher's LSD method. Thus, we do not need to change the setting.

11. Still in the Pairwise comparisons dialog box, click on the Reporting tab, then check the following two options, as shown in Figure 12.10:

   • Specify additional tables (default is effects table with confidence intervals)

   • Show effects table with confidence intervals and p-values

12. Click OK. The results should be displayed in the Results window.

**Figure 12.10**    Stata Dialog Box for Step 11

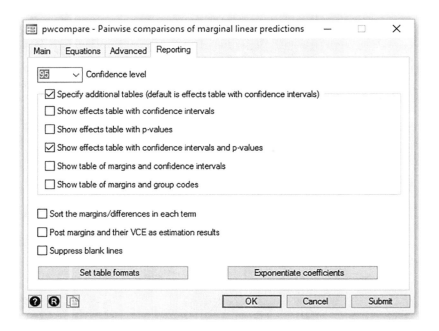

Alternatively, for Steps 8 to 11, we can use the following command line to conduct the post hoc analysis using Fisher's LSD method:

```
pwcompare groups, effects
```

The post hoc comparisons using Fisher's LSD in Table 12.12 label each group. The *p* value, which indicates a significant difference when *p* is less than .05, is given in the P > |t| column. These results clearly indicate that there is a significant difference between the Low and High Stress level groups, which confirms the conclusions we made in Example 12.1.

**Table 12.12**    Stata Results Table for the Post Hoc Comparisons Using Fisher's LSD Test

```
Pairwise comparisons of marginal linear predictions

Margins      : asbalanced
```

|  | Contrast | Std. Err. | Unadjusted t | Unadjusted P>|t| | Unadjusted [95% Conf. Interval] | |
|---|---|---|---|---|---|---|
| **groups** | | | | | | |
| Moderate vs Low | -.13 | .1746319 | -0.74 | 0.463 | -.488315 | .228315 |
| High vs Low | -.45 | .1746319 | -2.58 | 0.016 | -.808315 | -.091685 |
| High vs Moderate | -.32 | .1746319 | -1.83 | 0.078 | -.678315 | .038315 |

Additionally, we can also use Stata to generate the post hoc comparison using Tukey's HSD method:

1. Follow Steps 8 to 11 from the steps given for the Postestimation command.

2. In Step 10, instead of using the default choice for the Multiple comparisons box, select Tukey's method into the cell, as displayed in Figure 12.11.

3. Click OK. The results should be displayed in the Results window (see Table 12.13).

Alternatively, the Tukey's HSD test can also be conducted by using the following command line:

```
pwcompare groups, mcompare(tukey) effects
```

**Figure 12.11**  Dialog Box for Step 2

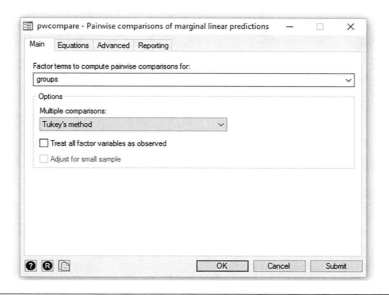

**Table 12.13**  Stata Results Table for the Post Hoc Comparisons Using Tukey's HSD Test

```
Pairwise comparisons of marginal linear predictions

Margins      : asbalanced
```

| | Number of Comparisons |
|---|---|
| groups | 3 |

| | Contrast | Std. Err. | Tukey t | Tukey P>|t| | Tukey [95% Conf. Interval] | |
|---|---|---|---|---|---|---|
| **groups** | | | | | | |
| Moderate vs Low | -.13 | .1746319 | -0.74 | 0.740 | -.5629854 | .3029854 |
| High vs Low | -.45 | .1746319 | -2.58 | 0.040 | -.8829854 | -.0170146 |
| High vs Moderate | -.32 | .1746319 | -1.83 | 0.178 | -.7529854 | .1129854 |

# 13.6 STATA IN FOCUS

## The One-Way Within-Subjects ANOVA

Privitera's *Statisics for the Behavioral Sciences,* Third Edition (p. 423)

In Example 13.1, we concluded that ratings of effectiveness for the three advertisements significantly varied, $F(2, 12) = 17.38$, $p < .05$. A Bonferroni procedure showed that participants rated the effectiveness of an ad with smoking-related cues higher compared to an ad with no cues and compared to an ad with generic cues. We will use Stata to confirm the calculations we computed in Example 13.1.

1. Click on the Data Editor (Edit) icon and bring up the Data Editor (Edit) window. Click on the Data tab and select Create or change data → Create new variable. Enter *person* in the Variable name box. In the Variable type box, select "str" from the drop-down list. Under Contents of variable, select Fill with missing value and click Submit. Repeat this procedure to create the *cue* variable, using "str" as the variable type, and then create the *value* variable using "int" as the variable type.

2. In the Data Editor (Edit) window, enter the data for each group in the appropriate column, as shown in Figure 13.7.

**Figure 13.7** Variables and Values

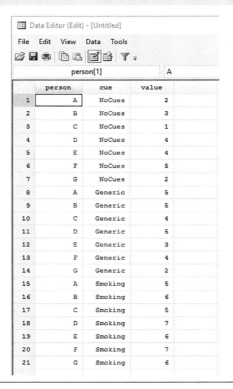

You may notice that the values under the *person* column and *cue* column are highlighted in red. That is because these two variables are string variables. In general, Stata is not good at processing string variables, so we need to convert these variables from string to numerical. One method to solve the problem is what we have done in previous chapters, by creating numerical variables, entering the numerical values, then creating and applying text labels for these numerical values. In the current example, the process of creating labels for two variables can be lengthy. Here, we introduce the other method—using the command line to convert the string variable to a numerical variable.

3. In the command window, input the following command line:
    - To convert *person* to numerical: *encode* person, gen(n_person)
    - To convert *cue* to numerical: *encode* cue, gen(n_cue)

These two commands generate two new numerical variables, *n_person* and *n_cue*, as shown in Figure 13.8.

**Figure 13.8** Step 3—New Variables Generated

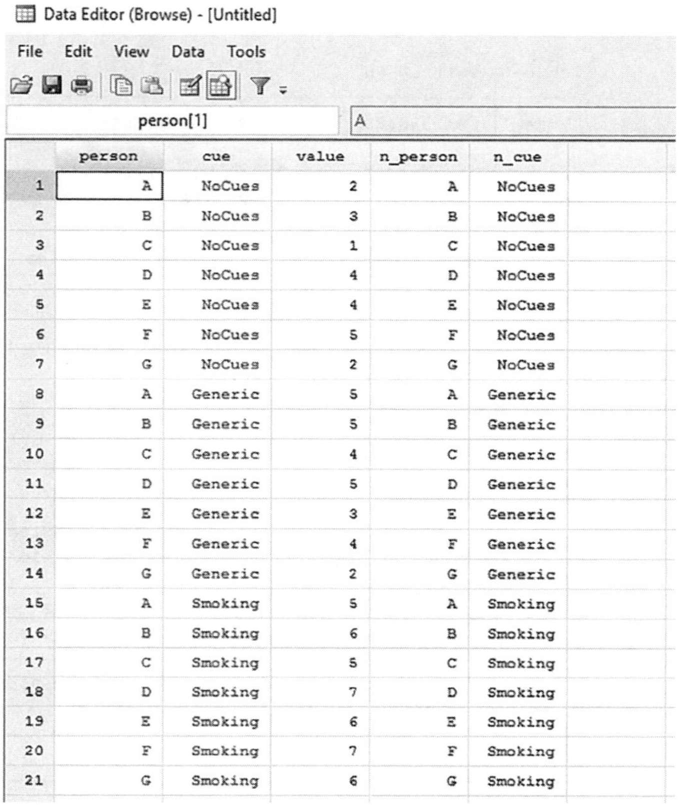


| | person | cue | value | n_person | n_cue |
|---|---|---|---|---|---|
| 1 | A | NoCues | 2 | A | NoCues |
| 2 | B | NoCues | 3 | B | NoCues |
| 3 | C | NoCues | 1 | C | NoCues |
| 4 | D | NoCues | 4 | D | NoCues |
| 5 | E | NoCues | 4 | E | NoCues |
| 6 | F | NoCues | 5 | F | NoCues |
| 7 | G | NoCues | 2 | G | NoCues |
| 8 | A | Generic | 5 | A | Generic |
| 9 | B | Generic | 5 | B | Generic |
| 10 | C | Generic | 4 | C | Generic |
| 11 | D | Generic | 5 | D | Generic |
| 12 | E | Generic | 3 | E | Generic |
| 13 | F | Generic | 4 | F | Generic |
| 14 | G | Generic | 2 | G | Generic |
| 15 | A | Smoking | 5 | A | Smoking |
| 16 | B | Smoking | 6 | B | Smoking |
| 17 | C | Smoking | 5 | C | Smoking |
| 18 | D | Smoking | 7 | D | Smoking |
| 19 | E | Smoking | 6 | E | Smoking |
| 20 | F | Smoking | 7 | F | Smoking |
| 21 | G | Smoking | 6 | G | Smoking |

5. Go to the menu bar and click Statistics, then select Linear models and related → ANOVA/ MANOVA → Analysis of variance and covariance to display the ANOVA dialog box.

6. In the Dependent variable box, click on the drop-down list and select *value*. Next, in the Model box, click on the drop-down list and select both *n_person* and *n_cue*. Also check Repeated-measure variable, and click on the drop-down list to select *n_person*.

7. Click OK. The results should be displayed in the Results window.

Alternatively, for Steps 4 and 5, we can use the following command line to conduct the analysis:

```
anova value n_person n_cue, repeated(n_person)
```

Table 13.8 displays the Stata results table for the ANOVA. As displayed in the table, the *F* value is 17.29, and the associated *p* value (.0003) is less than .05. These results are similar to Table 13.5, which we computed for Example 13.1.

**Table 13.8**   Stata Results *F* Table for Example 13.1

```
              Number of obs =        21    R-squared     =   0.8000
              Root MSE      =  .971825    Adj R-squared =   0.6667

     Source | Partial SS        df         MS          F     Prob>F

      Model | 45.333333          8    5.6666667      6.00    0.0031

   n_person | 12.666667          6    2.1111111      2.24    0.1111
      n_cue | 32.666667          2    16.333333     17.29    0.0003

   Residual | 11.333333         12    .94444444

      Total | 56.666667         20    2.8333333
```

```
Between-subjects error term:  n_cue
                    Levels:   3          (2 df)
      Lowest b.s.e. variable:  n_cue

Repeated variable: n_person
                              Huynh-Feldt epsilon       =   0.4842
                              Greenhouse-Geisser epsilon =  0.2204
                              Box's conservative epsilon =  0.1667

                              ----------- Prob > F -----------
     Source |   df     F    Regular    H-F      G-G       Box

   n_person |    6   2.24   0.1111   0.1879   0.2556    0.2735
   Residual |   12
```

We can also conduct the post hoc analysis using the command line introduced in Section 12.8. To conduct a post hoc estimation with the Bonferroni method, we can use the following command line:

```
pwcompare n_cue, mcompare(bonferroni) effects
```

Table 13.9 displays the Stata results table for the Bonferroni post hoc test. This display is similar to that for the post hoc test we computed using Stata in Chapter 12. The $p$ values for each pairwise comparison are given in the P > $|t|$ column. The display in Table 13.9 confirms the results we obtained for Example 13.1.

**Table 13.9** Stata Results Table for Post Hoc Comparisons Using the Bonferroni Procedure

```
Pairwise comparisons of marginal linear predictions

Margins      : asbalanced
```

|  | Number of Comparisons |
|---|---|
| n_cue | 3 |

|  | Contrast | Std. Err. | Bonferroni t | Bonferroni P>|t| | Bonferroni [95% Conf. Interval] | |
|---|---|---|---|---|---|---|
| **n_cue** |  |  |  |  |  |  |
| NoCues vs Generic | -1 | .5194625 | -1.93 | 0.235 | -2.443832 | .443832 |
| Smoking vs Generic | 2 | .5194625 | 3.85 | 0.007 | .556168 | 3.443832 |
| Smoking vs NoCues | 3 | .5194625 | 5.78 | 0.000 | 1.556168 | 4.443832 |

In Example 14.1, we tested whether levels of exposure to sugars interfered with the time it took participants to complete a computer task in the presence or absence of a buffet of sugary foods. We concluded that participants with more exposure to sugars took longer to complete the computer task when the buffet of sugary foods was present. Using the same data as in Example 14.1, we will use Stata to confirm the calculations that we computed for these data.

1. Click on the Data Editor (Edit) icon and bring up the Data Editor (Edit) window. Click on the Data tab and select Create or change data → Create new variable. Enter *buffet* in the Variable name box. In the Variable type box, select "int" from the drop-down list. Under Contents of variable, select Fill with missing value and click Submit. Repeat this procedure to create *exposure* and *times* variables.

2. In the row named *buffet*, click on the small gray box with three dots in the Values column. In the dialog box, enter 1 in the value cell and *absent* in the label cell, and then click Add. Then enter 2 in the value cell and *present* in the label cell, and then click Add. Select OK.

3. To code the *buffet* variable, still in the Data Editor (Edit) window, click on the Data tab and select Variable Manager to bring up the Variable Manager dialog box. Select the *groups* variable and, in the right panel, under Variable properties, locate the Variable label box and click on the Manage button. This will open up the Manage value labels dialog box. Click on Create label and bring up the Create label dialog box. Enter *buffet_status* in the Label Name box, then enter 1 in the value cell and *absent* in the label cell, and then click Add; enter 2 in the value cell and *present* in the label cell, and then click Add. Select OK.

4. Close the Manage value labels dialog box, and you should be at the Variable Manager dialog box now. With the *buffet* variable selected, again in the right panel, click on the drop-down list in the Value label box and select *buffet_status*, which we just created. Click Apply and close the Variable Manager dialog box.

5. Repeat Steps 3 and 4 to code the *exposure* variable, except use *exp_level* as the label name, and enter 1 for *low*, 2 for *moderate*, and 3 for *high*.

6. In the Data Editor (Edit) window, in the *buffet* column, enter 1 in the first 18 cells, then enter 2 in the next 18 cells.

7. In the *exposure* column, enter 1 in the first six cells, then enter 2 in the next six cells, then enter 3 in the next six cells. Repeat this: Enter 1 in the next six cells, enter 2 in the next six cells, and enter 3 in the next six cells. We have now set up the groups. For example, the first six cells read 1, 1; these codes identify the group with the buffet absent and low exposure to sugars.

8. In the *times* column, enter the data in the cells that correspond with the codes for each group listed in the first and second columns.

9. Go to the menu bar and click Statistics, then select Linear models and related → ANOVA/MANOVA → Analysis of variance and covariance to display the ANOVA dialog box.

10. In the Dependent variable box, click on the drop-down list and select *times*. In the Model box, click on the drop-down list and select both *buffet* and *exposure*. Now we have included both main effect variables in the model.

11. Next, we need to include the interaction term (i.e., *buffet * exposure*) in the model. Reselect those two main effect variables, but this time add a "#" sign between these two variables, as shown in Figure 14.1. The *buffet # exposure* represents the interaction term. *Tip: Because this is a full factorial model (i.e., both independent variables are categorical, and all possible interaction combinations are considered), we can simplify the Model box input as buffet ## exposure, instead of buffet exposure buffet # exposure.*

12. Click OK. The results should be displayed in the Results window.

Alternatively, for Steps 10 and 11, we can use the following command line to conduct the analysis:

```
anova times buffet exposure buffet # exposure
```

Or

```
anova times buffet ## exposure
```

**Figure 14.1**   Interaction Model for Steps 10 and 11

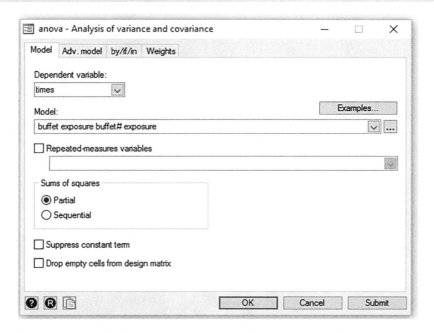

The Stata results table, shown in Table 14.19, confirms our conclusion that we have a buffet* exposure interaction and a main effect of exposure.

**Table 14.19**   Stata Results Table for Two-Way ANOVA

```
                    Number of obs =        36    R-squared      =  0.5763
                    Root MSE       =   2.23607    Adj R-squared =  0.5056

           Source | Partial SS        df         MS         F    Prob>F
        ----------+----------------------------------------------------
            Model |     204            5        40.8       8.16  0.0001
                  |
           buffet | 7.100e-30          1    7.100e-30      0.00  1.0000
         exposure |     150            2         75       15.00  0.0000
   buffet#exposure|      54            2         27        5.40  0.0099
                  |
         Residual |     150           30          5
        ----------+----------------------------------------------------
            Total |     354           35   10.114286
```

To identify where the difference is located exactly, we can input the command line introduced in Chapter 12 to perform the post hoc analysis using Tukey's HSD method:

```
pwcompare buffet exposure buffet#exposure, mcompare(tukey) effects
```

# 15.4 STATA IN FOCUS

## Pearson Correlation Coefficient

Privitera's *Statisics for the Behavioral Sciences,* Third Edition (p. 501)

In Example 15.1, we concluded that mood and eating were significantly correlated ($r = -.744$, $p < .05$) using the Pearson correlation coefficient. Let us confirm this conclusion using Stata.

1. Click on the Data Editor (Edit) icon and bring up the Data Editor (Edit) window. Click on the Data tab and select Create or change data → Create new variable. Enter *mood* in the Variable name box. In the Variable type box, select "int" from the drop-down list. Under Contents of variable, select Fill with missing value and click Submit. Repeat this procedure and create the *eating* variable this time.

2. In the Data Editor (Edit) window, enter the data for *mood* in the first column; enter the corresponding data for *eating* in the second column.

3. Go to the menu bar and click Statistics, then select Summaries, tables, and tests → Summary and descriptive statistics → Pairwise correlations to open up the Pairwise correlation of variables dialog box.

4. In the Variables box, click on the drop-down list. From the list, first select *mood,* then select *eating* (note that you can select multiple variables). Now you will see two variables in the Variables box, as shown in Figure 15.1. Also, check the following three options:

   - Print number of observations for each entry
   - Print significance level of each entry
   - Significance level for displaying with a star (by default, the value is 5, we shall keep this value; this option allows us to indicate the significant correlation with an asterisk, given the significance level)

5. Click OK. The results should be displayed in the Results window.

**Figure 15.1** Pairwise Correlation of the Variables Dialog Box for Step 5

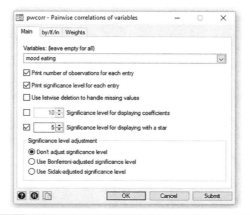

Alternatively, for Steps 3 and 4, we can use the following command line to conduct the correlation test:

```
pwcorr mood eating, obs sig star(5)
```

The Stata results table, shown in Table 15.3, gives the results of a two-tailed test at a *.05* level of significance. The Stata results table is set up in a matrix with *mood* and *eating* listed in the rows and columns. The cell next to *eating* in the matrix gives the direction and strength of the correlation ($r = -.7439$ for mood and eating; this value is shown with an asterisk for significant correlations); the significance ($p = .0343$) is shown in the second row of the same cell; and the sample size ($N = 8$) is given as well. To find the coefficient of determination, square the correlation coefficient.

**Table 15.3**   Stata Results Table for Example 15.1

|        | mood     | eating |
|--------|----------|--------|
| mood   | 1.0000   |        |
|        | 8        |        |
| eating | -0.7439* | 1.0000 |
|        | 0.0343   |        |
|        | 8        | 8      |

# 15.8 STATA IN FOCUS

## Spearman Correlation Coefficient

Privitera's *Statisics for the Behavioral Sciences,* Third Edition (p. 512)

In Example 15.2, we concluded that a significant correlation was evident between the order of ranks on each task ($r_s = .768$, $p < .05$) using the Spearman correlation coefficient. Let us confirm this conclusion using Stata.

1. Click on the Data Editor (Edit) icon and bring up the Data Editor (Edit) window. Click on the Data tab and select Create or change data → Create new variable. Enter *food* in the Variable name box. In the Variable type box, select "int" from the drop-down list. Under Contents of variable, select Fill with missing value and click Submit. Repeat this procedure and create the *water* variable this time.

2. In the Data Editor (Edit) window, enter the original ranks for the *food* task and *water* task in the appropriate columns. You can enter the tied ranks, but entering the original ranks is easier because Stata will average the tied ranks by default. Hence, for the *food* task, enter 1, 1, 3, 4, 5, 6, 7, and 8 down the first column. For the *water* task, enter 1, 3, 2, 6, 4, 7, 8, and 5 down the second column.

3. Go to the menu bar and click Statistics, then select Summaries, tables, and tests → Nonparametric tests of hypotheses → Spearman's rank correlation to open up the Spearman's rank correlation coefficients dialog box.

4. In the Variables box, click on the drop-down list. From the list, first select *food,* then select *water* (note that you can select multiple variables). Now you will see two variables in the Variables box, as shown in Figure 15.16.

5. Under List of statistics, check all three options:

   • Display correlations coefficient (default)

   • Display number of observations

   • Display significance level. Under Display adjustment, check Significance level for displaying with a star.

6. At the bottom of the dialog box, also check Force matrix table output.

7. Click OK. The results should be displayed in the Results window.

**Figure 15.16**   The Dialog Box in Steps 4 and 5

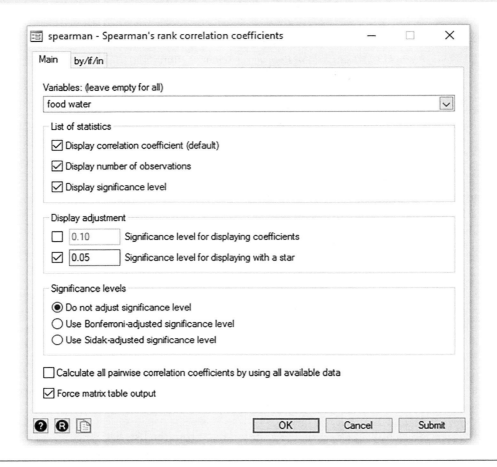

Alternatively, for Steps 3 to 5, we can use the following command line to conduct the correlation test:

```
spearman food water, stats(rho obs p) star(0.05) matrix
```

The Stata results table, shown in Table 15.6, shows the value of the correlation coefficient ($r_s$ = .7665; this is slightly different from our calculation due to rounding error); the $p$ value ($p$ = .0265); and the sample size ($N$ = 8) for this test. If you enter values for each factor that are not ranks, such as the actual times it took subjects to complete the food and water tasks, Stata will automatically convert the values to ranks and average the tied ranks before computing the Spearman correlation coefficient. To compute the coefficient of determination, square the correlation coefficient. To compute the coefficient of determination, square the correlation coefficient.

**Table 15.6**   Stata Results Table for Example 15.2

```
┌─────────────────────────┐
│ Key                     │
├─────────────────────────┤
│   rho                   │
│   Number of obs         │
│   Sig. level            │
└─────────────────────────┘
```

```
                     food     water
         ──────────────────────────────
         food     1.0000
                       8


        water     0.7665*   1.0000
                       8         8
                  0.0265
```

# 15.10 STATA IN FOCUS

## Point-Biserial Correlation Coefficient

Privitera's *Statisics for the Behavioral Sciences,* Third Edition (p. 517)

To compute a point-biserial correlation coefficient using Stata, we first code the dichotomous factor and then compute the Pearson correlation coefficient. Because the point-biserial correlation coefficient is derived mathematically from the Pearson correlation coefficient, the value we obtain using Stata will be identical to that obtained for a point-biserial correlation.

In Example 15.3, we concluded that a correlation between sex and duration of laughter was not significant ($r_{pb} = -.163$, $p > .05$) using the point-biserial correlation coefficient. Let us confirm this conclusion using Stata.

1. Click on the Data Editor (Edit) icon and bring up the Data Editor (Edit) window. Click on the Data tab and select Create or change data → Create new variable. Enter *sex* in the Variable name box. In the Variable type box, select "int" from the drop-down list. Under Contents of variable, select Fill with missing value and click OK. Repeat this procedure and create the *laughter* variable this time.

2. To code the dichotomous variable, still in the Data Editor (Edit) window, click on the Data tab and select Variable Manager to bring up the Variable Manager dialog box. Select the *sex* variable and, in the right panel, under Variable properties, locate the Variable label box and click on the Manage button. This will open up the Manage value labels dialog box. Click on Create label and bring up the Create label dialog box. Enter *sex_status* in the Label Name box, then enter 1 in the value cell and *men* in the label cell, and then click Add. Then enter 2 in the value cell and *women* in the label cell, and then click Add. Select OK.

3. Close the Manage value labels dialog box, and you should be at the Variable Manager dialog box now. With the *sex* variable selected, again in the right panel, click on the drop-down list in the Value label box and select *sex_status*, which we just created. Click Apply and close the Variable Manager dialog box.

4. In the Data Editor (Edit) window, in the *sex* column, enter 1 five times and 2 seven times. In the *laughter* column, enter the data for laughter for men and women across from the corresponding code (i.e., enter the data for men next to a code of 1 and the data for women next to a code of 2).

5. Go to the menu bar and click Statistics, then select Summaries, tables, and tests → Summary and descriptive statistics → Pairwise correlations to open up the Pairwise correlation of variables dialog box.

6. In the Variables box, click on the drop-down list. From the list, first select *sex,* then select *laughter* (note that you can select multiple variables). Also, check the following three options:

   • Print number of observations for each entry
   • Print significance level of each entry

- Significance level for displaying with a star (By default, the value is 5, and we shall keep this value; this option allows us to display the significant correlation with an asterisk, given the significance level.)

7. Click OK. The results should be displayed in the Results window.

Alternatively, for Steps 5 and 6, we can use the following command line to conduct the correlation test:

```
pwcorr sex laughter, obs sig star(5)
```

The Stata results table, shown in Table 15.9, shows the value of the correlation coefficient ($r = .1633$), the $p$ value ($p = .6121$), and the sample size ($N = 12$) for this test. Again, the sign of the correlation is not meaningful for the point-biserial correlation. As long as you code the dichotomous variable, the Pearson and the point-biserial correlation coefficients will be identical. To compute the coefficient of determination, square the correlation coefficient.

**Table 15.9**   Stata Results Table for Example 15.3

```
                        |    sex laughter
               ---------+----------------
           sex |        1.0000
               |
               |            12
               |
      laughter |        0.1633    1.0000
               |        0.6121
               |            12        12
               |
```

There is no embedded command in Stata to compute a phi correlation coefficient (but you can always use the findit command to discover user-generated functions). To compute a phi correlation coefficient using Stata, we first code each dichotomous factor and then compute a Pearson correlation coefficient, weighted by the proper variable. Because the phi correlation coefficient is derived mathematically from the Pearson correlation coefficient, the value we obtain using Stata will be identical to that obtained for a phi correlation.

In Example 15.4, we concluded that a correlation between employment and happiness was significant ($r_\phi = .40, p < .05$) using the phi correlation coefficient. We can confirm this conclusion using Stata.

1. Click on the Data Editor (Edit) icon and bring up the Data Editor (Edit) window. Click on the Data tab and select Create or change data → Create new variable. Enter *employment* in the Variable name box. In the Variable type box, select "int" from the drop-down list. Under Contents of variable, select Fill with missing value and click OK. Repeat this procedure and create the *happiness* and *count* variables.

2. We will code each variable with 0s and 1s to identify each cell in Table 15.11. To code the *employment* variable, still in the Data Editor (Edit) window, click on the Data tab and select Variable Manager to bring up the Variable Manager dialog box. Select the *employment* variable and, in the right panel, under Variable properties, locate the Variable label box and click on the Manage button. This will open up the Manage value labels dialog box. Click on Create label and bring up the Create label dialog box. Enter *emp_status* in the Label Name box, then enter 0 in the value cell and *unemployed* in the label cell, and then click Add. Then enter 1 in the value cell and *employed* in the label cell, and then click Add. Select OK.

3. Close the Manage value labels dialog box, and you should be at the Variable Manager dialog box now. With the *employment* variable selected, again in the right panel, click on the drop-down list in the Value label box and select *emp_status*, which we just created. Click Apply and close the Variable Manager dialog box.

4. Repeat Steps 2 and 3 to code the *happiness* variable. Use *happy_level* as the label name, enter 0 in the value cell and *unhappy* in the label cell, then click Add. Then enter 1 in the value cell and *happy* in the label cell, then click Add. Apply *happy_level* to the *happiness* variable in the Variable Manager dialog box.

5. In the Data Editor (Edit) window, for the *employment* variable, enter 0, 0, 1, and 1. For the *happiness* variable, enter 0, 1, 0, and 1. For the *count* variable, enter 14, 6, 6, and 14 down the column.

6. Go to the menu bar and click Statistics, then select Summaries, tables, and tests → Summary and descriptive statistics → Pairwise correlations to open up the Pairwise correlation of variables dialog box.

7.  In the Variables box, click on the drop-down list. From the list, first select *employment,* then select *happiness* (note that you can select multiple variables). Also, check the following three options:

    -   Print number of observations for each entry
    -   Print significance level of each entry
    -   Significance level for displaying with a star (By default, the value is 5, and we shall keep this value; this option allows us to display the significant correlation with an asterisk, given the significance level.)

8.  Click on the Weights tab on the top of the Pairwise correlation of variables dialog box, select Frequency weights as the weight type, then select *count* from the drop-down list into the Frequency weights cell, as shown in Figure 15.17.

9.  Click OK. The results should be displayed in the Results window.

**Figure 15.17**    The Dialog Box in Step 8

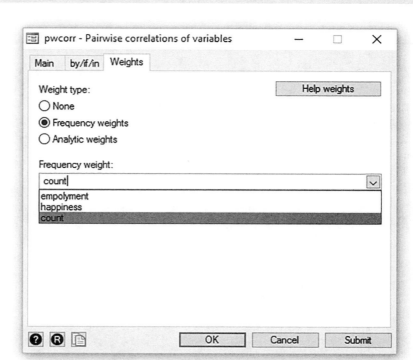

Alternatively, for Steps 6 to 8, we can use the following command line to find the phi correlation:

```
pwcorr employment happiness [fweight = count], obs sig star(5)
```

The Stata results table, shown in Table 15.14, shows the value of the correlation coefficient ($r = .400$), the $p$ value ($p = .0105$), and the total number of participants observed ($N = 40$) for this test. As long as you code and weight the dichotomous factors, the Pearson and phi correlation coefficients will be identical. To compute the coefficient of determination, square the correlation coefficient.

**Table 15.14**   Stata Results Table for Example 15.4

|  | employ~t | happin~s |
|---|---|---|
| employment | 1.0000 | |
| | 40 | |
| happiness | 0.4000* | 1.0000 |
| | 0.0105 | |
| | 40 | 40 |

# 16.7 STATA IN FOCUS

## Analysis of Regression

Privitera's *Statisics for the Behavioral Sciences,* Third Edition (p. 551)

To illustrate how all of our calculations are completed in Stata, let us compute the data in Example 16.3 in Stata. The data for Example 16.3 are reproduced in Table 16.5 from data originally given in Figure 16.5. We will compare how our analysis computed by hand matches the analysis computed using Stata.

**Table 16.5** A Table Showing the Number of Sessions Eight Patients ($n = 8$) Attended and the Number of Symptoms They Expressed

| Number of Sessions (X) | Number of Symptoms (Y) |
|:---:|:---:|
| 9 | 0 |
| 5 | 3 |
| 8 | 2 |
| 2 | 5 |
| 6 | 3 |
| 3 | 4 |
| 5 | 2 |
| 4 | 3 |

1. Click on the Data Editor (Edit) icon and bring up the Data Editor (Edit) window. Click on the Data tab and select Create or change data → Create new variable. Enter X in the Variable name box. In the Variable type box, select "int" from the drop-down list. Under Contents of variable, select Fill with missing value and click OK. Repeat this procedure and create the Y variable.

2. In the Data Editor (Edit) window, enter the data for Example 16.3 in the columns for X and Y. Enter the data for number of sessions in the column labeled X; enter the data for number of symptoms in the column labeled Y.

3. Go to the menu bar and click Statistics, then select Linear models and related → Linear regression to open up the Linear regression dialog box.

4. In the Dependent variable box, click on the drop-down list. From the list, select $Y$, then in the Independent variables box, click on the drop-down list and select $X$ into the cell, as shown in Figure 16.7.

5. Click OK. The results should be displayed in the Results window.

**Figure 16.7**   Stata Dialog Box for Steps 3 and 4

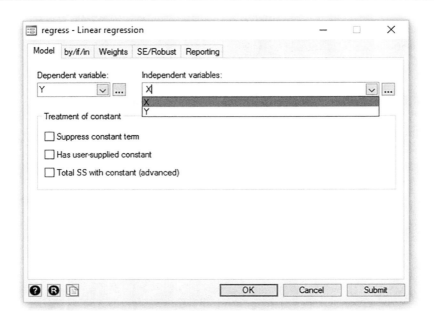

Alternatively, for Steps 3 and 4, we can use the following command line to conduct the regression analysis:

```
regress Y X
```

Please note that Stata is case sensitive, so we have to input capital letters $Y$ and $X$ to exactly match the variable names that we created in Step 1. Sometimes it is better to use all lowercase letters to name variables.

The Stata results, shown in Table 16.6, give the value of the slope (in the bottom table, *Coef.* column; $b = -0.5696$); the coefficient of determination (on the right of the top table; $R$-squared = .8269); and the $F$ value ($F = 28.66$), which are the same as those we computed by hand, give or take rounding. The decision for this test is to reject the null hypothesis, same as the decision we made for this test. The Stata results also give the *standard error of estimate* (in the bottom table, *Std. Err.* column; Std. Err. = 0.1064), which is described in the next section.

**Table 16.6** Stata Results Table for the Analysis of Regression in Example 16.3

| Source | SS | df | MS | | | |
|---|---|---|---|---|---|---|
| | | | | Number of obs | = | 8 |
| | | | | F(1, 6) | = | 28.66 |
| Model | 12.8164557 | 1 | 12.8164557 | Prob > F | = | 0.0017 |
| Residual | 2.6835443 | 6 | .447257384 | R-squared | = | 0.8269 |
| | | | | Adj R-squared | = | 0.7980 |
| Total | 15.5 | 7 | 2.21428571 | Root MSE | = | .66877 |

| Y | Coef. | Std. Err. | t | P>|t| | [95% Conf. Interval] | |
|---|---|---|---|---|---|---|
| X | -.5696203 | .1064095 | -5.35 | 0.002 | -.8299948 | -.3092457 |
| _cons | 5.740506 | .6066272 | 9.46 | 0.000 | 4.256143 | 7.22487 |

# 16.13 STATA IN FOCUS

## Multiple Regression Analysis

Privitera's *Statisics for the Behavioral Sciences*, Third Edition (p. 566)

While the many levels of computation and the many coefficients computed to perform an analysis of multiple regression might seem overwhelming, it can help to see how these values are summarized in the Stata results table. To illustrate how all of our calculations are computed in Stata, let us use Stata to compute the data in Example 16.4. The data for Example 16.4 are reproduced in Table 16.13 from data originally given in Table 16.8. We will compare how our analysis computed by hand matches the analysis reported in the Stata results table for multiple regression.

1. Click on the Data Editor (Edit) icon and bring up the Data Editor (Edit) window. Click on the Data tab and select Create or change data → Create new variable. Enter *age* in the Variable name box. In the Variable type box, select "int" from the drop-down list. Under Contents of variable, select Fill with missing value and click OK. Repeat this procedure to create the *education* and *sales* variables.

2. In the Data Editor (Edit) window, enter the data for Example 16.4 in each corresponding column, same as it is entered in Table 16.13.

**Table 16.13** Data for the Age, Education Level, and Sales Among Six Patrons

| Age (years) $X_1$ | Education (years) $X_2$ | Sales (dollars) Y |
|---|---|---|
| 19 | 12 | 20 |
| 21 | 14 | 40 |
| 26 | 13 | 30 |
| 28 | 18 | 68 |
| 32 | 17 | 70 |
| 30 | 16 | 60 |

3. Go to the menu bar and click Statistics, then select Linear models and related → Linear regression to open up the Linear regression dialog box, similar to Figure 16.7.

4. In the Dependent variable box, click on the drop-down list. From the list, select *sales*, then in the Independent variables box, click on the drop-down list and select *age* and *education* (note that you can select multiple variables).

238

5. On the top of the Linear regression dialog box, click on the Reporting tab, then check Standardized beta coefficients, as shown in Figure 16.8.

6. Click OK. The results should be displayed in the Results window.

**Figure 16.8** Stata Dialog Box for Step 5

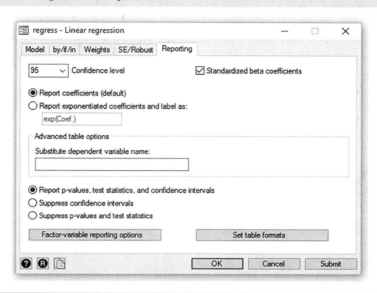

Alternatively, for Steps 3 to 5, we can use the following command line to conduct the multiple regression analysis:

```
regress sales age education, beta
```

The Stata results, shown in Table 16.14, gives the $F$ value, which is identical to the $F$ table we completed by hand in Table 16.10 in Section 16.10. The Stata results also include the unstandardized beta coefficients (computed in Section 16.10), the standardized beta coefficients (identified in Section 16.11), and each test for the relative contribution of each predictor variable (computed in Section 16.12).

**Table 16.14** Stata Results Table for the Analysis of Multiple Regression in Example 16.4

| Source | SS | df | MS | | Number of obs | = | 6 |
|---|---|---|---|---|---|---|---|
| | | | | | F(2, 3) | = | 73.66 |
| Model | 2156.09581 | 2 | 1078.0479 | | Prob > F | = | 0.0028 |
| Residual | 43.9041916 | 3 | 14.6347305 | | R-squared | = | 0.9800 |
| | | | | | Adj R-squared | = | 0.9667 |
| Total | 2200 | 5 | 440 | | Root MSE | = | 3.8255 |

| sales | Coef. | Std. Err. | t | P>|t| | | Beta |
|---|---|---|---|---|---|---|
| age | .7904192 | .5538194 | 1.43 | 0.249 | | .19214 |
| education | 7.359281 | 1.193331 | 6.17 | 0.009 | | .8302389 |
| _cons | -82.94012 | 10.9574 | -7.57 | 0.005 | | . |

# 17.3 STATA IN FOCUS

## The Chi-Square Goodness-of-Fit Test

Privitera's *Statisics for the Behavioral Sciences,* Third Edition (p. 586)

In Example 17.1, we concluded from the chi-square goodness-of-fit test that the frequency of dream recall during REM sleep was similar to what was expected, $\chi^2(2) = 3.06$, $p > .05$. Let us confirm this result using Stata. Stata does not have an embedded function to compute the chi-square goodness-of-fit, so we need to use the findit command to find other user-created functions.

1. In the command window, input:

   ```
   findit chitesti
   ```

   and the Stata Viewer window will open up, as shown in Figure 17.3.

**Figure 17.3** Stata Viewer Window for Chitesti

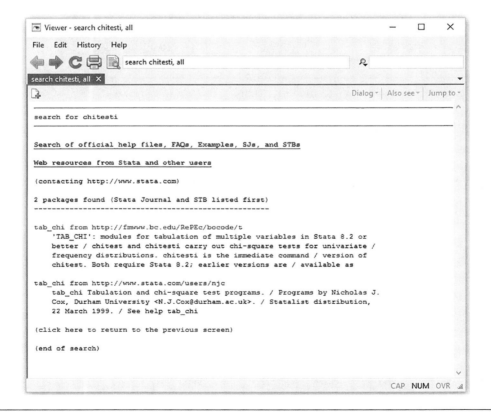

2. Click on the first result. You will be directed to the installation page, as displayed in Figure 17.4.

**Figure 17.4**   Stata Dialog Box for Step 4

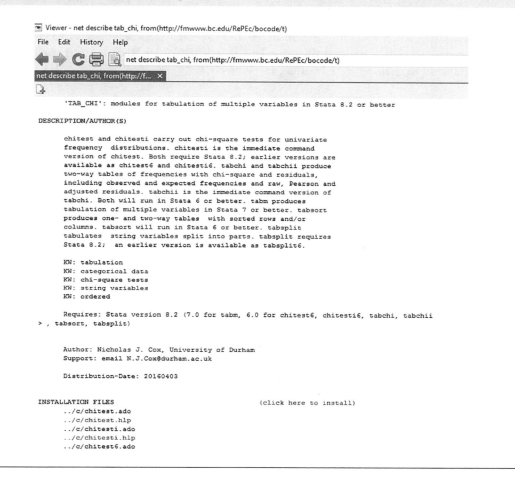

3.  Click on click here to install. The chitesti function should be installed.

4.  Chitesti requires two sets of values: the observed frequencies and the expected frequencies. These values can be found in Table 17.2.

**Table 17.2**   The Observed Frequency of Dreams Recalled and the Expected Frequency Based on Proportions in Each Category That Were Reported in Previous Studies

|  | **Dream Recall** | | | |
|---|---|---|---|---|
|  | **Did Recall** | **Did Not Recall** | **Unsure** | |
| $f_o$ | 58 | 12 | 10 | |
| $f_e$ | 80(.80) = 64 | 80(.10) = 8 | 80(.10) = 8 | |
|  | | | | $N = 80$ |

5. In the command window, input the following command line:

   ```
   chitesti 58 12 10\64 8 8
   ```

   Please note: When you input the observed and expected values, they have to be aligned. In other words, the observed values for Did Recall, Did Not Recall, and Unrecall have to correspond to their expected values, respectively.

The Stata results table displays two *p* values, which are both shown in Table 17.5. Here, we look at the Pearson chi2 value. These data match the values we computed for Example 17.1.

**Table 17.5**   The Stata Output for the Chi-Square Goodness-of-Fit Test

```
observed frequencies from keyboard; expected frequencies from keyboard

             Pearson chi2(2) =    3.0625    Pr =  0.216
    likelihood-ratio chi2(2) =    2.7750    Pr =  0.250
```

| observed | expected | obs - exp | Pearson |
|---|---|---|---|
| 58 | 64.000 | -6.000 | -0.750 |
| 12 | 8.000 | 4.000 | 1.414 |
| 10 | 8.000 | 2.000 | 0.707 |

# 17.9 STATA IN FOCUS

## The Chi-Square Test for Independence

Privitera's *Statistics for the Behavioral Sciences,* Third Edition (p. 601)

In Example 17.2, a 2 × 2 chi-square test for independence showed a significant relationship between type of counseling and outcome of counseling, $\chi^2(1) = 5.386$, $p < .05$. Let us confirm this conclusion using Stata.

1. Click on the Data Editor (Edit) icon and bring up the Data Editor (Edit) window. Click on the Data tab and select Create or change data → Create new variable. Enter *row* in the Variable name box. In the Variable type box, select "int" from the drop-down list. Under Contents of variable, select Fill with missing value and click OK. Repeat this procedure to create the *column* and *frequency* variables.

2. To code the *row* variable, still in the Data Editor (Edit) window, click on the Data tab and select Variable Manager to bring up the Variable Manager dialog box. Select the *row* variable and, in the right panel, under Variable properties, locate the Variable label box and click on the Manage button. This will open up the Manage value labels dialog box. Click on Create label and bring up the Create label dialog box. Enter *con_env* in the Label Name box, then enter 1 in the value cell and *family* in the label cell, and then click Add. Then enter 2 in the value cell and *individual* in the label cell, and then click Add. Select OK.

3. Close the Manage value labels dialog box, and you should be at the Variable Manager dialog box now. With the *row* variable selected, again in the right panel, click on the drop-down list in the Value label box and select *con_env*, which we just created. Click Apply and close the Variable Manager dialog box.

4. Repeat Steps 2 and 3 to code the *column* variable. Use *completion_status* as the label name, and enter 1 in the value cell and *completion* in the label cell, then click Add. Then enter 2 in the value cell and *premature termination* in the label cell, then click Add. Apply *completion_status* to the *column* variable in the Variable Manager dialog box.

5. In the Data Editor (Edit) window, in the *row* column, enter 1, 1, 2, and 2 in the first four cells. For the column labeled *column*, enter 1, 2, 1, and 2 in each cell respectively. Enter the corresponding observed frequencies in the *frequency* column: 22, 12, 31, and 45, respectively.

6. Go to the menu bar and click Statistics, then select Summaries, tables, and tests → Frequency tables → Two-way table with measures of association to open up the Two-way table dialog box.

7. In the Row variable box, click on the drop-down list and select *row* into the cell. In the Column variable box, click on the drop-down list and select *column*. Under Test statistics, check the following two options:

   - Pearson's chi-squared
   - Cramer's *V*

8. Click on the Weights tab on the top of the Two-way table dialog box, select Frequency weights as the weight type, and then select *frequency* from the drop-down list in the Frequency weights cell.

9. Click OK. The results should be displayed in the Results window.

Alternatively, for Steps 6 to 8, we can use the following command line to conduct the chi-square test for independence:

```
tabulate row column [fweight = frequency], chi2 V
```

Table 17.15 shows the Stata results table for the chi-square test for independence. The frequency table shows the observed and expected frequencies. The first row under the frequency table lists the value of the chi-square test statistic, the degrees of freedom (the value 1 in the parentheses), and the *p* value (Pr = 0.020) for the test. The effect size value using Cramer's *V* is also provided. The values in the Stata output tables are the same as those we computed by hand for Example 17.2, give or take rounding.

**Table 17.15**    Stata Results for the Chi-Square Frequency Table With the Chi-Square Test for Independence and Effect Size Using Cramer's *V*

|  | column | | |
| --- | --- | --- | --- |
| row | completio | premature | Total |
| family | 22 | 12 | 34 |
| individual | 31 | 45 | 76 |
| Total | 53 | 57 | 110 |

```
Pearson chi2(1) =    5.3818    Pr = 0.020
      Cramér's V =    0.2212
```

# 18.3 STATA IN FOCUS

## The Related-Samples Sign Test

Privitera's *Statistics for the Behavioral Sciences,* Third Edition (p. 621)

Based on data given in Table 18.2 in Example 18.2, we concluded that outbursts were more common in a class taught by a substitute teacher compared to a class taught by a full-time teacher, $x = 9$, $p < .05$. Let us confirm this conclusion using Stata.

1. Click on the Data Editor (Edit) icon and bring up the Data Editor (Edit) window. Click on the Data tab and select Create or change data → Create new variable. Enter *substitute* in the Variable name box. In the Variable type box, select "int" from the drop-down list. Under Contents of variable, select Fill with missing value and click Submit. Repeat this procedure and create the *fulltime* variable this time.

2. In the Data Editor (Edit) window, enter the number of outbursts for each variable that is listed in the middle two columns of Table 18.3.

3. Go to the menu bar and click Statistics, then select Summaries, tables, and tests → Nonparametric tests of hypotheses → Test equality of matched pairs. Select *substitute* from the drop-down list in the Variable cell, and type *fulltime* in the Expression cell.

4. Click OK. The results should be displayed in the Results window.

Alternatively, for Step 3, we can use the following command line to conduct the sign test:

```
signtest substitute = fulltime
```

The Stata results table, shown in Table 18.4, shows the number of positive differences, negative differences, and ties. The *p* value can be found under Two-sided test, which is .025. The results here are consistent with our conclusion.

**Table 18.4**  Stata Results Table for the Related-Samples Sign Test

| sign | observed | expected |
|---|---|---|
| positive | 9 | 5 |
| negative | 1 | 5 |
| zero | 1 | 1 |
| all | 11 | 11 |

```
One-sided tests:
  Ho: median of substitute - fulltime = 0 vs.
  Ha: median of substitute - fulltime > 0
      Pr(#positive >= 9) =
        Binomial(n = 10, x >= 9, p = 0.5) =  0.0107

  Ho: median of substitute - fulltime = 0 vs.
  Ha: median of substitute - fulltime < 0
      Pr(#negative >= 1) =
        Binomial(n = 10, x >= 1, p = 0.5) =  0.9990

Two-sided test:
  Ho: median of substitute - fulltime = 0 vs.
  Ha: median of substitute - fulltime != 0
      Pr(#positive >= 9 or #negative >= 9) =
        min(1, 2*Binomial(n = 10, x >= 9, p = 0.5)) =  0.0215
```

# 18.5 STATA IN FOCUS

## The Wilcoxon Signed-Ranks *T* Test

Privitera's *Statisics for the Behavioral Sciences,* Third Edition (p. 626)

Based on data given in Table 18.5 in Example 18.3, we concluded that patients significantly reduced their cigarette use six months following diagnosis of heart disease, $z = -2.28$, $p < .05$. Let us confirm this conclusion using Stata.

1. Click on the Data Editor (Edit) icon and bring up the Data Editor (Edit) window. Click on the Data tab and select Create or change data → Create new variable. Enter *before* in the Variable name box. In the Variable type box, select "int" from the drop-down list. Under Contents of variable, select Fill with missing value and click Submit. Repeat this procedure and create the *after* variable this time.

2. In the Data Editor (Edit) window, enter the data from Table 18.8. Make sure that values for before diagnosis and after diagnosis are paired up correctly.

3. Go to the menu bar and click Statistics, then select Summaries, tables, and tests → Nonparametric tests of hypotheses → Wilcoxon matched-pairs signed-rank test. In the Wilcoxon test dialog box, select *after* from the drop-down list in the Variable cell. In the Expression cell, type *before*.

4. Click OK. The results should be displayed in the Results window.

Alternatively, for Step 3, we can use the following command line to conduct the Wilcoxon Signed-Ranks *T* Test:

```
signrank after = before
```

The Stata results table, shown in Table 18.7, displays the number of positive and negative ranks, and the sum of ranks. The test statistics in which we are interested are the normal approximation of this test and the $p$ value (Prob > $|z| = 0.029$). These results confirm the conclusion that patients reduce their cigarette use after diagnosis.

Table 18.7   Stata Results Table for the Wilcoxon Signed-Ranks *T* Test

```
Wilcoxon signed-rank test

        sign |    obs    sum ranks    expected

    positive |     2          10           39
    negative |    10          68           39
        zero |     0           0            0

         all |    12          78           78

unadjusted variance      162.50
adjustment for ties        0.00
adjustment for zeros       0.00

adjusted variance        162.50

Ho: after = before
           z =   -2.275
    Prob > |z| =   0.0229
```

Based on data given in Table 18.8 in Example 18.4, we concluded that job satisfaction was significantly greater among day-shift compared to night-shift employees, $U = 2$, $p < .05$. Let us confirm this conclusion using Stata.

1. Click on the Data Editor (Edit) icon and bring up the Data Editor (Edit) window. Click on the Data tab and select Create or change data → Create new variable. Enter *groups* in the Variable name box. In the Variable type box, select "int" from the drop-down list. Under Contents of variable, select Fill with missing value and click Submit. Repeat this procedure and create the *scores* variable this time.

2. To label the *groups* variable, still in the Data Editor (Edit) window, click on the Data tab and select Variable Manager to bring up the Variable Manager dialog box. Select the *groups* variable and, in the right panel, under Variable properties, locate the Variable label box and click on the Manage button. This will open up the Manage value labels dialog box. Click on Create label and bring up the Create label dialog box. Enter *shifts* in the Label Name box, then enter 1 in the value cell and *day shift* in the label cell, and then click Add. Then enter 2 in the value cell and *night shift* in the label cell, and then click Add. Select OK.

3. Close the Manage value labels dialog box, and you should be at the Variable Manager dialog box now. With the *groups* variable selected, again in the right panel, click on the drop-down list in the Value label box and select *shifts*, which we just created. Click Apply and close the Variable Manager dialog box.

4. In the Data Editor (Edit) window, enter the data from Table 18.8. In the *groups* column, enter 1 five times and 2 five times below that. In the *scores* column, list the scores that correspond to each group code. Hence, the scores 88, 72, 93, 67, and 62 should be listed next to a code of *day shift*; the scores 24, 55, 70, 60, and 50 should be listed next to a code of *night shift* in the second column.

5. Go to the menu bar and click Statistics, then select Summaries, tables, and tests → Nonparametric tests of hypotheses → Wilcoxon rank sum test. Select *scores* as the outcome variable and *groups* as the variable defining group.

6. Please note: The Wilcoxon rank sum test used here is identical to the Mann-Whitney *U* test (independent samples) and should be distinguished from the Wilcoxon matched-pairs signed-rank test (related samples), which we used in the Section 18.5 Stata in Focus.

7. Click OK. The results should be displayed in the Results window.

Alternatively, for Step 5, we can use the following command line to conduct the Wilcoxon rank-sum test:

```
ranksum scores, by(groups)
```

As we can see, the Stata results table, shown in Table 18.11, indicates that the Wilcoxon rank-sum test is essentially the Mann-Whitney $U$ test. The test statistics show the number of participants and sum of ranks for each group. The results also list the $z$ score for the normal approximation and the $p$ value for a two-tailed test (Prob > $|z|$ = 0.0283).

**Table 18.11**   Stata Results Table for the Mann-Whitney $U$ Test

```
Two-sample Wilcoxon rank-sum (Mann-Whitney) test

        groups |    obs    rank sum    expected
---------------+--------------------------------
     day shift |     5          38        27.5
   night shift |     5          17        27.5
---------------+--------------------------------
      combined |    10          55          55

unadjusted variance        22.92
adjustment for ties         0.00
                         --------
adjusted variance          22.92

Ho: scores(groups==day shift) = scores(groups==night shift)
            z =    2.193
    Prob > |z| =  0.0283
```

# 18.9 STATA IN FOCUS

## The Kruskal-Wallis *H* Test

Privitera's *Statisics for the Behavioral Sciences,* Third Edition (p. 637)

Based on data given in Table 18.12 in Example 18.5, we concluded that rankings of three safe driving video clips were significantly different, $H = 7.28$, $p < .05$. Let us confirm this conclusion using Stata.

1. Click on the Data Editor (Edit) icon and bring up the Data Editor (Edit) window. Click on the Data tab and select Create or change data → Create new variable. Enter *categories* in the Variable name box. In the Variable type box, select "int" from the drop-down list. Under Contents of variable, select Fill with missing value and click Submit. Repeat this procedure and create the *ratings* variable this time.

2. Next, we need to label the *groups* variable. Still in the Data Editor (Edit) window, click on the Data tab and select Variable Manager to bring up the Variable Manager dialog box. Select the *groups* variable and, in the right panel, under Variable properties, locate the Variable label box and click on the Manage button. This will open up the Manage value labels dialog box. Click on Create label and bring up the Create label dialog box. Enter *clips* in the Label name box, then enter 1 in the value cell and *Clip A* in the label cell, and click Add. Then enter 2 in the value cell and *Clip B* in the label cell, and then click Add. Then enter 3 in the value cell and *Clip C* in the label cell, and then click Add. Select OK.

3. Close the Manage value labels dialog box, and you should be at the Variable Manager dialog box now. With the *groups* variable selected, again in the right panel, click on the drop-down list in the Value label box and select *clips*, which we just created. Click Apply and close the Variable Manager dialog box.

4. In the Data Editor (Edit) window, enter the data from Table 18.12. In the *groups* column, enter 1 five times, 2 five times below that, and 3 five times below that. In the ratings column, list the scores that correspond to each group code.

5. Go to the menu bar and click Statistics, then select Summaries, tables, and tests → Nonparametric tests of hypotheses → Kruskal-Wallis rank test. In the Kruskal-Wallis test window, select *ratings* as the outcome variable and *groups* as the variable defining group.

6. Click OK. The results should be displayed in the Results window.

Alternatively, for Step 5, we can use the following command line to conduct the Kruskal-Wallis rank test:

```
kwallis ratings, by(groups)
```

The Stata results table, shown in Table 18.14, shows the number of participants and rank sum per group. Note that because we have a tied rank here (i.e., Clip A and Clip C), we need to consult the results highlighted in the rectangle: chi-square test statistic with degrees of freedom (chi-squared with ties = 7.260 with 2 d.f.), and the *p* value (probability = .0265).

**Table 18.14**   Stata Results Table for the Kruskal-Wallis *H* Test

```
Kruskal-Wallis equality-of-populations rank test
```

| groups | Obs | Rank Sum |
|--------|-----|----------|
| Clip A | 5 | 29.00 |
| Clip B | 5 | 62.00 |
| Clip C | 5 | 29.00 |

```
chi-squared =      7.260 with 2 d.f.
probability =      0.0265
```

```
chi-squared with ties =       7.260 with 2 d.f.
probability =      0.0265
```

# 18.11 STATA IN FOCUS

## The Friedman Test

Privitera's *Statisics for the Behavioral Sciences,* Third Edition (p. 641)

Based on the data given in Table 18.15a in Example 18.6, we concluded that there are no significant differences in the number of office visits made by women in each trimester of their pregnancy, $R^2(2) = 2.658$, $p > .05$. Let us confirm this conclusion using Stata.

1. Click on the Data Editor (Edit) icon to open up the Data Editor (Edit) window. Click on the Data tab and select Create or change data → Create new variable. Enter *first* in the Variable name box. Go to the Variable type box and select "int" from the drop-down list. Under Contents of variable, select Fill with missing data and click Submit. Repeat these steps to create another two variables, using *second* and *third* as the variable names, respectively.

2. In the Data Editor (Edit) window, enter the data from Table 18.15a. Enter the number of visits for the first, second, and third trimesters in the appropriately labeled columns.

3. By default, Stata does not have Friedman Test installed. Therefore, we need to install the Friedman Test package. In the command window, input

   ```
   findit friedman
   ```

   to open up the Stata Viewer window. Here, we install the package titled "SJ-5-2 snp2_1" (should be the fourth result), created by Richard Goldstein.

4. In order for the Friedman Test command to function appropriately, we must transpose our original data, in other words, changing variables into observations and observations into variables. This can be achieved by using the command:

   ```
   xpose, clear
   ```

5. The command clear is required, which is used to remind you that untransposed data will be lost. After transpose, our data should look like Figure 18.1.

**Figure 18.1** Data After Transpose

| | v1 | v2 | v3 | v4 | v5 | v6 | v7 |
|---|---|---|---|---|---|---|---|
| 1 | 3 | 6 | 2 | 4 | 4 | 4 | 8 |
| 2 | 5 | 4 | 0 | 3 | 6 | 3 | 6 |
| 3 | 8 | 7 | 5 | 2 | 9 | 7 | 5 |

In the command window, input the following command to conduct the Friedman Test:

```
friedman v1-v7
```

Here, "v1-v7" means all variables in our data, from variable "v1" to variable "v7" (in other words, all variables should be included in the test). Alternatively, we can input each variable name individually (i.e., v1 v2 v3 v4 v5 v6 v7). Clearly, this is not as efficient as using "v1-v7."

The Stata output table, shown in Table 18.16, shows the chi-square test statistic (Friedman = 2.5714), and the $p$ value (P-value = .2765). These results indicate that there are no differences between groups, therefore confirming our conclusion.

**Table 18.16**   Stata Results Table for the Friedman Test

Friedman = 2.5714
Kendall = 0.1837
P-value = 0.2765

# General Instruction Guide

The General Instruction Guide (GIG) for using Stata provides standardized instructions for using Stata to enter and analyze data. The instructions provided in the GIG are also given in the *Statistics for the Behavioral Sciences,* Third Edition textbook. Every chapter except Chapter 8 gives at least one step-by-step Stata in Focus section. These sections provide step-by-step instructions for using Stata to enter data and compute the statistics taught in each chapter. For each Stata in Focus section, please follow the "point-and-click" directions given for each example. This guide also provides one place where you can find all the code you will need to help you complete any Stata in Focus section in this book. You can use these instructions to complete each exercise and refer to the Stata examples in the textbook to clear up any points of confusion.

The instructions here are organized by exercise in this guide make it easier for you to find the appropriate instructions to complete each Stata exercise. The instructions for each exercise are given with a reference for which Stata in Focus section provides an example for following the steps.

## Exercise 1.1: Entering and Defining Variables

This exercise is illustrated in Chapter 1, Section 1.7 (Stata in Focus).

Follow the point-and-click directions given in Stata in Focus Section 1.7. No code is needed.

## Exercise 2.1: Frequency Distributions for Quantitative Data

This exercise is illustrated in Chapter 2, Section 2.4 (Stata in Focus).

1. Follow the point-and-click directions given in Stata in Focus Section 2.4 to enter the data.

2. To conduct the analysis, we can use the following command line:

```
tabulate complaints, sort
```

## Exercise 2.2: Frequency Distributions for Categorical Data

This exercise is illustrated in Chapter 2, Section 2.7 (Stata in Focus).

1. Follow the point-and-click directions given in Stata in Focus Section 2.7 to enter the data.

2. To conduct the analysis, we can use the following command line:

```
tabulate categories [fweight = frequencies]
```

## Exercise 2.3: Histograms, Bar Charts, and Pie Charts

This exercise is illustrated in Chapter 2, Section 2.12 (Stata in Focus).

1. Follow the point-and-click directions given in Stata in Focus Section 2.12 to enter the data.

2. To conduct the analysis, we can use the following command line:

```
histogram numbers, discrete width(0.5) frequency
```

## Exercise 3.1: Mean, Median, and Mode

This exercise is illustrated in Chapter 3, Section 3.6 (Stata in Focus).

1. Follow the point-and-click directions given in Stata in Focus Section 3.6 to enter the data.

2. We can use the following command line to find the mean and median values:

```
summarize creativity, detail
```

3. In order to find mode, we need to use egen to create a new mode variable:

```
egen creativity_mode = mode (creativity)
```

4. In case there are multiple modes, if we want the smaller mode value:

```
egen creativity_mode = mode(creativity), minmode
```

or

```
egen creativity_mode = mode(creativity), maxmode
```

for the larger mode value.

## Exercise 4.1: Range, Variance, and Standard Deviation

This exercise is illustrated in Chapter 4, Section 4.11 (Stata in Focus).

1. Follow the point-and-click directions given in Stata in Focus Section 4.11 to enter the data.

2. To conduct analysis, we can use the following command line:

```
summarize creativity, detail
```

## Exercise 5.1: Probability Tables

This exercise is illustrated in Chapter 5, Section 5.6 (Stata in Focus).

1. Follow the point-and-click directions given in Stata in Focus Section 5.6 to enter the data.

2. Use the following command line to construct the probability table:

```
tabulate hospital insurance [fweight = frequencies]
```

## Exercise 6.1: Converting Raw Scores to Standard $z$ Scores

This exercise is illustrated in Chapter 6, Section 6.8 (Stata in Focus).

1. Follow the point-and-click directions given in Stata in Focus Section 6.8 to enter the data.

2. Use the following command line to generate $z$ scores:

```
egen ZSAT = std(SAT), mean(0) std(1)
```

## Exercise 7.1: Estimating the Standard Error of the Mean

This exercise is illustrated in Chapter 7, Section 7.7 (Stata in Focus).

1. Follow the point-and-click directions given in Stata in Focus Section 7.7 to enter the data.

2. Use the following command line to find the standard error:

```
mean reaction
```

## Exercise 9.1: One-Sample $t$ Test

This exercise is illustrated in Chapter 9, Section 9.6 (Stata in Focus).

1. Follow the point-and-click directions given in Stata in Focus Section 9.6 to enter the data.

2. Use the following command line to conduct the one-sample $t$ test:

```
ttest health == 77.43
```

## Exercise 9.2: Two-Independent-Sample *t* Test

This exercise is illustrated in Chapter 9, Section 9.9 (Stata in Focus).

1.  Follow the point-and-click directions given in Stata in Focus Section 9.9 to enter the data.
2.  Use the following command line to conduct the two-sample *t* test:

```
ttest intake, by(groups)
```

## Exercise 10.1: The Related-Samples *t* Test

This exercise is illustrated in Chapter 10, Section 10.4 (Stata in Focus).

1.  Follow the point-and-click directions given in Stata in Focus Section 10.4 to enter the data.
2.  Use the following command line to conduct the related-samples *t* test:

```
ttest present == absent
```

## Exercise 11.1: Confidence Intervals for the One-Sample *t* Test

This exercise is illustrated in Chapter 11, Section 11.5 (Stata in Focus).

1.  Follow the instructions in Exercise 9.1 to enter the data.
2.  Then use the following command line to conduct the one-sample *t* test:

```
ttest health == 77.43, level(90)
```

## Exercise 11.2: Confidence Intervals for the Two-Independent-Sample *t* Test

This exercise is illustrated in Chapter 11, Section 11.7 (Stata in Focus).

1.  Follow the instructions in Exercise 9.2 to enter the data.
2.  Use the following command line to conduct the two-sample *t* test:

```
ttest intake, by(groups) level(90)
```

## Exercise 11.3: Confidence Intervals for the Related-Samples *t* Test

This exercise is illustrated in Chapter 11, Section 11.9 (Stata in Focus).

1. Follow the instructions in Exercise 10.1 to enter the data.

2. Use the following command line to conduct the related-samples *t* test:

```
ttest present == absent, level(90)
```

## Exercise 12.1: The One-Way Between-Subjects ANOVA

This exercise is illustrated in Chapter 12, Section 12.8 (Stata in Focus). Compute this test using the One-Way ANOVA command:

1. Follow the point-and-click directions given in Stata in Focus Section 12.8 to enter the data.

2. Use the following command line to conduct the ANOVA analysis:

```
anova length group
```

For post hoc analysis:

3. Use the following command line to conduct the post hoc analysis using Fisher's LSD method:

```
pwcompare groups, effects
```

4. To generate the post hoc comparison using Tukey's HSD method, use the following command line:

```
pwcompare groups, mcompare(tukey) effects
```

## Exercise 13.1: The One-Way Within-Subjects ANOVA

This exercise is illustrated in Chapter 13, Section 13.6 (Stata in Focus).

1. Follow the point-and-click directions given in Stata in Focus Section 13.6 to enter the data.

2. Use the following command line to conduct the analysis:

```
anova value n_person n_cue, repeated(n_person)
```

For post hoc analysis:

3. Use the following command line to conduct the post hoc analysis using the Bonferroni method:

```
pwcompare n_cue, mcompare(bonferroni) effects
```

## Exercise 14.1: The Two-Way Between-Subjects ANOVA

This exercise is illustrated in Chapter 14, Section 14.8 (Stata in Focus).

1. Follow the point-and-click directions given in Stata in Focus Section 14.8 to enter the data.

2. Use the following command line to conduct the analysis:

```
anova times buffet exposure buffet # exposure
```

Or

```
anova times buffet ## exposure
```

For post hoc analysis:

3. Use the following command line to conduct the post hoc analysis using Tukey's HSD method:

```
pwcompare buffet exposure buffet#exposure, mcompare(tukey) effects
```

## Exercise 15.1: Pearson Correlation Coefficient

This exercise is illustrated in Chapter 15, Section 15.4 (Stata in Focus).

1. Follow the point-and-click directions given in Stata in Focus Section 15.4 to enter the data.

2. Use the following command line to conduct the correlation test:

```
pwcorr mood eating, obs sig star(5)
```

## Exercise 15.2: Spearman Correlation Coefficient

This exercise is illustrated in Chapter 15, Section 15.8 (Stata in Focus).

1. Follow the point-and-click directions given in Stata in Focus Section 15.8 to enter the data.

2. Use the following command line to conduct the correlation test:

```
spearman food water, stats(rho obs p) star(0.05) matrix
```

## Exercise 15.3: Point-Biserial Correlation Coefficient

This exercise is illustrated in Chapter 15, Section 15.10 (Stata in Focus).

1. Follow the point-and-click directions given in Stata in Focus Section 15.10 to enter the data.

2. Use the following command line to conduct the analysis:

```
pwcorr sex laughter, obs sig star(5)
```

## Exercise 15.4: Phi Correlation Coefficient

This exercise is illustrated in Chapter 15, Section 15.12 (Stata in Focus).

1. Follow the point-and-click directions given in Stata in Focus Section 15.12 to enter the data.

2. Use the following command line to find the phi correlation:

```
pwcorr employment happiness [fweight = count], obs sig star(5)
```

## Exercise 16.1: Analysis of Regression

This exercise is illustrated in Chapter 16, Section 16.7 (Stata in Focus).

1. Follow the point-and-click directions given in Stata in Focus Section 16.7 to enter the data.

2. Use the following command line to conduct the regression analysis:

```
regress Y X
```

## Exercise 16.2: Multiple Regression Analysis

This exercise is illustrated in Chapter 16, Section 16.13 (Stata in Focus).

1. Follow the point-and-click directions given in Stata in Focus Section 16.13 to enter the data.

2. Use the following command line to conduct the multiple regression analysis:

```
regress sales age education, beta
```

## Exercise 17.1: The Chi-Square Goodness-of-Fit Test

This exercise is illustrated in Chapter 17, Section 17.3 (Stata in Focus).

Because Stata does not have an embedded function to compute the chi-square goodness-of-fit, we need to use the findit command to find other user-created functions:

1. In the command window, input:

   ```
   findit chitesti
   ```

   and the Stata Viewer window will open.

2. Click on the first result. You will be directed to the installation page.

3. Click on click here to install. The chitesti function should be installed.

4. The chitesti requires two sets of values: the observed frequencies and the expected frequencies.

5. In the command window, input the following command line:

   ```
   chitesti 58 12 10\64 8 8
   ```

## Exercise 17.2: The Chi-Square Test for Independence

This exercise is illustrated in Chapter 17, Section 17.9 (Stata in Focus).

1. Follow the point-and-click directions given in Stata in Focus Section 17.9 to enter the data.

2. Use the following command line to conduct the chi-square test for independence:

   ```
   tabulate row column [fweight = frequency], chi2 V
   ```

## Exercise 18.1: The Related-Samples Sign Test

This exercise is illustrated in Chapter 18, Section 18.3 (Stata in Focus).

1. Follow the point-and-click directions given in Stata in Focus Section 18.3 to enter the data.

2. Use the following command line to conduct the sign test:

   ```
   signtest substitute = fulltime
   ```

## Exercise 18.2: The Wilcoxon Signed-Ranks $T$ Test

This exercise is illustrated in Chapter 18, Section 18.5 (Stata in Focus).

1. Follow the point-and-click directions given in Stata in Focus Section 18.5 to enter the data.

2. Use the following command line to conduct the Wilcoxon Signed-Ranks $T$ Test:

   ```
   signrank after = before
   ```

## Exercise 18.3: The Mann-Whitney *U* Test

This exercise is illustrated in Chapter 18, Section 18.7 (Stata in Focus).

1. Follow the point-and-click directions given in Stata in Focus Section 18.7 to enter the data.

2. Use the following command line to conduct the Wilcoxon rank-sum test:

```
ranksum scores, by(groups)
```

## Exercise 18.4: The Kruskal-Wallis *H* Test

This exercise is illustrated in Chapter 18, Section 18.9 (Stata in Focus).

1. Follow the point-and-click directions given in Stata in Focus Section 18.9 to enter the data.

2. Use the following command line to conduct the Kruskal-Wallis rank test:

```
kwallis ratings, by(groups)
```

## Exercise 18.5: The Friedman Test

This exercise is illustrated in Chapter 18, Section 18.11 (Stata in Focus).

1. Follow the point-and-click directions given in Stata in Focus Section 18.11 to enter the data.

2. By default, Stata does not have the Friedman Test installed. Therefore, we need to install the Friedman Test package. In the command window, input

```
findit friedman
```

to open up the Stata Viewer window. Here, we install the package titled "SJ-5-2 snp2_1" (should be the fourth result), created by Richard Goldstein.

3. Transpose our original data using the command:

```
xpose, clear
```

4. Use the following command to conduct the Friedman Test:

```
friedman v1-v7
```

# References

Centers for Disease Control and Prevention. (2013). *Adult BMI calculator: English*. Retrieved from http://www.cdc.gov/healthyweight/assessing/bmi/adult_bmi/english_bmi_calculator/bmi_calculator.html

Chatterjea, R. G., & Mitra, A. (1976). A study of brainstorming. *Manas, 23*, 23–28.

Piffer, D. (2012). Can creativity be measured? An attempt to clarify the notion of creativity and general directions for future research. *Thinking Skills and Creativity, 7*, 258–264. doi:10.1016/j.tsc.2012.04.009

Privitera, G. J. (2016). Health psychology. In C. McCarthy, M. DeLisi, A. Getzfeld, G. J. Privitera, C. Spence, J. Walker, . . . C. Youssef-Morgan (Eds.), *Introduction to applied behavioral science* (pp. 32–54). San Diego, CA: Bridgepoint Education.

Privitera, G. J. (2018). *Statistics for the behavioral sciences* (3rd ed.). Thousand Oaks, CA: Sage.

# Index